# Breaking the Pendulum

# Breaking
# the Pendulum

*The Long Struggle Over
Criminal Justice*

PHILIP GOODMAN
JOSHUA PAGE
and
MICHELLE PHELPS

OXFORD
UNIVERSITY PRESS

# OXFORD
UNIVERSITY PRESS

Oxford University Press is a department of the University of Oxford. It furthers
the University's objective of excellence in research, scholarship, and education
by publishing worldwide. Oxford is a registered trade mark of Oxford University
Press in the UK and certain other countries.

Published in the United States of America by Oxford University Press
198 Madison Avenue, New York, NY 10016, United States of America.

© Oxford University Press 2017

CIP data is on file at the Library of Congress

ISBN 978-0-19-997605-8 (hbk)
ISBN 978-0-19-997606-5 (pbk)

1 3 5 7 9 8 6 4 2

Paperback printed by Webcom, Inc., Canada

Hardback printed by Bridgeport National Bindery, Inc., United States of America

*To our parents, with love*

# Contents

# *Preface*

ON JULY 16, 2015, Barack Obama visited the El Reno Federal Correctional Institution in Oklahoma, becoming the first sitting president to visit a federal prison. A few days earlier, he had publicly questioned the United State's massive criminal justice system: "We have to consider whether this is this smartest way for us both to control crime and to rehabilitate individuals."[1] Though measured, this statement was remarkable—just several years earlier it would have been practically unthinkable.

A little over a year before Obama made history, the *New York Times* ran an editorial with the declarative title, "End Mass Incarceration Now."[2] The piece boldly insisted that the country's penal polices were deeply harmful, especially to poor minority communities:

> The severity is evident in the devastation wrought on America's poorest and least educated, destroying neighborhoods and families. From 1980 to 2000, the number of children with fathers in prison rose from 350,000 to 2.1 million. Since race and poverty overlap so significantly, the weight of our criminal justice experiment continues to fall overwhelmingly on communities of color, and particularly on young black men.

To end the "insanity," the editorial urged lawmakers to reduce the length of prison sentences, increase rehabilitation opportunities, and facilitate former prisoners' transition back into the community.

The president's prison tour and the *Times* editorial indicated a shift in the criminal justice landscape. Statistics supported this view too: after decades of unprecedented growth, the nation's prison population finally leveled off in 2010, leading some to wonder if the era of "mass incarceration" was coming to an end.[3] With the tide beginning to change, pundits and academics increasingly suggested that the penal "pendulum" was swinging away from "tough on crime" and toward "smart on crime." This swing, we were told, would shrink the carceral state and ameliorate its most harmful aspects.

Proclamations about this "pendulum swing" seemed intuitive. For one thing, the politics and rhetoric around criminal justice had been distinctly harsh since the 1980s. It seemed during the 1990s and the first decade of the twenty-first century that the rates of people behind bars and under community supervision (particularly for young African Americans and Latinos) would continue to grow in perpetuity. At the same time, images of irredeemable criminal predators pervaded popular culture, and policymakers and private actors (such as landlords and employers) often framed "offenders" as pariahs—semi-citizens, at best. In this context, reforms designed to cut into penal populations, increase services and programs for people serving time, remove barriers to prisoner reentry, and improve police-community relations seemed like a major rupture.

While the pendulum view has a certain appeal, we argue that it badly distorts the nature and process of penal change. For example, developments in the last 10 or so years have been piecemeal, with important laws, discourses, and institutions left untouched or, at best, softened at the edges. American punishment remains very punitive and managerial. And as we move back in time, the pendulum view works no better. It assumes, for instance, that "rehabilitation" died during the 1980s and '90s and is now making a comeback. That assumption is patently false; rehabilitative programs definitely changed in previous decades, becoming more disciplinary and focused on cost-effectiveness, but efforts to correct people remained and, in some cases, grew stronger. Rehabilitation was reconfigured, not rolled back. Likewise, during the late 1940s, '50s, and '60s, when rehabilitation supposedly reigned supreme, correctional programs were typically managerial and punitive.

As the three of us discussed misconceptions about the nature and scope of current penal developments, we became increasingly convinced of the limits of the pendulum perspective (and, more generally, pendular logic). We concluded that the pendulum perspective *always* distorts how and why criminal justice changes (or does not change). Punishment expands, contracts, and morphs because of struggle between real people in concrete contexts, not because of a mechanical "swing" of the pendulum. As we show throughout the book, this was true with the birth of the American penitentiary centuries ago, and it remains so today.

More than a critique, *Breaking the Pendulum* offers an alternative approach to conceptualizing penal development. The agonistic perspective we develop and employ proposes that struggle between people is the motor force of criminal justice history.[4] Situating contestation within concrete social-structural and institutional contexts, this perspective encourages us not to lose sight of the broader conditions in which people spar. This alternative framework, we believe, is far more accurate and empowering than approaches that ignore or downplay the importance of contestation in shaping criminal justice.

WE WOULD LIKE to express gratitude to some of the many people who helped make this book a reality. The following scholars and colleagues shaped our thinking on criminal justice and penal change (and, in some instances, gave generously of their time in reading drafts and providing useful suggestions and critiques): Hadar Aviram, Vanessa Barker, Katherine Beckett, Michael Campbell, Jennifer Carlson, Randol Contreras, Amy Cooter, Alessandro De Giorgi, Benjamin Fluery-Steiner, David Garland, Marie Gottschalk, Kelly Hannah-Moffat, Elizabeth Hinton, John Irwin, Valerie Jenness, Candace Kruttschnitt, Issa Kohler-Hausmann, Chrysanthi Leon, Amy Lerman, Mona Lynch, Paula Maurutto, Rebecca McLennan, Heather McCarty, Fergus McNeill, Lisa Miller, Vivien Miller, Marc Mauer, Devah Pager, Keramet Reiter, Ashley Rubin, Danielle Rudes, Joachim Savelsberg, Heather Schoenfeld, Christopher Seeds, Jonathan Simon, Joe Soss, Richard Sparks, Brett Story, Heather Ann Thompson, Christopher Uggen, Loïc Wacquant, Sara Wakefield, and Vesla Weaver.

We are also grateful to the anonymous reviewers for their challenging, insightful, and generative feedback. James Cook at Oxford skillfully and very patiently steered this project from inception to completion. We could not ask for a better steward. Letta Page edited the entire manuscript with exceptional zeal, acumen, and care. Alexandra Hunter, Kaleigh Scott, and Alexandra Wilson offered further assistance with the notes and bibliography, and Robert Stewart helped compile examples for several chapters.

Although it may be unorthodox, we want to also thank one another. This truly collaborative work[5] has been a labor of love, and we are both excited and saddened to see it end. We hope readers will learn as much from the final product as we did researching and writing it.

Finally, we extend unbound gratitude to our families, who contributed to the *long struggle* to finish this book in more ways than they know. Our partners (Dan Myers, Jackie Goodman, and Letta Page) and children (Theo, Ryken, and Nyella) generously listened to us discuss this book for years, helped us hone our analysis, and provided much-needed respite and daily joy. Thank you. We love you.

# Breaking the Pendulum

# *I*

# *Penal Development and Plate Tectonics*

IN HIS WIDELY acclaimed, posthumously published book, *The Collapse of American Criminal Justice*, eminent legal scholar William J. Stuntz argued that "a kind of pendulum justice took hold in the twentieth century's second half, as America's justice system first saw a sharp decline in the prison population—in the midst of a record-setting crime wave—then saw that population rise steeply. In the late 1960s and early 1970s, the United States had one of the most lenient justice systems in the world. By century's end, that justice system was the harshest in the history of democratic government."[1] This swinging back and forth, Stuntz maintained, generated major instability and "dysfunction" in penal institutions.

Stuntz's argument about the negative consequences of radical ruptures in criminal justice was novel.[2] However, his depiction of the system as a pendulum that mechanically swings back and forth between distinct orientations and regimes of practice was—and remains—quite common. As it is usually portrayed, the penal pendulum's first major swing occurred in the early 1800s, when deprivation of liberty (that is, incarceration) in penitentiaries (rather than capital and corporal punishments) became the preferred way in the United States to sanction offenders. After quickly swinging back toward the punitive side of the ledger, criminal justice thrust back to reformation during the Progressive Era. The penal system then hardened during World War I and the Great Depression, before swinging back to reform after World War II as the "rehabilitative era" transformed punishment into a "correctional" system. Between the late 1960s and the 1980s, a combination of retribution and containment replaced rehabilitation as the standard purpose of the criminal justice system. And today, with some states implementing new sentencing, prison, and parole reforms, commentators increasingly believe the pendulum is "swinging back" to an emphasis on rehabilitation and leniency.

As the three of us drew on the pendulum metaphor in our own teaching and research, we became increasingly uneasy with this characterization of change. To tell the pendulum story, we had to ignore the complexity we found in our own research and that of other scholars, findings that belied the existence of a single, pervasive penal orientation in *any* historical period, let alone any dramatic "rupture" moments demarcating them. For example, the rehabilitative ideal was *never* as widespread as indicated by the pendulum perspective, whether in theory or practice. Nor has there been a clean break into a punitive era since the 1970s or a cataclysmic realignment in 2010. In addition to mischaracterizing the "what" of change, the pendulum metaphor also made the problematic assumption of a natural evolution from one dominant narrative to the other, with the pendulum providing its own internal force or momentum toward change. This evolutionary perspective obscured the important struggles we saw among actors, which ultimately shape criminal justice.

To be clear, our critique is not about use of the pendulum to describe abrupt shifts in penal trends, such as rapid growth of imprisonment rates or new sentencing laws. One can reasonably describe, for example, the increase of imprisonment in the 1980s and 1990s as a pendulum shift, if one means that rates swung from low to high (though using the metaphor to describe trends may incorrectly suggest that the trends occurred because of a mechanical process, rather than actors and social forces). Our critique focuses on the use of the metaphor to describe radical swings in "criminal justice regimes."[3] By this, we mean the prevailing *orientation* of the penal field[4] (dominant goals of criminal justice institutions; understandings of crime, punishment, and justice; and visions of lawbreakers) and related *policies* and *practices*. All too often, pundits, scholars, and activists insist that the country (or its individual states) swings from one criminal justice regime to another—for example, from rehabilitative and lenient to punitive or managerial. Commentators conclude from trends (such as growth of imprisonment or correctional programs) that we have swung into a new era. The historical record, however, shows that claims of radical regime change (or swinging) are misleading and blind us to the blending of penal orientations, policies, and practices, as well as the struggle between actors within and beyond the penal field that limits wholesale transformations in regimes.

As we began this project, we quickly realized that much of our critique of the pendulum view of penal change also applied to important scholarship within the sociology of punishment (including some of our own). Major studies that do not explicitly mention the "pendulum" nonetheless implicitly rely on a similar logic. For instance, scholars may argue that social forces (especially economic) generate radical swings in criminal justice. These swings, in turn, produce major ruptures in which punishment changes wholesale from one orientation to another. In these accounts, change is predictable and mechanical—punishment swings *behind the backs* of social actors, to paraphrase sociologist Harold Garfinkel.[5] What happens "on the ground" is overlooked, and agitation for change is of limited consequence. Thus, our critique of the pendulum model of criminal justice calls attention to tendencies within the sociology of punishment to distort how and why criminal justice does and does not change, and seeks to reinstate social power over historical inevitability.

This book argues that the pendulum model of criminal justice history (and more broadly, pendular logic itself) is satisfying but ultimately misleading. It's time to "break" the pendulum and develop a new way of thinking about the processes of criminal justice development. (We use the term "development" to refer to the unfolding of punishment—which sometimes produces sharp changes and, at other times, reinforces existing policies, practices, and priorities. We do not use the term to describe a movement toward an *ideal* state of punishment.) We propose, instead, an agonistic perspective, positing that actors (or "agonists") with varying resources and differing visions of how to prevent and sanction crime continually contest punishment. This contestation shapes the deep variations across place (as local actors shape implementation of policies) and ultimately produces the penal change that outsiders describe as a pendulum swing driven by macro-level changes in the economy, politics, culture, and intergroup relations. While periods of relatively less explosive conflict or change appear, on the surface, as moments of stability or consensus, we argue that they are, instead, characterized by quieter contestation, paving the road for the next penal pivot. Struggle is the motor of penal change.

## *The Pendulum in Action*

The pendulum metaphor is common in popular, policy, and academic discussions of criminal justice, and it serves a variety of useful purposes. Journalists and pundits use the imagery to situate events, policy changes, judicial decisions, or statistics (such as declines in the prison population) within larger penal trends. Along these lines, the *New York Times* maintained in August

2013: "Two decisions Monday, one by a federal judge in New York and the other by Attorney General Eric H. Holder Jr., were powerful signals that the pendulum has swung away from the tough-on-crime policies of a generation ago."[6]

College textbooks are chock full of the pendulum metaphor, too. One proclaims: "Over the past two hundred years, ideas about punishment have moved like a pendulum from far in one direction to far in another."[7] Another reads:

> The dualities within the system might be viewed as existing on the arc of a pendulum, with crime control, rigid adherence to policy, conservative crime control policies, and a view of justice as retribution at the right end of the pendulum's arc. At the left end of the arc are due process, use of discretion, liberal crime control policies, and a view of justice as restorative. Sometimes the pendulum slows and is near the middle, but at other times it swings more heavily to one side or the other.[8]

In this view, the pendulum is like a continuum, and criminal justice practices swing toward one pole or the other.

These swings are then used to classify the history of criminal justice into discrete eras. One textbook divides US punishment into seven, mutually exclusive "epochs": Colonial (1600s–1790s), Penitentiary (1790s–1860s), Reformatory (1870s–1890s), Progressive (1890s–1930s), Medical (1930s–1960s), Community (1960s–1970s), and Crime Control (1970s–2000s).[9] Separating history into ideal typical periods can be useful for summarizing change and continuity. However, textbooks and research manuscripts tend to treat these ideal types as *real* things, rather than approximations. They suggest that criminal justice is fundamentally "rehabilitative" *or* "retributive" in a way that it is the same everywhere and wholly different from earlier or later periods, rather than a novel combination of the two at any given time.

Likewise, policy scholars often argue that the pendulum swings between retribution and rehabilitation because practitioners implement policies that "don't work" or live up to expectations. Renowned criminal justice expert Joan Petersilia said in a 2013 interview:

> I've been around the criminal justice policy world since the 1970s, and, in the 1980s, 1990s, and now 2000 and the next decade, we have seen these huge shifts in terms of endorsing tough-on-crime and building

up prisons or endorsing probation and community alternatives, and we just seem to go back-and-forth and back-and-forth. . . . I think for both sides of the coin, if you think about the coin being this pendulum swing—community corrections, soft-on-crime versus prisons, tough-on-crime—we just simply go back-and-forth because we don't really have solid evidence that would allow us to choose one option over the other.[10]

For policy scholars such as Petersilia, policy success or failure—and the lack of evidence and systematic research to make sense of it—is what pushes the pendulum from one side to the other.

Academic analyses also use the pendulum model to describe and explain penal change. For their part, Edward Rhine and colleagues write:

> The field of corrections is experiencing a reawakening interest in reha-bilitation driven by a notable commitment to offender reentry. . . . The new ideas and programs energizing this latest swing of the criminal jus-tice pendulum are based on an impressive body of literature providing considerable empirical evidence that rehabilitation efforts can and do work to reduce offender recidivism.[11]

So the pendulum will continue to swing—yet, echoing policy researchers, the authors suggest that the direction of movement depends on whether cor-rectional programs "work" to reduce recidivism. Again, this is a mechanical view of change: policy success or failure automatically drives change across a homogenous "system."

The logic of the pendulum is also present in scholarly works that do not explicitly use the metaphor. Academics routinely describe ruptures in crim-inal justice as characterized by sweeping shifts from one penal orientation to another. This narrative is clearest in descriptions of the "punitive turn" in the 1980s and 1990s. One of us (Page) employed the rupture narrative to set up a book on the California prison officers' labor union and the politics of imprisonment, positing a wholesale transformation (or "flip") in criminal jus-tice. The introduction to *The Toughest Beat* states: "It was not long, however, before the Golden State flipped from a leader in *correctional* incarceration to a forerunner in *retributive* confinement."[12] This kind of pendular language asserts (or implies) that one orientation and its attendant policies and pro-grams are rolled back as a whole new regime takes its place. Sociologist Jill McCorkel, to take another example, writes in the introduction of *Breaking*

*Women*, "'Get tough' turned penal welfarism on its head at virtually every conceivable level within the criminal justice system. . . . Educational, vocational, and rehabilitative programming all but disappeared."[13]

The mechanistic logic of the pendulum perspective has deep roots within the sociology of punishment. Émile Durkheim famously argued that changes in social solidarity (that is, the norms and relationships that hold society together) automatically and autonomously drive penal change.[14] Similarly, Georg Rushe and Otto Kirchheimer posited a direct relationship between the labor market and punishment, so that shifts in society's economic base produce concurrent changes in penal forms.[15] These accounts read as if people, organizations, and institutions are largely inconsequential to (or, at best, secondary in) penal development. On this point, David Rothman argues, "The more one understands the alterations within the [penal] system, the more one explores motives, designs, and alliances, the less an air of inevitability hangs over the practice of punishment and the less compelling arguments of economic determinism become."[16]

Even one of the most sophisticated, influential analyses of contemporary punishment, David Garland's *Culture of Control*, advances a somewhat mechanical view of penal development.[17] Arguing that "late modern" developments in the economy, politics, and culture drove incredible penal changes in the United States and the United Kingdom in the last several decades of the twentieth century, Garland downplays contingency and struggle—somewhat surprising given that his earlier work on the development of welfarist criminal justice in Great Britain focused so centrally on them. In *Punishment and Welfare* (1985), he argued, "Reformed penal practices, ideologies and institutions must always be the product of specific struggles, calculated according to their political and ideological effects as well as their penological efficacy."[18] Responding to critics of *Culture of Control*, Garland acknowledged that his method of analysis in that book pays insufficient attention to "the place of ongoing conflict and contestation," and thus:

> tends to understate the importance of the actors whose preferences and policies lost out in the current conjuncture but who continue to be a presence in the field and to exert a pressure for change. In doing so, it tends to misrepresent the real nature of the field, which is composed not of fully settled practices and firmly established policies but rather of competing actors and ongoing struggles, often with delicately balanced forces and power ratios whose equilibria are subject to change.
> . . . A greater emphasis on these ongoing "counter-doxic" struggles,

and upon the distributions of power and prestige that sustain them, would have provided not just a fuller sense of the present, but also a more adequate basis for thinking about future possibilities.[19]

Garland is right that focusing on contestation illuminates less powerful actors and policies that lose out in the political arena. But insufficient concentration on diverse actors and conflict also is why Garland and others[20] see sudden rupture where we and others do not.[21]

In sum, we view several interrelated problems with the pendulum metaphor and analyses that employ pendular logic:

(1) *Rupture*: The notion of rupture assumes that one criminal justice regime is replaced wholesale with another.[22] This logic is most pronounced in discussions of the fall of rehabilitation and rise of "tough on crime" during the last several decades of the twentieth century. Yet, this "before and after" tale is inaccurate: rehabilitative programming, for example, did not vanish as a result of a "punitive turn." Research shows instead that punishment is "braided" (alternatively called "variegated," "assembled," or "hybridized"), combining various penal logics and practices as actors build on and adapt what came before.[23] The rupture framework hinders us from asking *how* and *why* the logics and practices of punishment morph—distorting the processes of historical development, focusing too much on the period of transformation, ignoring antecedent processes that facilitate change, and often mistaking radical shifts in *rhetoric* for radical shifts in *practice*.[24]

(2) *Mechanical*: A pendulum moves back and forth, driven by internal energy. There is no contingency, no variation, no struggle. Descriptions of penal change (especially those that employ the pendulum metaphor) advance this mechanistic view. Shifts in crime, sensibilities, labor markets, and other structural factors produce predictable, major changes in criminal justice. As explained in the following section, we agree that macro-level developments affect penal outcomes but argue that punishment does not change mechanically. People and organizations make it move.

(3) *Homogeneity*: There is a tendency to treat American criminal justice as a monolithic "system" and to describe penal trends as national and system-wide. These national-level analyses highlight trends that are very important, and they illuminate broad shifts in rhetoric, logic, and practice. However, views of penal homogeneity (perhaps especially in the United States) obscure variation across and within regions and states. Research demonstrates that there are major differences across states, in areas such

as imprisonment rates, sentencing policies, community supervision rates, probation and parole revocation rates, and spending on corrections.[25] Pendulum views gloss over these and other variations—after all, there is only *one* pendulum—and reinforce the false notion that there is *a* criminal justice system that swings, as a unit, between punishment, rehabilitation, or some other dominant orientation. In doing so, they ignore and fail to explain critical differentiation.

## *An Agonistic Perspective*

This book offers an alternative vision of penal development that we believe is more accurate and useful. Our agonistic perspective consists of a set of principles (or axioms) that seek to remedy the problems outlined above. We use the adjective "agonistic" because it simultaneously refers to competition, striving, and combative behavior—all of which are central to our view of penal development. In this section, we lay out this perspective's key elements, which will guide our analytical history in chapters 2 through 5.

It is important to first note that other scholars also emphasize the importance of politics, actors, and struggle in understanding the unfolding of criminal justice. For example, criminologists Ian Loader and Richard Sparks argue, "A properly historical sociology of the crime control field would . . . seek to discern the intentions of the array of actors—politicians, civil servants, practitioners, campaigners, think tanks, editorialists, social scientists—who struggle to shape the contours of crime control and criminal justice."[26] They then "insist upon a method that sees political *combat* as pivotal in determining the character of crime control under late modern conditions, rather than epiphenomenal to the master patterns of structural change."[27] Although they may not argue as forcefully as Loader and Sparks (or us, for that matter) about the centrality of struggle, a host of other scholars show that contestation within and beyond the political and penal fields drives the unfolding of criminal justice (albeit within concrete social-structural contexts, as we explain below).[28] Our agonistic perspective should be viewed as part of a collective effort to highlight and understand the role of contestation in transformations of penal orientations, policies, and practices.

The agonistic framework centers on the following axiom: *Penal development is the product of struggle between actors with different types and amounts of power.* Throughout the book, we use the terms "struggle" and "contestation" synonymously. We periodically use the term "conflict" when discussing struggle of a distinctly contentious nature (that is, where there is heated confrontation). However, as we discuss in this section, not all struggle is explicitly conflictual (as when academics engage in symbolic struggle to define the nature and consequences of social problems such as crime). In short, we do not assume that struggle is openly antagonistic.

Drawing on the work of Pierre Bourdieu, we view struggle as endemic to social life. Bourdieu's collaborator, Loïc Wacquant, writes of the late sociologist's agonistic social ontology:

> Like Max Weber, Bourdieu's vision of society is fundamentally agonistic: for him, the social universe is the site of endless and pitiless competition, in and through which arise the differences that are the stuff and stake of social existence. Contention, not stasis, is the ubiquitous feature of collective life that his varied inquiries aim at making at once visible and intelligible. Struggle, not "reproduction," is the master metaphor at the core of his thought.[29]

Bourdieu argues that social actors compete to accumulate and employ resources to advance their positions in organizations and fields and to impose or support their particular visions of how things should be.[30] Drawing on this view, we propose that individuals and organizations that operate within and beyond the penal field struggle over status and the ability to define and implement their conceptions of justice.[31]

Criminal justice is replete with struggle, in part, because punishment (by definition) demands that people succumb to coercive pressures—this is true whether the state sentences a person to pay a fine, go to treatment, or serve a prison, jail, or probation term. Struggle is particularly evident inside prisons, which impose severe deprivations (most notably, the deprivation of liberty).[32] Contrary to classic studies and popular thinking, prisons are not "total institutions" that thoroughly discipline individuals and crush individuality. Prisoners often struggle—sometimes implicitly and quietly, sometimes explicitly and loudly—to assert autonomy, obtain goods and services, have intimate relations, and protest conditions of confinement.[33] As we show in later chapters, collective action, individual refusals, and other acts of contestation within penal institutions can have major effects on the development of criminal justice.

The modernization of punishment in the United States and other industrialized democracies has contributed greatly to the persistence and intensity of struggle. (As discussed in chapter 3, for instance, the process of rationalization accelerated greatly during the Progressive Era with the diversification, centralization, and professionalization of criminal justice.) Drawing on the work of Max Weber, Garland links rationalization and struggle, noting that as more of those involved in criminal justice are paid professionals (embedded in various bureaucracies), so too is there "an elaborate division of labour . . . in which specialized agencies and functionaries carve up the various tasks of penological work, often coming into conflict with one another in the process." The end result is "a complex, differentiated process, involving a series of agencies, each displaying a distinctive set of concerns and objectives, and often drawing upon different sources of social support."[34] Modernization, then, has produced a diversified field with numerous positions that ensures constant struggle over the purpose, character, and implementation of penal policies and programs.

There are a couple of factors that make criminal justice in the United States especially contested. The federalist structure facilitates struggle because policy is made and implemented at the national, state, and local levels.[35] There is often contestation both between and within jurisdictions, which tend to have unique cultures, institutional arrangements, and histories of intergroup relations (this is especially true when we consider variation across states). We see this in the extreme when the federal government attempts to impose (via legislation, funding mandates, or Supreme Court decisions) policy changes on states that disagree with the changes, as well as when counties and cities subvert the intent of state laws or administrative mandates.[36]

The relatively democratic and political nature of penal policymaking in this country also facilitates struggle. Whereas western European countries have professional, somewhat buffered processes for making sentencing law, selecting judges and prosecutors, and deciding similarly important justice issues, the United States (with some variation across states) typically leaves these matters to legislators, executives (e.g., governors, mayors, or presidents), or citizens (via ballot initiatives or popular vote).[37] This relatively open system of decision making invites high-stakes struggle among interest groups, political parties, and grassroots organizations.[38] And research shows that the presence of well-organized and well-financed interest groups motivates and enhances the political salience of and conflict over criminal justice issues.[39] Highly politicized decision making can (and often does) produce policies that put major constraints on the people and organizations responsible for carrying out those directives; therefore, penal actors often subvert the intention of policies for practical reasons—that is, so that they can do their jobs as they understand them.[40] Of course, they may also oppose and subvert directives on ideological grounds.

As should already be clear, we conceive of struggle broadly.[41] Most obviously, struggle refers to *conventional political behavior* such as lobbying, contributing campaign funds, door knocking, phone banking, coalition building, informational pickets, and rallies. It also includes *subversion*—that is, patterned refusal to implement or adhere to policies and programs or implementation of mandates in ways that pervert or reject their original intent (thus potentially undermining the policies). We emphasize "patterned" subversion because individual acts of subversion may cause friction, but they generally do not produce serious changes in criminal justice regimes.[42] However, individual acts of subversion may lead to collective action that does shake up the status quo and produce transformations.

Struggle also may take the form of *disruption*. Political scientist Frances Fox Piven argues that society is organized "through networks of specialized and interdependent activities. . . . Networks of cooperation and interdependence inevitably give rise to contention, to conflict, as people bound together by social life try to use each other to further their often distinctive interests and outlooks." These interdependencies "generate widespread power capacities to act on these distinctive interests and outlooks." Disruption occurs when subordinate actors withdraw cooperation, refusing to follow the script and do "their part."[43] Examples include work strikes, prison riots, boycotts, and hunger strikes. Disruption upsets "a pattern of ongoing and institutionalized cooperation" and forces those in power to respond with meaningful action (typically concessions, repression, or a combination of the two).[44]

*Symbolic struggle* is also central to our view of contestation. Bourdieu and Wacquant argue, "Classes and other antagonistic social collectivities are continually engaged in a struggle to impose the definition of the world that is most congruent with their interests." [45] This is certainly true of punishment: actors struggle to shape ideas, collective representations, and sentiments about crime, punishment, and related issues. As Loader and Sparks argue, "certain key terms of political discourse—order, authority, liberty, justice—are mobilized in such struggles . . . disputes over criminal justice encode in miniature a wider contest between . . . visions of how the good society should be organized and governed."[46] So, for example, social scientists fight to enhance the legitimacy of "evidence-based practices" and to gain power to implement their ideas in penal institutions. In this view, even scientific enterprises that claim objectivity can become political weapons in contests over penal policy. Much of the struggle in this area takes place at the level of representation.[47]

Since it encompasses many strategies, the struggle over criminal justice includes a diversity of actors (the particular array depends on the specific struggle). But these actors are not equally equipped to participate or ulti-mately prevail in competitions over penal outcomes. Individuals and groups have different amounts and compositions of resources. Which types of resources are most useful will depend on the type of struggle: economic capi-tal, for example, is very important in struggles over ballot initiatives that deal with sentencing policies. Political capital is essential when trying to pass penal policy in legislatures. And cultural capital is useful when fighting battles at the level of public opinion. Axes of inequality (e.g., race, gender, sexuality, and immigration status) greatly affect the hierarchical distribution of capital and, therefore, actors' capacity to shape penal outcomes.

The penal game is tilted toward those with the most resources and the greatest desire to maintain the status quo (the "incumbents") and away from actors with fewer resources who seek to reform or radically alter existing prac-tice (the "challengers").[48] As actors achieve dominance, their policies produce "feedback effects" that tend to entrench their positions.[49] For example, when politicians created parole and probation in the early 1900s, they simultane-ously created groups of workers (probation and parole officers) who devel-oped professional associations and struggled to advance their professions. This feedback effect strengthened the hand of actors who wanted to maintain and extend community corrections.[50]

Elites in the penal field also benefit from what Bourdieu calls "symbolic power." Incumbents use their dominant positions to define issues and con-strict possible alternatives to addressing them. Here we are reminded of E. E. Schattschneider's famous claim: "*The definition of the alternatives is the supreme instrument of power*; the antagonists can rarely agree on what the issues are because power is involved in the definition. [She] who determines what pol-itics is about runs the country, because the definition of alternatives is the choice of conflicts, and the choice of conflicts allocates power."[51] Symbolic power is the capacity to define what is possible about a given issue and to force players in the game to conceive of issues with a limited set of categories. So, after World War II, when correctionalists cemented their privileged positions in certain states, actors increasingly felt pressure to characterize penal policies and programs as "rehabilitative." Similarly, in the 1980s and 1990s, as retribu-tivists gained power across the United States, actors increasingly highlighted the punitive qualities of policies, even those that sought to shrink the penal system or spread rehabilitation (e.g., drug courts). This power of incumbents to define "reality" puts challengers at a severe disadvantage.

Incumbents' accrued advantages help explain why major changes in crim-inal justice occur over extended periods of time (a fact that rupture narratives distort). Struggles over punishment are long and laborious, and challengers often feel like they are pushing Sisyphus's boulder up the hill. Nevertheless, tireless contestation often pays off over the long haul. It creates fissures in the penal landscape that help generate larger shifts under the right conditions. Likewise, we demonstrate that struggle is a major cause of variegation—the mixing and meshing of penal logics and practices. Through political mobilization and subversive acts, challengers routinely rework and reroute criminal justice directives and programs.

The second axiom of our agonistic perspective builds on the first: *Contestation over how (and who) to punish is constant; consensus over penal orientations is illusory.* There is a tendency to describe periods of general consensus over penal orientations and practices, and, conversely, to make a case for periods of major transformation. We argue that even in times where the penal landscape seems settled (that is, when a criminal justice regime appears stable), consensus is illusory. Even when there is not open "warfare" and one side appears to have "won," opponents of the status quo continue their efforts to shape public and political opinion in ways that favor their positions. Perhaps more provocatively, we contend that this subterranean struggle is critical in shaping criminal justice regimes and paving the road for the next penal pivot.

A further complication is that powerful actors supporting winning policies in one era may be weaker actors supporting fading policies in another, but those stances and their champions do not simply appear and disappear. Imagine a series of regular snapshots showing only the dominant players and practices: actors and their favored practices would seem to pop into focus and then disappear almost as suddenly. The evidence from case studies suggests otherwise: groups and ideas dominant at one time almost always existed earlier but occupied less powerful positions (perhaps these would be the people in the back row of the photo). Likewise, when groups lose some of their power, they rarely disappear—they are pushed to the edge of the frame. To see the proper nature of the field and the role of actors requires studying each frame more carefully, looking beyond dominant actors, and stringing frames together such that shifts can be identified more accurately.

Our third and final axiom relates our perspective back to the macro-level theorizing about national and international trends that shape criminal justice: *Large-scale trends in the economy, politics, social sentiments, intergroup relations, demographics, and crime affect (or condition)—but do not determine—struggles over punishment and, ultimately, penal outcomes.* As sociologists argue, agents construct social reality, but they do so within particular structural contexts.[52] Objective conditions impinge on our "freedom" to shape the social world. Macro-level theorists of punishment astutely identify structural factors that contribute greatly to penal trends. These conditions, however, do not directly shape punishment; they are filtered through national, state, or local penal fields.[53] They are also filtered through organizations, which can be viewed as mini-fields.[54] Struggle can be thought of as nested, with social-structural conditions filtering first through fields (e.g., penal, political, bureaucratic, and juridical) and then through organizations (e.g., departments of corrections, state legislatures, and court systems). This axiom forces us to analyze contestation on the ground, and within the context of large-scale social processes that shrink or expand opportunities for transformation and affect the shape of struggle.[55]

Along with social-structural developments that typically build over a long period of time, critical events and processes also affect the nature and outcomes of struggle. Here we are thinking of wars, economic depressions, heinous crimes that help spawn moral panics, massive shake-ups in Congress or state legislatures, major judicial decisions, and acts of terrorism. Events can provide "windows of opportunities" for subordinate actors to improve their positions in the penal and political fields. They may also reinforce dominant actors' power, as when moral panics about violent crime in the 1990s helped governors, district attorneys, and law enforcement leaders pass sentencing laws consistent with their "law and order" perspectives and interests.[56] As detailed in following chapters, contingent events (like social-structural developments) have been instrumental in shaping struggle over criminal justice regimes.

THE AGONISTIC PERSPECTIVE we propose helps account for the somewhat cyclical nature of penal development. Contrary to the pendulum model, however, we do not view punishment as *ever* "swinging back" to a previous penal approach. Struggles over criminal justice produce new and different configurations of thought and practice, but old ideas and practices are regularly recycled (even if they are adapted to fit current preferences and contexts). Instead of simply declaring *that* recycling occurs (or claiming that one or several social forces causes it), our framework also tries to explain *why* penal "reforms" are often resurrected and reshaped from previous eras.

As suggested above, advocates of particular penal orientations do not simply go away once their preferred penal perspective falls out of favor. They keep struggling. In criminal justice, the opposition is never vanquished—but it may be forced into abeyance and reinvention.[57] By suggesting that there are wholesale transformations in criminal justice regimes, the pendulum model obscures the extent to which the old guard continues to fight and influence criminal justice regimes; it is this fighting that perpetuates the unsettled and kaleidoscopic nature of punishment—which the pendulum model also misses. Similarly, categorizing a period as simply "rehabilitative," "punitive," "managerial," or something else masks ongoing struggles by groups that are active but currently lack the power and opportunities needed to institute their vision of penal change.

Breaking the pendulum means disposing with a popular, intrinsically satisfying way of representing change in criminal justice. Therefore, we propose an alternative metaphor, which we hope is useful—albeit more complicated. The agonistic process we propose is somewhat analogous to *plate tectonics*: As tectonic plates in the earth constantly rub against each other, they produce varying degrees of friction and occasional dramatic shifts. The settling of the earth represents a dominant orientation in criminal justice.[58] By this, we mean that criminal justice professionals and scholars describe punishment as predominantly reformative, punitive, or managerial (or a combination of these orientations). The dominant orientation is the *prevailing representation* of criminal justice. For example, after World War II, prison administrators, journalists, and academics represented criminal justice as "corrections" (and renamed prisons as "correctional institutions," prison officers as "correctional officers," and community supervision as "community corrections"). However, dominant orientations (like "settled" earth) hide fissures and building pressure. The reality of criminal justice regimes is far more complex and differentiated than it may appear on the surface, and it differs from place to place, just as the ground beneath us is uneven and quietly moving. Like the earth's plates, criminal justice is never permanently settled; it is always changing, however subtly and slowly.

Like the rubbing of tectonic plates, individuals, groups, and organizations that struggle over punishment constantly bump up against the ideologies and practices of others; there is continual (though sometimes low-impact and low-visibility) friction as well as occasional explosive conflict over how to prevent and respond to crime and criminals. Furthermore, just as major earthquakes are simultaneously dramatic *and* foregrounded by many smaller seismic events, so too is penal change both the product of an immediate set of catalysts (including contemporaneous struggles in other arenas and locales)[59] and the result of struggles with long historical roots.[60] And, like earthquakes, major changes in criminal justice often have ripple effects in other locales.

It is important that we note what the agonistic perspective is *not*. Ours is a mid-level account of *how* and *why* penal practices change in given times and places through the lens of contestation. The result is a richer picture of criminal justice and the actors, ideas, and contexts that shape it. We are interested, for example, in how the social, political, and economic contexts of the Progressive Era provided actors opportunities and challenges during that period and how the resulting conflicts shaped penal practices later. What we do not provide is a grand narrative about why those larger contexts shifted in the ways they did at those moments (e.g., the account of late modernity provided by David Garland's *Culture of Control*). Nor is our account one in which we "prove" one social-structural account over another (e.g., Durkheimian vs. Marxist theories). *Breaking the Pendulum* is designed to take these lessons and augment (rather than replace) them by highlighting the struggle that shapes penal outcomes—the deep, long-term shifts, grinding, and upheaval that reshape the landscape of punishment in small and large ways.

## *The Terrain*

In developing *Breaking the Pendulum*, we had to make some hard choices regarding the terrain to cover. To keep the manuscript concise and accessible, we settled on several boundaries. First, we focus on adult criminal justice and discuss the juvenile system only in passing. Although we are confident that our perspective applies to juvenile justice, extending our analysis to the youth system (which displays a distinct historical trajectory) would necessitate two parallel narratives and a much longer text. Second, we concentrate on punishment in the United States. Although criminal justice in this country has similar features to systems in other regions of the world (especially Canada, the U.K., and western Europe), punishment in the United States is unique enough historically, structurally, and culturally to warrant its own analysis. As outlined in the conclusion, we hope that scholars will employ the agonistic perspective to analyze penal development outside the United States.

A third, softer boundary is that we focus disproportionately on sentencing law and three institutions: prisons, probation, and parole (the three Ps), which are the main forms of punishment for felons in the United States.[61] The pendulum metaphor has most commonly been used in relationship to prisons, and the vast majority of scholarship focuses on penal institutions (especially prisons). This means that the research we are drawing on (and our focus) is skewed first toward studies of imprisonment and second toward analyses of probation and parole. However, we seek to include enough examples beyond sentencing and the three Ps to justify our claim that the book is about "criminal justice."

Like the book's focus, the state and local punishment examples we draw on are selective. Our goal is to build from existing case study research to demonstrate the value of our agonistic approach (and the limitations of the pendulum perspective).[62] In each chapter, we begin by reviewing the "standard narrative" about the period. We then turn to case studies, documenting variation to make a larger point about that historical moment. In most chapters, we begin by examining a case that is seen as "ground zero" for the era in question—for example, New York during the Progressive Era, California during the 1950s and 1960s, or Arizona during the 1990s—and show how even in these idealized locations, the rhetoric and practices were much more complex than pendulum perspectives suggest. We then consider a counter-example such as Texas during the Progressive Era—that shows how the dominant orientation influenced criminal justice in that time and place, and reveals some limits of the standard narrative.[63] In doing so, we highlight and help explain the variation seen across the country. Throughout the case studies, we describe how different configurations of local and state-level actors within and beyond the penal field struggled in the context of changing social circumstances to shape penal practices.

The following five chapters put our agonistic perspective to work. Chapter 2 analyzes the development of the "penitentiary ideal" and the battles over imprisonment in the North and the South. It shows that elites with an array of resources, in the context of widespread social anxiety about dramatic societal transformations, overcame opposition from less powerful competitors who viewed the prison as anti-republican, anti-labor, and anti-religion. We highlight the role of struggle and local culture in circumscribing the penitentiary ideal and braiding punishment. The chapter concludes that the decline of the penitentiary ideal was not a sudden rupture, but a subtle shift in the penal landscape. The onset of the Civil War would further entrench that penal pivot.

Chapter 3 focuses on criminal justice during the Gilded Age and Progressive Era, arguing first that progressive punishment did not arise mechanically or represent an immediate, all-encompassing break from the past. It shows that a range of actors fought in the Gilded Age against harsh, exploitative penal practices, producing major fissures in the penal terrain. Macro-level changes in the early twentieth century produced political openings for competitors to spread what became known as the "new penology," designed both to reform and repress. The chapter then turns to case studies of New York and Texas, showing that national and local factors shaped the nature of struggle in those states, and, consequently, the scope, character, and timing of "progressive" punishment.

Chapter 4 focuses on the struggle for "correctionalist" criminal justice in the decades following the Second World War. It shows that social-structural developments provided critical opportunities for correctionalists—who, along with a range of other actors, had fought against harsh, exploitative punishment in the interwar years—to gain power at the national level and within individual states. In California, widely understood as the epicenter of the rehabilitative ideal, correctionalists faced intense opposition that limited their success and created enormous friction that would later fuel the Golden State's establishment of a more punitive and managerial penal regime. The chapter ends with analysis of Florida, showing that influential actors there strategically employed the rhetoric of rehabilitation to bureaucratize and professionalize criminal justice. Although states such as Florida did not substantially implement the socio-medical model of rehabilitation, their use of correctionalist *language* helps us understand claims that the rehabilitative ideal dominated penal practice during this period.

Chapter 5 argues that the significant changes to criminal justice in the later part of the twentieth century (such as the rise of mass imprisonment) were not the product of sudden rupture. Macro-level developments created opportunities for previously subordinate actors to enact reforms that fueled the development of a larger, harsher carceral state. The chapter then shows that the story of wholesale transformation from a relatively lenient, rehabilitative criminal justice to one that was harsh and exclusively punitive (or managerial) is misleading; this period was marked, instead, by the repackaging and reformulating of existing penal logics and practices. Rehabilitation did not die off; it transformed, becoming increasingly neo-liberal and neo-conservative as actors worked to keep their correctionalist vision alive.

Further, we argue that throughout the 1980s and 1990s and into the early twenty-first century, actors struggled against the hardening of punishment in areas such as sentencing laws and the expanding use of solitary confinement. Contestation produced fissures that expanded as the economy tanked, crime rates steadily declined, and politicians on both sides of the aisle embraced reform. The campaign to reform the Rockefeller Drug Laws in New York provides a case study for how this process unfolded. We conclude that while major reforms are reshaping punishment in the 2010s, there is no consensus on rolling back the carceral state. In addition, some of the strategic decisions made to undercut harsh penal policies in earlier years (such as the policy emphasis on low-level drug offenders) now make it difficult to achieve major transformations.

The concluding chapter explores the implications of the agonistic perspective for teachers, researchers, practitioners, and activists. We focus in particular on how the agonistic perspective can help us to see the possibilities and limitations of present-day reform efforts in the United States, as well as how our perspective might inform related topics and penal developments in other countries. The book ends on an encouraging note, arguing that struggle matters greatly in determining the shape and outcome of criminal justice. Ultimately, the pendulum model is disempowering. The following statement, made in 1989 by legendary penal reformer Jerome Miller, captures this sentiment:

> Rehabilitation is, for the most part, now absent from contemporary American corrections. Harsher sentences, warehouse prisons, and corrections establishment which militantly rejects the idea of salvaging offenders has become the rule of the land. We must now wait for the swing of the pendulum. I fear it will be a long wait.[64]

What Miller neglected to recognize was that people and organizations were *not* waiting. At the local, state, and national levels, they were fighting against the growth and hardening of punishment. In fact, Miller and the organization he co-founded the National Center on Institutions and Alternatives, were at the forefront of that struggle. People always struggle, and struggle shapes penal development. But because it takes years—sometimes even decades— for results to materialize, scholars, pundits, and even activists downplay the importance of contestation. *Breaking the Pendulum* seeks to right that wrong.

## 2

## *The Pain of Penitence in the Early Republic*

IN MOST ACCOUNTS, the first major swing of the penal pendulum occurred in the late eighteenth or early nineteenth century as the country increasingly replaced corporal and capital punishments with imprisonment. In practice, this meant states would now seek to "correct" convicted felons, not just punish them. Serving their sentences in silence, prisoners would pay penance (hence the name "penitentiary"), while hard work, personal reflection, and moral guidance would mold well-ordered men out of ill-disciplined ruffians.[1] This vision of reform was the "penitentiary ideal."

Incarceration was not entirely new: it had existed in the United States and Europe well before the penitentiary ideal took hold. During the colonial era, when public shaming, physical punishments such as flogging, and execution were the primary means of criminal sanction, localities used jails (sometimes called "prisons") as a form of containment to hold debtors, vagrants, witnesses, the condemned, and petty offenders. It was not until after the American Revolution that imprisonment became a bona fide penal sanction.

The turn *toward* imprisonment was simultaneously a turn *away* from corporal and capital punishment. For many contemporary American elites, sanguinary punishments smacked of a monarchial despotism unseemly to their newly established democracy. Public displays of brute, physical force produced political and social problems, as commoners increasingly identified with the punished rather than the punishers.[2] Moreover, judges and juries became reluctant to send low-level offenders to the stocks, pillories, whipping posts, or gallows.[3] This uneven, irrational application of punishment undercut justice and government authority (as well as individuals' attachment to the law) and seemed to enable crime more than prevent it.

Inspired by Enlightenment thinkers such as Cesare Beccaria and Jean-Jacques Rousseau, leaders in the United States such as Benjamin Rush and Thomas Jefferson advocated new penal codes to eliminate excessively brutal punishments.[4] Although it seemed merciful by comparison, incarceration was a serious punishment, depriving individuals of perhaps the most fundamental value of the new republic: liberty. Legislatures could calibrate prison terms to correspond to the perceived severity of crimes and the perceived culpability of those who committed the acts, making punishment appear more proportionate, just, and rational (all important Enlightenment ideals).[5] The penitentiary thus represented the government's commitment to "non-violent, regulated, uniform" punishment doled out in a "controlled and lawful manner," and demonstrated that the state would hold up its side of the tenuous social contract of the new country.[6]

Reformers, most notably surgeon and "founding father" Rush, also believed that imprisonment could *reform* criminals into well-ordered citizens, thereby strengthening the young, democratic nation. As legal historian Lawrence Friedman notes, "a republican society had different needs and demands: self-discipline, moderation, sobriety."[7] In theory, sequestered within a "house of repentance," convicts would peer into their souls and repent for their sins. Communication between convicts would be forbidden—both to facilitate reflection and avoid cross-contamination, as it were. Working long hours, prisoners would learn discipline and indirectly help pay for their own incarceration. Through this almost monastic process, criminals would become industrious citizens with deep humility and respect for religious and secular authority.

Acknowledging the major changes in penal rhetoric and practice that occurred in the late 1700s through the mid-1800s, this chapter challenges the commonly held view of a radical swing of the penal pendulum between the Revolutionary and Civil Wars. As we have already begun to argue, ignoring contestation obscures variability and leads us to misrepresent both *how* and *why* change happens. As in other eras, we see significant, ongoing contestation as well as considerable variability across place and time.

First we examine the development of the penitentiary ideal and early attempts to implement it, in what sociologist Ashley Rubin refers to as "proto-prisons."[8] We show that imprisonment (more precisely, the deprivation of liberty as a primary means of punishment) was borne of considerable social anxiety and a search for order in a fledgling federalist republic. In this struggle, actors with extensive social, cultural, and political resources overcame significant opposition from less well-equipped and less organized competitors who viewed imprisonment as anti-republican, anti-labor, and antireligious. Even as one side seemingly "won," major conflict inside and outside the proto-prisons severely limited implementation of the ideal and the early penitentiaries came to be viewed as polluted sites that produced disorder, rather than reformed citizens.[9]

The second section demonstrates that Jacksonian-Era reformers and their political allies did not give up the struggle for reformative criminal justice; instead, they skillfully took advantage of continued social upheaval to resuscitate and expand the penitentiary ideal. Despite the failure of proto-prisons, elite reformers such as Rush argued that "real" penitentiaries would live up to their promise to instill order in a chaotic republic. This struggle ultimately led to the establishment of two competing models of imprisonment: the "solitary system" in Pennsylvania and the "congregate system" in New York. Digging into the epic battle between the systems' respective proponents, we show that the models (and their particular visions of the penitentiary ideal) developed in competition and in response to pressures inside and outside the prisons. Contestation shaped these famous prisons from their outset.

The third section shows that even at Eastern State Penitentiary in Philadelphia (the symbolic heart of the solitary model), practice quickly diverged from lofty rhetoric, as subversion inside the walls and ongoing struggles across political and class lines outside the walls took their tolls. Operations at New York's Auburn prison also changed in response to strident opposition, especially from free laborers and their supporters. In the decades leading up to the Civil War, penitentiaries everywhere began to merge in their practice: economic exploitation and secure control won through brutal repression of prisoners.

In the fourth section, we travel south to investigate whether and how the penitentiary ideal spread in the slave states. By 1860, many southern states (Georgia, Alabama, Mississippi, Louisiana, Texas, Tennessee, Kentucky, Missouri, Arkansas, and Virginia) had built congregate-style penitentiaries. These set out to discipline criminals and communicate progress and "civility" in the face of claims that the southern states were "backward."[10] Governors and state legislators led the push for modern imprisonment in the Confederacy, overcoming opposition from fellow politicians, religious leaders, free workers, and print media. Moreover, because the penitentiary ideal applied specifically to white men (especially younger white men), southern states' adoption of modern prisons reinforced, rather than undercut, white privilege and the exploitation of black labor.

We conclude that the decline of the penitentiary ideal was no earthquake, but instead, a shift in the surface of the penal landscape. Racism, sexism, classism, and intense opposition from political, religious, labor, and humanitarian actors (not to mention prisoners) had limited implementation of the ideal from the start (even where it supposedly was strongest). With the onset of the Civil War, that shift toward prisons designed to control, exploit the labor of, and warehouse criminals would become even more fully entrenched.

## Proto-prisons in a New Nation

On March 9, 1787, Benjamin Rush attended a meeting of the "Society for Promoting Political Inquiries" at the Philadelphia home of Benjamin Franklin. At this gathering of influential locals committed to exploring "new modes of governance in a republican setting,"[11] Rush presented a passionately reasoned critique of the death penalty and other public punishments. After detailing the individual and social harms caused by executions, public hard labor, communal whippings, and the like, Rush sketched an enlightened alternative: incarceration in "houses of repentance."

Assuring his compatriots that he had no desire to abolish punishments, Rush proclaimed, "I wish only to change the *place* and manner of inflicting them, so as to render them effectual for the reformation of criminals and beneficial to society."[12] According to Rush's vision (which drew inspiration from British reformer John Howard), incarceration would "consist of BODILY PAIN LABOUR, WATCHFULNESS, SOLITUDE, and SILENCE," "joined with CLEANLINESS and a SIMPLE DIET." To "render these physical remedies more effectual," they would "be accompanied by regular instruction in the principles and obligations of religion."[13] Imprisonment, then, would serve the utilitarian goals of reforming criminals and generating revenue for the state (through prisoners' hard labor).

Rush's vision was not one of a gentler, softer punishment. The renowned physician asserted, "personal liberty is so dear to all men that loss of it, for an indefinite time, is a punishment so severe that death has often been preferred to it." He believed that hard labor, anxiety, loneliness, and austerity in the "abode of misery" would both inspire reform and deter future crime.[14] Physical and psychological pain, in Rush's vision, paved a path toward personal and social betterment. Imprisonment would restore "the vicious part of mankind to virtue and happiness" and eliminate "a portion of vice from the world." Whereas public punishments "leave scars which disfigure the whole character," reformation through incarceration would wash away the stain of crime.[15]

Once reformed, former prisoners would reenter the community as full members of the body politic. Rush imagined intimate reentry reunions:

> Methinks I already hear the inhabitants of our villages and townships counting the years that shall complete the reformation of one of their citizens. I behold them running to meet him on the day of his deliverance. His friends and family bathe his cheeks with tears of joy; and the universal shout of the neighborhood is, "This our brother was lost as is found—was dead, and is alive."[16]

Rather than hang or suffer public humiliation, criminals would be born again in the privacy of prisons.

Rush's vision of penitential justice (and the movement to transform punishment that it would inspire) reflected and bolstered emerging conceptions of social ills and their remedies. Historian Michael Meranze explains:

> Whether the target was poverty, criminality, delinquency, prostitution, or idleness, reformers and officials believed that social problems could best be contained through the transformation of individual character, that individual character could best be transformed through the careful supervision of individual regimen, and that the supervision of individual regimen could best take place within an environment where time and space were carefully regulated. These *laboratories of virtue* . . . sought to inculcate the habits of labor, personal restraint, and submission to the law. . . . Penitentiaries were only the most fearsome embodiment of a widespread strategy to regulate and regularize moral life and create citizens and workers for the new liberal, capitalist societies of the nineteenth century.[17]

The penitential ideal developed, then, as part of a larger strategy of governance: the new democracy required a disciplined, self-monitored, and productive citizenry; prisons would help build it.

In the month following Franklin's gathering, Rush's essay was published as a pamphlet. A new reform organization, the Philadelphia Society for Alleviating the Miseries of Public Prisons, led efforts to institute Rush's vision. Heavily influenced by the Quaker faith and American Enlightenment, the Society "fused Christian charity and political advocacy."[18] The organization of distinguished Philadelphians achieved a major victory when, in 1790, the Pennsylvania legislature authorized the restructuring of the Walnut Street Jail into the nation's first "house of penitence."[19]

Walnut Street was the country's first genuine state prison, designed to confine prisoners sentenced to incarceration (rather than death or corporeal punishment).[20] Surely to Rush's great pleasure, offenders were sent to the facility for hard labor. They were to work silently as a means of reformation (and to pay for the facility's upkeep) and to spend time alone reflecting on their immoral behavior. Unlike earlier jails, Walnut Street also sought to classify and separate criminals according to sex, age, sentence length, and criminality. The system was designed to keep the prisoners from "contaminating" one another.

Reformation was the watchword at Walnut Street. By the "labor of the hardest and most servile kind" (in the words of Pennsylvania law), convicts were to be taught a lesson, and their toil would ease the burden of their sin.[21] Imprisonment now sought to change wayward boys and men into reliable workers and, by extension, "good citizens." There was to be both reform *and* punishment at Walnut Street and later prisons built in its image. Indeed, what scholars now artificially separate into "rehabilitation" versus "punishment," "treatment" versus "incapacitation," or "reform" versus "retribution" practices were understood at the time as inseparable goals. Not only was it clear to many reformers at the time that *multiple* impulses animated imprisonment, it was also believed that punishment and reform ought to work together in producing the disciplined worker-citizens needed in a liberal republic.[22]

Following Pennsylvania's lead, 17 other states (throughout the North and the South) authorized houses of penitence that resembled Walnut Street's intent and organization.[23] By 1810, imprisonment was a common penal sanction,[24] but these proto-prisons were far from Rush's ideal. In fact, they failed in almost every imaginable way. First, they did not keep convicts separate or silent. Walnut Street, for example, used its mere 16 solitary rooms for punishing (not reforming) recalcitrant prisoners.[25] Even though reformers had wanted desperately to avoid the spread of vice (what Meranze calls "mimetic corruption"), illicit activity was common.[26] Prisoners worked, slept, and ate in large open spaces and communicated at will. Life on the inside was unstructured and disorderly. Second, despite the invention of ingenious, often cruel technologies such as the original treadmill (on which prisoners were forced to walk for hours, grinding grain as they plodded), early penitentiaries failed to instill industriousness among the vast majority of prisoners. "Convicts worked slowly and sloppily, shirking whenever they could," historian David

Rothman explains. "Lacking incentive and close supervision, they were neither reliable nor efficient."[27]

Subversion and disruption were rampant. Convicts set fires, escaped, rioted (or "mutinied," as the early republican press described the uprisings), sabotaged machinery, and went on periodic labor strikes. Sometimes hostages were taken, and sometimes militias stepped in to restore order.[28] Guards, who generally did not adopt the lofty republic-building rhetoric of the penitentiary ideal, often fell back on the corporal punishments imprisonment had allegedly replaced—including whipping and restraining disorderly prisoners.[29]

Opposition to reformatory imprisonment came from outside the facilities as well. Religious fundamentalists "charged that incarceration offended morality because it presumed to operate upon souls of mortals. The spiritual work of curing and cleansing souls was—and ought to be—strictly reserved to the Lord of God."[30] Free laborers argued that the new system was just another form of involuntary servitude that might be expanded to them.[31] They challenged the claim that penitentiary justice was republican: it seemed that locking people up and forcing them to work for the state was fundamentally anti-democratic, even tyrannical.

By the late 1810s, the penitentiary movement was in a deep crisis of legitimacy.[32] The facilities suffered poor management, technical limitations, and inadequate organizational structures (for example, a lack of solitary cells). Worse still, there was evidence at Walnut Street and its offshoots that the penitentiary ideal was being sabotaged from the inside out—by those guards who reverted to corporal punishment, among others. In a statement that exemplifies the agonistic perspective, historian Rebecca McLennan explains, "What is critical to grasp is that the administration of the penitentiary was, in large part, 'ineffective' because convicts, families, friends, workmates, the keepers, and even some of the higher ranking administrators to whom lawmakers entrusted the running of the penitential system were able to, and did in fact, render it so."[33] Partially in response to these problems, elites increasingly believed that the proto-prisons were criminogenic—despite their intentions, the facilities actually *produced* crime and disorder by promoting bonds among prisoners that fortified antisocial attitudes and sharpened illicit skills.[34] Opposition to the penitential ideal, embraced just a dozen years earlier, became so widespread that legislatures in the Northeast reconsidered the model. Some lawmakers and critics even called for abolishing the houses of penitence. Others floated alternatives such as banishment, confinement in penal colonies, or a return to hard labor on public work crews.[35]

BY 1820, THE penitentiary ideal was on life support. Many would predict the end of imprisonment, but for the persistence of influential reformers such as Rush. With extensive cultural, political, and social resources, they refused to give up on the penitentiary ideal, even using the extraordinary failures of the proto-prisons to breathe new life into their cause. Consider, for example, the situation at Walnut Street. Between about 1815 and 1820, the prison was "a cauldron of discontent."[36] Its many problems—disease, violence, overcrowding, idleness, prisoners' black-market trade, collusion between keepers and kept, and high recidivism—seemed to have reached new levels of crisis. In May of 1820 a riot occurred, requiring intervention from the militia and armed civilians.[37]

After the Walnut Street riot, a diverse set of actors used the catastrophe to argue for an expanded and improved system of prisons, rather than an abandonment the penitentiary ideal. "The Board of Inspectors and the Philadelphia Society for Alleviating the Miseries of Public Prisons argued the case for radical reform," Meranze explains. "In addition, James Mease, a student and friend of Benjamin Rush, published a series of essays attacking the existing prison system and calling for solitary confinement."[38] In this time of struggle, the legislature and governor mandated the construction of a new prison to impose solitary confinement. Social elites such as Mease and organizations such as the Philadelphia Society effectively used the failure of proto-prisons as an opportunity to push for the creation of what they saw as *real* penitentiaries in the 1830s and beyond.

Before delving into the second wave, it is important to note that the survival of the penitentiary ideal in the early part of the 1800s was due not only to reformers' persistence, but also to certain key, large-scale developments in the Jacksonian Era. This was a period of great flux, movement, and opportunity. Advances in transportation—including railroads and steam-powered ships—facilitated large-scale movement to cities and to the western frontier, where people hoped to earn money as wage laborers in the emerging manufacturing economy or as prospectors of land and natural resources. Literal boatloads of western Europeans immigrated to the United States, producing extensive ethnic and cultural diversity, particularly in the urban centers of the Northeast. Working-class and poor white men gained the right to vote, and the battle over slavery escalated. Massive, compressed change and turmoil fueled perceptions of widespread disorder.[39]

Social elites argued that modern developments loosened the influence that traditional institutions of church, school, and family had over individuals, leaving room for the insidious creep of crime, insanity, pauperism, and corruption. Dorothea Dix, renowned Jacksonian reformer, pithily summarized the popular view of social problems: "It is to the defects of our social organization, to the multiplied and multiplying temptations to crime that we chiefly owe the increase of the evil doers."[40] The revived penitentiary, it was hoped, would instill order in a world increasingly marked—at least in the eyes of elites—by disorder. The *idea* of the penitentiary and its associated ability to impose order continued to resonate with elites, especially politicians and state executives. But, again, this idea did not spread by itself; reformers with extensive resources and organizational capacity vigorously struggled to sustain, fund, and implement the reformative ideal.

## The Great Debate

Renewed efforts to implement the penitentiary ideal led to the establishment of new institutions in the Northeast. Upper-crust reformers' persistence—particularly that of the Philadelphia Society for Alleviating the Miseries of Public Prisons—led the Pennsylvania legislature to approve two new prisons.[41] The more famous of these, Eastern State Penitentiary, was located on a cherry orchard near Philadelphia. Opened in 1829, Eastern (as it is sometimes called) became synonymous with the "separate system" of imprisonment. It eventually contained 500 cells and resembled a medieval castle, symbolizing the facilities' heady mission and social import.

Ideally, prisoners would serve their entire sentence alone—they would eat, sleep, pray, read the Bible, and perform craft-style labor in their austere cells.[42] A small, private yard connected to the cell would provide prisoners' only respite from their cavernous existence, and their only human contact would be with penitentiary staff, spiritual advisers, and local elites assisting in the convicts' moral and educational training. Convicts could not receive letters, periodicals, or other texts containing information about life beyond the walls. Instead, isolation would inspire reflection and prevent nefarious influences from obstructing prisoners' path toward righteousness. Moreover, anonymity (prisoners were known by numbers, not names, and wore hoods when moving through the penitentiary) would keep staff and fellow prisoners from recognizing and stigmatizing prisoners after release. Supporters of "the Pennsylvania model" insisted this approach was a pure, effective, and humane means of reforming criminals.

A competing model developed concurrently in New York. As Pennsylvania doubled down on the penitentiary ideal, the Empire State diverged in several key ways. Implemented first at the newly built Auburn State Prison,

New York's model was initially two tiered. Older, "hardened" prisoners were separated from the general population and remained in a state of forced idleness; along with keeping these troublemakers from corrupting their fellows, isolation would theoretically facilitate self-reflection and personal transformation.[43] The other prisoners spent evenings in single cells but manufactured together during the days. Because prisoners (except the "hard cases") ate and worked together, New York's model of incarceration became known as the "congregate" system.

After several years, administrators at Auburn ended the two-tiered system. Solitary confinement appeared to make the "hard cases" insane, and the lack of mobility harmed them physically. From that point forward, all convicts spent evenings in their own cells and congregated during the days. Solitary confinement became a punishment for breaking prison rules, rather than a de facto form of imprisonment.[44]

The New York model sought to reform convicts through hard labor and strict discipline. Although prisoners were to remain silent at all times (even sharing glances was forbidden), solitary reflection and penitence were but secondary goals.[45] To express and reinforce discipline, the administration instituted military measures, such as requiring prisoners to march in lockstep, wear striped uniforms, shear their hair, and stick to a rigid timetable. The staff at Auburn used whippings and other physical sanctions to instill order, maintain silence, and spur industriousness among the captives—ironic, given that imprisonment had been meant to *replace* corporal punishment.

The differences between the solitary and congregate systems may appear minor. But their respective proponents viewed the distinctions both as vast and critical. In fact, symbolic struggle between the two camps, which occurred primarily through written documents such as pamphlets and reports, was so heated and extensive that Rothman compares it to the contestation over slavery in the decades leading up to the Civil War.[46]

Supporters of the Pennsylvania system claimed that isolation greatly helped prisoners (and, by extension, society), while Auburn proponents characterized it as torture that harmed convicts psychologically and physically. Denying man's social nature through solitary confinement, Pennsylvania's opponents charged, was just as inhumane as the corporal punishments that imprisonment supposedly replaced. Auburn's backers also charged that the rival system was impractical and prohibitively expensive because each prisoner required a sizeable cell, and their handiwork (deemed inefficient in the emerging industrial economy) could never cover prison expenses, much less earn a profit.[47] Rubin contends that these arguments against Pennsylvania's separate system took on a "powerful myth-like status,"[48] through the dogged efforts of a well-connected coterie of influential actors who convinced key decision makers of the validity of their claims.

As Auburn's backers became evermore strident and powerful, supporters of the Pennsylvania system pushed back. Acknowledging that their system was expensive, they insisted that reform did not come cheap and, unlike their rivals in New York, that they were not focused on the financial bottom line. In short, their mission was moral, not pecuniary. Boosters of the solitary system denied that convicts were tortured by isolation, because prisoners had regular contact with religious counselors and moral reformers. Additionally, staff did not use the whip (as guards did in New York) to maintain order or "motivate" convict laborers.[49] To them, cruelty was inherent in the Auburn model, putting prisoners in proximity during work and meals and then harshly punishing them when they succumbed to temptation and communicated with each other.[50] The Pennsylvania system, its backers claimed, was more reformatory *and* gentler than its counterpart.

Advocates for each system dug in their heels, and it was a protracted, often nasty battle lasting well into the 1840s. Some believed that the Auburn system tweaked the penitentiary ideal to make it workable—a realistic, financially sustainable alternative to a quixotic Pennsylvania model. Those backing Eastern retorted that for the sake of convenience and profit, New York had abandoned the penitentiary ideal altogether; worse, their bastardized system was criminogenic. Exploitative labor and harsh discipline embittered convicts, making men even less tied to the rule of law, and the congregate style of imprisonment allowed men to corrupt each other while working and eating. In short, each side felt that its status and survival depended on the dismissal and failure of the other. For these reformers, the fight for penal predominance was a zero-sum game.[51]

## A Compromised Ideal

Contestation shaped operations inside the attention-grabbing penitentiaries and altered how their backers framed and demonstrated their preferred model's superiority. Even in the facility that strove hardest and longest to implement the penitential ideal—Eastern State Penitentiary—struggle molded internal operations. Rubin documents the blending of logics and practices at Eastern, which developed in the context of struggle between backers of the Pennsylvania system (especially Eastern's administrators) and critics within and beyond the state, including influential figures such as Charles

Dickens, who, after touring Eastern, described "solitary horrors," "torture," and "agony" that "no man has the right to inflict upon his fellow creature."[52] For Eastern's leadership, it was especially problematic to see elite reformers associated with the Philadelphia Society for Alleviating the Miseries of Public Prisons—the very group that had originally lobbied for the legislation to establish Eastern—pressuring the facility's administration for change. The protests sought to alter Eastern's system to limit negative effects on prisoners' physical and mental health, to promote reformation, and to make the prison economically sustainable.[53]

Persistent challenges came from multiple fronts, and Eastern's officials took measures to protect the reputation of the Pennsylvanian system.[54] For example, to address the "insanity problem" (that is, the charge that long periods without human interaction drove prisoners to madness), officials broke the cardinal rule of the solitary system and experimented with double celling well before overcrowding was a pressing concern. They allowed some prisoners to labor outside their cells, despite seeing the fears of inmate interaction come to fruition: prisoners socialized, gained access to contraband (including liquor), and even escaped.[55] Guards routinely talked with prisoners and allowed convicts to communicate with each other.[56]

In another apparent breach of the penitentiary ideal, prison leaders allowed black prisoners to go outside to perform manual labor, such as chopping wood. This was due to racist beliefs about black people's inherent need to spend time outdoors, as well as notions that black men and women were especially susceptible to communicable disease and that black people were "made" for hard labor. This is to say, the penitentiary ideal essentially did not apply to blacks—imprisonment, after all, was supposed to restore wayward *white* men to citizens in full standing. As an inspector's report indicates, blacks were unwelcome aliens at Eastern: "The coloured prisoners are a burthen [*sic*] to the system, both because it does not and cannot operate as beneficially on them as on the white prisoners, and because they are more diseased, and less capable of being made profitable in confinement."[57]

With respect to concerns that the model was fiscally unstable, Eastern's leaders responded by grasping for the moral high ground. *Reform*, they insisted, was far more important than filling state coffers. "In practice, however, the economic logic that inmates defray the cost of their confinement frequently dominated the penal logic in which inmates receive beneficial training in a useful trade," Rubin explains.[58] Thus, while a "useful trade" was supposed to help prisoners reintegrate into society (by making them more attractive to an employer), this educational effort more typically meant putting prisoners to work in unskilled, manual labor projects that would generate revenue for the prison but do little to train the men in a trade.

Economic considerations also trumped reform when it came to female prisoners. As was the case with black male prisoners, Eastern's leaders viewed female prisoners as, at best, bothersome, and, at worst, as a serious problem inimical to reform and security efforts. When pressed to shore up the institution's financial situation, prison officials wondered whether they could get rid of the female population all together. When it became clear that the small trickle of women sentenced to the institution every year would not dry up, prison officials continued to house the women in their own sequestered section of the prison.[59] By 1835, prison officials conceded the "problem" was not going away, and they hired a "matron" to supervise the women.[60] Because the penitential ideal literally targeted poor white men, white women—like all blacks—were portrayed as costly drags on the institution.

As seen in these examples, Eastern's leadership frequently braided penal, managerial, and economic logics to fend off criticism, maintain order, and prolong the Pennsylvania system.[61] While Eastern's leaders remained committed to the penitentiary ideal, at least in theory, they continually made decisions and concessions that undercut their model. Extensive variegation developed as administrators sought to make their model work in the context of struggle within and beyond the prison and state borders.

Pennsylvania's main competitor, New York, implemented a more practical model of imprisonment; although less committed to the idea of reformation via solitary penance, the Empire State nonetheless held up reform as its main penal project. Reformation was to come through hard work, strict discipline, austere conditions, and, when necessary, harsh physical repression. New York's congregate system refrained from compelling convicts to repent their sins in favor of more technical, administrative objectives. Most important among these was the enforcement of order, making the penitentiaries self-sufficient and breaking prisoners' rebellious spirits.[62] Coercion and hard labor were the lynchpins of reform and institutional order.

By design, economics shaped prison operations at Auburn. For example, administrators established disciplinary measures that would attract private businesses reluctant to set up shop inside the walls, and prisoners' daily routines revolved around employers' needs. Manufacturing took off, with a captive labor force that suffered the lash for not following strict orders.[63] By 1830, the congregate model had matured; legislators and elite reformers (some of whom were previously critical of what they saw as New York's perversion of the purity of the penitential ideal) applauded Auburn's economic progress and strict discipline.[64] In this context, "reforming" prisoners was in no way antithetical to subjecting them to an exploitative labor regime.

Just as prisoners and staff at Eastern subverted the ideals of the separate system, at Auburn prisoners violated rules, including the prohibition against communication, and enjoyed contraband (such as alcohol, tobacco, and playing cards) that guards, contractors, and foremen snuck into the institution.[65] The daily realities of the Auburn system invited and facilitated rule violations, McLennan explains: "The organization of the prisoners into production often necessitated that the supreme rule of the prison—prisoners' perpetual silence—be broken so that the business of production could proceed. Foremen often needed to communicate with prison laborers, and prison laborers needed to communicate with each other."[66]

It is important to note that Auburn appears to have been one of the most disciplined congregate-style prisons.[67] Auburn's followers in the Mid-West and West were decidedly more disorderly. Regarding Ohio's penitentiary in the 1840s, for example, Rothman notes that convicts "enjoyed an almost free run of the place, communicating at will and controlling much of their routine."[68] To gain the compliance of their prisoners, the Ohio guards resorted to bribing them with food and clothing, a move that surely would have revolted the pioneers of the penitentiary ideal.

The main source of contestation around penitentiaries during the mid-nineteenth century came from the emerging labor movement.[69] As they had early in the 1800s, free laborers worried about income and the status of labor more generally; penal servitude, they argued, benefited monarchial, aristocratic regimes and slavery, not a free, democratic country. Prison labor, in the eyes of many free laborers, was a clear-cut example of the state and capitalists colluding to profit at the expense of the "little man."[70]

In protest, mechanics, stonecutters, and other artisans organized strikes and petitioned state legislatures to end the practice of using convicts for trade labor. The craft workers galvanized public support and pressured state legislators.[71] Changes designed to pacify the protesting laborers, such as limiting the length of contracts and the types of trades inside prisons, were enacted, but viewing the reforms as insufficient, laborers in New York continued their opposition. Soon it spread across state borders.

The struggle against convict labor led to legislative investigations and laws that further curtailed industrial production inside the walls. New York disallowed the prison system from "putting convicts to work in any trade other 'than that which the convict has learned and practiced previous to his conviction.' . . . Prisoners were put to unskilled labor, such as railroad building and fur-cutting, of the sort that was unlikely to provoke the ire of skilled, organized workers."[72] There was even an effort to open a new prison in which all prisoners would labor at iron smelting, precisely because so few unionized workers in New York toiled in that industry.[73]

Administrators and wardens at penitentiaries far beyond Auburn adapted to similar contestation by turning to industries that skilled workers did not oppose (and that were permitted by new laws). They did so to maintain economic productivity and institutional order—not because these adaptations facilitated prisoner reformation. Hard labor backed by brute force was the primary source of discipline not just in New York, but throughout most of the United States for the entire nineteenth century. The rhetoric of reform justified the exploitative system, but it was a gloss, especially from the 1840s forward.

## The Poor White Man's Prison

The penitentiary was, as we have seen, a northern invention produced in a period in which the common historical generalization is of an increasingly large gap between "free" and "slave" states in the run-up to the Civil War. So it is perhaps surprising that even states in the South built congregate-style prisons. As was true up north and out west, elites (rather than the general public) led southern states to adopt penitentiaries. Specifically, building modern prisons was a way for these states to shake off a reputation for being backward. Historian Robert Perkinson explains that "legislators, governors, and newspaper editors . . . [were] aware that the rest of the Anglo-American world increasingly looked upon the slave South as a throwback to a part of a common past best forgotten."[74] In Texas, leaders claimed that a penitentiary would put the state "on the map"[75]; David Oshinsky argues that "The Walls," Mississippi's prison, was considered by many in the nineteenth century to be the state's "most impressive civic reform."[76] Thus, while the political contexts were very different, southern states built prisons for reasons similar to why northern states did: politicians and state executives sought to demonstrate enlightened progress and instill social order.[77]

Throughout the South (as well as the North), states built prisons that were based on the congregate model. Unlike the solitary system with its cell-based craftwork, this model reflected the burgeoning capitalist economy through its emphasis on factory labor and industrial discipline. Prison labor would transform convicts into "good workers."[78] But economics do not sufficiently explain the rapid diffusion of the congregate system. Again, struggle is key: Reform organizations that advocated for the Auburn system (especially the Boston Prison Discipline Society, which included prison officials in other states as "corresponding members") were more organized and better connected than their counterparts.[79] Leaders of these organizations capitalized on their social networks to gain an upper hand in the symbolic struggle, casting the adoption of the Pennsylvania model as risky and unwise and making the Auburn model seem sensible by comparison. Uncertain about the longevity and feasibility of penitentiary incarceration (especially in light of the failure of proto-prisons such as Walnut Street), governors and legislators throughout the South (as in the North) were swayed toward what seemed to be the safer of the two options.[80]

Southern governors led the charge, primarily because establishing penitentiaries would make them look like leaders of progress (and incidentally, of course, created patronage they might dole out). According to historian Edward Ayers, state legislators who promoted the prisons "numbered themselves among 'the best people' from their counties. They were wealthier than most of their constituents, of course, and owned a greater stake in social order. This may have been incentive enough for many lawmakers to vote for a penitentiary."[81] Ayers further explains how the penitentiary indirectly served class interests: "it 'proved' the benevolence of the men who ruled, demonstrated that fair and equitable punishment flourished under their aegis, showed the world that the slave south was not the barbaric land its detractors claimed."[82] Demonstrating that this was no benevolent largess; in Alabama, for instance, support for building a penitentiary came from a governor and state legislature that paid careful attention to letters from colleagues in the North reporting that their state penitentiaries, especially once they were in operation for a few years, often turned a profit for the state.[83] Adopting penitentiaries seemed to communicate enlightenment and civilization and cost them little, if anything, in return.[84]

Despite the appeal of penitentiaries as a top-down project in state development, governors and their allies faced stiff resistance. Significant opposition came from non-elite whites, who strongly distrusted state power and saw imprisonment as anti-republican, far too similar to slavery.[85] While the penitentiaries might have increased the legitimacy of state governments in the South (somewhat ironically, by enhancing the reputation of southern public officials in the eyes of northerners), they generated opposition from many members of the voting public.[86]

Ayers writes that, as in the North, "town and city workers fought bitterly against penitentiary labor. Although these workmen attacked the penitentiary ideal in the familiar language of republicanism, their rhetoric often sounded far more like the equal rights demands of Northern workers."[87] Many legislators and prison officials gave up trying to manufacture "simple goods in steady demand" (such as shoes or bricks), which greatly limited the prisons' scale of production.[88] Soon the penitentiaries' lack of financial stability led prison managers to plead for state monies, affirming critics' claims that the institutions drained public coffers and harmed the public good.[89]

In addition (and related) to this opposition were the realities of southern penitentiaries. There was a chasm between how such institutions were discussed and imagined by political elites and how they actually operated. First and foremost, southern penitentiaries were explicitly designed for lower-class white men. In Alabama before the Civil War, the state penitentiary had never held more than four blacks at a time; enslaved blacks were, as throughout the South, punished by their "masters," not by the state.[90] This allowed elite whites to establish their political and social credentials as the protectors of social order: to police (and, where necessary, punish) the conduct of their less refined (lower-class) compatriots, while doing nothing to disrupt the economic and social realities of slavery and the exploitation of black labor.[91]

The "problem" for elites in punishing free blacks, however, was thornier. States varied in their approaches. In some southern states such as Virginia and Maryland, many free blacks convicted of crimes were sent to state prison, which upset both supporters and opponents of the penitentiary model. "Blacks' presence in the penitentiary seemed to destroy whatever reformatory effect the institution might exert on either race, prison officials felt, for it destroyed white men's feelings of pride while dangerously inflating that of blacks," explains Ayers.[92] One common solution was to segregate black prisoners within the penitentiaries. At least one state (Virginia) addressed this problem by selling free blacks convicted of serious crimes *into* slavery.[93] Eventually, southern and some frontier states, such as California, would solve the issue by leasing black convicts to private employers. In the meantime, entrenched racism meant that the presence of free blacks both challenged the ostensible "purity" of the republican penitentiary and upset those charged with carrying out the reformation of wayward white men.

The few women who received prison sentences in the pre–Civil War era posed another challenge for southern penitentiaries (as was the case in the North). Because white women were viewed as "virtuous" and "pure," legal actors went to great lengths to keep them out of prisons.[94] This actually contributed to the dreadful conditions faced by the unlucky few who did end up behind bars: "Women in Southern penitentiaries generally suffered much more than their male counterparts. Since no cells had been built for them, women often languished in small, dirty, and unventilated buildings within the penitentiary walls. Not surprisingly, sexual abuse created the worst terror of their imprisonment."[95] As with free blacks, prison administrators preferred not to manage female convicts (although some profited by using female convicts as domestic servants).[96]

Southern states, too, had to contend with making their penal institutions financially sustainable. Constrained by the objections of free laborers and with relatively small prison populations, southern penitentiaries lacked manpower for large-scale manufacturing or large-scale public works projects (as in some midwestern and western states). Georgia's prison, for example, never held more than 245 convicts; Alabama's penitentiary throughout the 1840s held about 120 prisoners, rising to only 206 by 1855.[97] Along with the problem of its small labor pool, Georgia (like many other southern prisons) had a geographic disadvantage—located in the "heart of the plantation belt," it struggled to sell the goods its prisoners did produce and it paid high prices for imported materials.[98] As a result, southern penitentiaries were never self-sustaining. Their insolvency fed opposition from laborers, the public, and critics in the legislature.

In a fundamental and symbolic failure, penitentiaries in the South were also unable to reform poor white men—their primary selling point.[99] Convicts routinely caused serious disruption such as setting fires, making penal administrators' claims about reforming their charges seem hollow, at best. Moreover, persistent brutality and exploitation further shattered the facade of reform in southern penitentiaries.[100] The use of the lash in some prisons was particularly scandalous, since whipping—the quintessential sanction on slave plantations—suggested that white prisoners were slaves of the state.[101] (The periodic leasing of white convicts to private employers in Texas and elsewhere would elicit similar reactions.) Critics charged that these penitentiaries were unrepublican, with high walls concealing the harsh, exploitative punishment of white citizens.

Unending opposition, logistical challenges, and operational failures undermined southern administrators' efforts to establish functioning modern prisons. In Georgia, legislators simply refused to allocate funds for its penitentiary for a couple years.[102] Strident opposition led state officials and administrators to place economic efficiency and profit above all else; if the facilities proved self-sustaining, at least proponents could fend off some critics. Reforming convicts quickly became an afterthought—if it happened, it would be a nice byproduct of prison labor. Meanwhile, critiques opened space for the consideration of alternative penal sanctions, including returning to corporal punishment and the convict leasing that would become common throughout the South.[103] In summary, despite some southern elites' support of the penitentiary model, from which they stood to benefit in myriad ways, intense opposition and a limited base of support meant that the "roots of the penitentiary were shallow in the South."[104]

---

TEXT BOX

### Congregate Slave Labor in Texas

The Lone Star State developed a solution to the problem of economic sustainability by making its penitentiary, also nicknamed "The Walls," a site for textile production. In 1856, Texas built a cotton mill inside The Walls, creating the largest factory in the state. Fueled by convict labor, the mill pumped out volumes of cotton and wool fabric, turning a handsome profit for the state. By the mid-1860s, The Walls was, in fact, Texas's main source of revenue.[105]

The Walls' prison mill played a vital role during the Civil War, weaving fabric for uniforms and other essential supplies for the Confederacy. However, the prison did not have sufficient labor to keep pace with demand. Administrators considered supplementing the workforce with free laborers (in fact, the state legislature authorized The Walls to bring in contract workers); ultimately though, Texas decided that free laborers might compromise the imprisoned workforce's obedience and docility.

Instead, the prison brought in slaves to work alongside convicts. "The mingling of slave and convict labor confirmed the original fears of southern penitentiary opponents—that imprisonment would ultimately break down the sacred barrier between honor and dishonor, freedom and bondage, white and black," Perkinson points out. "Indeed, by 1863, white men convicted of criminal offenses were not only laboring, like slaves, without pay under the threat of the lash, but they were doing so shoulder-to-shoulder with actual slaves. *The prison at Huntsville thus became the state's first racially integrated public institution, not by bestowing rights on bondsmen but by stripping them from citizens.*"[106] The labor arrangement at The Walls highlights an obscured fact about congregate-style prisons in both the South and the North (especially after the 1840s): involuntary penal servitude was often more about exploitation than it was about reform. In Texas, it was literally slave labor.

## Conclusion

Given the reality of imprisonment in the nineteenth century, it is tempting to view penal reformers, legislators, and prison administrators as malevolent schemers who used the rhetoric of reform to implement brutal, exploitative penal practices. But that view is too simple. Although they had various motives for inventing the penitentiary, these actors appear to have believed that incarceration could actually reform individuals and promote order in a rapidly changing and, from the perspective of elites, undisciplined society. They viewed harsh discipline and austere conditions as part and parcel of transforming prisoners. This belief, in practice, justified extreme, even pitiless, methods of maintaining order behind the walls.

Penal reform in the Jacksonian Era was primarily championed by political, economic, and social elites. But penal practitioners adapted the reformers' visions as they juggled persistent challenges inside and outside the penitentiaries—most notably, by convicts (the alleged beneficiaries of reform) and laborers. Contestation between the proponents of the two dominant models of incarceration—the solitary and congregate systems—greatly influenced the shape that those models took in practice. In general, changes that developed amid this roiling struggle intensified economic and managerial concerns and practices, while making the goal of reforming prisoners less and less important.

To look back on the nineteenth century as a period of reformative justice—as is common in the criminological literature—is inaccurate. It was a time of harsh punishment, involuntary servitude, and exploitation, alongside genuine, if limited, moral reform. In this regard, legal scholar James Whitman writes:

> The penitentiary became a place of forced labor and corporal punishment, the forms of "unrepublican" treatment most strongly associated with slavery in the United States; and by the time of the Thirteenth Amendment [which permitted involuntary servitude as punishment for a crime] the identification of prisoners with slaves effectively became a part of American constitutional law. Indeed, in the age of liberal revolutions, American became the prime example of a country that did not abolish low-status punishment.[107]

And lest we romanticize northern penitentiaries as more "civilized" than their southern counterparts, Ayers reminds us: "In virtually every facet of their antebellum history the penitentiaries in the North and South were far more similar than different. . . . The major difference between penitentiaries in the South and the rest of America before the Civil War lay only in the ambitious dreams and rhetoric of Northern reformers."[108]

Recall also that, in general, men of color and women (of all racial categorizations) were not part of the reform picture as it was imagined and talked about by elite reformers.[109] The penitentiaries were designed to instill discipline in poor white men. Focusing on the incarceration of women in Jacksonian-Era prisons, Nicole Rafter notes a divergence from the (stated) goals of male penitentiary discipline: "Women were punished in nineteenth-century prisons, but few officials tried to transform them into obedient citizens through seclusion and rigorous routines."[110] This made women prisoners "probably lonelier and certainly more vulnerable to sexual exploitation, easier to ignore because so few in number, and viewed with distaste by prison officials." Much like black male convicts of the period, "women in custodial units were treated as the dregs of the state prisoner population."[111]

Despite many limitations, subversions, and multiple (and sometimes contradictory) impulses—and despite considerable heterogeneity in how punishment was actually carried out—reformation of (some) convicts nonetheless persisted as a goal of imprisonment until the Civil War. Aside from some lingering, sporadic attempts to revive elements of the "reformatory impulse" in late 1860s and 1870s,[112] the war effectively washed away the penitentiary ideal. Marie Gottschalk explains that after many southern penitentiaries were damaged, "Most states of the old Confederacy opposed building new penitentiaries or repairing existing ones after the war. . . . The collapse of state finances, the weakening of state governments, the rise in lawlessness, growing apprehension about the control of blacks with the end of slavery, and the demands of economic development and modernization prompted the South to adopt an alternative means of punishment—the convict-lease system."[113]

As detailed in the next chapter, during and after the Civil War, those running or providing political support for congregate-style prisons in New York and elsewhere became more committed to the economic imperative that prisons ought to cost the state as little money as possible. Many penitentiaries used convicts to produce materials for the war effort, and they tended to concentrate prisoners' labor into just a few industries that could flourish with unskilled labor.[114] The Civil War, in short, accelerated and entrenched economic exploitation; the notion of reforming convicts withered during these years, in rhetoric and practice, in the North and the South alike.

By the end of the Civil War in 1865, only administrators at Eastern State remained committed to the Pennsylvania model. All others had moved toward the congregate model; the debate over the rival systems was effectively over. Eastern was overcrowded as crime escalated after the war, and soon solitary confinement (the cornerstone of the system) became impossible. By the 1870s, Eastern "was virtually unrecognizable." It was not until 1913, however, that legislative authorization for the Pennsylvania system finally ceased.[115] The solitary system was relegated to the dustbin of history; however, solitary confinement would live on as a form of punishment inside penal facilities.

In sum, during the mid-nineteenth century, imprisonment changed dramatically, as lawmakers, prison administrators and staff, reform organizations, worker organizations, and others struggled over the purpose and character of criminal justice. Although those struggles produced shifts in the penal terrain (most notably the birth of modern imprisonment), punishment did not swing like a pendulum toward reformation, not even in the epicenters of the penitentiary ideal, New York and Pennsylvania. Rather, contestation shifted the landscape in complex and contradictory ways, producing friction and fissures of varying depth and representing varying combinations of economic exploitation, harsh punishment, and moral reform. In the years after the Civil War, new penal regimes would resurrect old battles and inspire new ones.

# 3

# Reform and Repression in the Progressive Era

THE SPIRIT OF punishment in the years following the Civil War was bleak. In an ambitious summer 1865 tour (redolent of the one taken half a century earlier by Gustave de Beaumont and Alexis de Tocqueville), renowned penologists E. C. Wines and Theodore Dwight visited and studied prisons across 18 states, covering much of New England, the Mid-Atlantic, and the Appalachian Midwest (only one state, Missouri, was west of the Mississippi River, and the scholars traveled only as far south as Maryland and West Virginia).[1] In their 1867 *Report on the Prisons and Reformatories of the United States and Canada*, the commissioners captured this darkness: "There is not a state prison in America in which the reformation of the convicts is the one supreme object of the discipline, to which everything else must bend. . . . There is not a prison system in the United States, which . . . would not be found wanting. There is not one, we feel convinced . . . which seeks the reformation of its subjects as a primary object."[2] Amid clear signs of failure all around, the already weakened penitentiary ideal—especially the belief that institutionalization led naturally (even automatically) to reformation—was nearly extinct.

The situation was worse in what had been the Confederacy. Southern punishment was not just bleak; it was brutal. After the Civil War, states passed "Black Codes" targeting former slaves, aiming "to control the labor supply, to protect the freedman from his own 'vices,' and to ensure the superior position of whites in southern life."[3] In an effort to effectively reenslave free blacks, legislatures and businessmen had developed a new penal form: convict leasing. This legal process allowed public officials to lease prisoners to business owners, essentially making convicts the property of private actors.

Leasing was allowed under the Thirteenth Amendment of the United States Constitution, which outlawed slavery but permitted involuntary servitude for convicted criminals. As discussed below, this exploitative practice—in key respects "worse than slavery"—was essential to the development of the New South.[4]

Approximately four decades after the end of the Civil War, the spirit of punishment (especially in the North) seemed to have transformed from hopeless to hopeful. The common narrative suggests that during the "Progressive Era" (ca. 1890 to 1920), the "pendulum" swung forcefully toward the reformative side of the penal ledger.[5] In this chapter, we make several arguments that, together, highlight the standard narrative's limitations and the benefits of our agonistic framework.

First, we argue that progressive punishment did not arise mechanically, and it did not represent a sudden, all encompassing rupture from the past. The first section shows that a range of actors—prisoners, humanitarian reformers, editorialists, and labor groups—fought in the Gilded Age against harsh, exploitative forms of punishment, producing major fissures in the penal landscape. At the same time, influential penologists and their political allies struggled, in the last decades of the nineteenth century, for an alternative vision of criminal justice focused on the reformation of offenders. The second section shows that macro-level changes in the early twentieth century produced political openings for the penologists (and their successors) to spread what became known as the "new penology," which was designed both to reform and repress; for the mostly white, middle-class, Protestant reformers who led the struggle for change, these were complementary (if even distinguishable) penal objectives. The penal shift in the Progressive Era, we conclude, was due to a long struggle against harsh, exploitative punishment and for *correctional* criminal justice that bore fruit amid major social transformations at the end of the 1800s and beginning of the 1900s.

In the third and fourth sections, we turn to case studies of imprisonment in New York, the epicenter of Progressive Era punishment, and Texas, a surprising site of reform, arguing that struggle within and beyond prisons in these states limited the development of "treatment communities" inside the walls while reinforcing social control and producing major fissures in the penal landscape. These case studies highlight national and local factors that shaped the nature of struggle in those two states, and, consequently, the scope, character, and timing of "progressive" punishment. Penal development in this period was just as heterogeneous and contested as in the penitentiary era.

## Grappling in the Gilded Age

In the immediate aftermath of the Civil War, reformers sought to brighten the dark state of punishment outlined in Wines and Dwight's report. On the morning of October 12, 1870, a group of experts (later dubbed the "new penologists") gathered in Cincinnati, Ohio, for the *National Congress of Penitentiary and Reformatory Discipline*. For the better part of six days, 130 delegates (representing 24 US states, Canada, and Colombia) reaffirmed their commitment to the "reformation in disposition and conduct of the criminal" and detailed concrete steps toward that goal.[6] The participants articulated their vision in a "Declaration of Principles," a truly remarkable (and, when viewed in context, quite radical) document that addressed a wide range of issues, including executive pardons, prison architecture, sentencing, prisoner reentry, statistics for measuring organizational performance, compulsory education for children (to prevent crime), centralization of state penal systems, and the inclusion of women in penal administration.[7]

Simultaneously condemning the existing state of punishment and pointing toward a brighter future, the declaration asserted that the "supreme aim" of incarceration should be "the reformation of criminals, not the infliction of vindictive suffering." Departing from the penitentiary ideal of the late eighteenth and early nineteenth centuries, this congress of new penologists advocated for a more nuanced, discretionary, and individualized approach to imprisonment. For example, the declaration proposed a "progressive classification of prisoners" (borrowing heavily from the Irish "mark system"), in which inmates would move through different stages with increased responsibilities and liberties on the basis of their behavior.[8] The declaration also demanded indeterminate sentencing so that the "prisoner's destiny" would be "placed, measurably, in his own hands." Like the mark system, open-ended sentencing would spark convicts' "regulated self-interest," inspiring them to embrace personal betterment. Lastly, in a move that would come to characterize many Progressive Era reforms (inside and outside the criminal justice system), women, youth, and racial and ethnic minorities were cast as distinct categories—people with particular needs and "characters." Following this logic, prisoners should be "classified or graded" (including separating out groups such as the "untried" and the "incorrigible") and, in some cases (especially women and youth), segregated in dedicated facilities.

Reform, for these penologists, required going beyond religious instruction and hard labor. It meant including education and vocational training that might transform wayward prisoners into productive, virtuous citizens capable of participating in the quickly industrializing democracy. The penal system should "make upright and industrious free men, rather than orderly and obedient prisoners," they declared. To continue the reformative process once convicts hit the street, the declaration proposed "providing [ex-prisoners] with work and encouraging them to redeem their character and regain their lost position in society."

To make punishment "scientific, uniform, and successful," the document explained, prison work must be "raised to the dignity of a profession." Prison officers should receive "special training" and have a "serious conviction" that criminals are "capable of being reformed." Further, the successful implementation of a professional, reformatory punishment required the creation of a centralized, bureaucratic penal system. A national prison society would compile statistics to evaluate the effectiveness of the states' various penal systems. In short, the proposal envisioned a bureaucratically rational penal system.

Emphases on individualization, discretion, education, institutional specialization, professionalization, and bureaucratization all distinguished the new penologists' vision from that of their predecessors. Yet, in advocating for reformative punishment (and pushing against demoralizing, brutal sanctions that denied convicts' dignity), E. C. Wines, Zebulon Brockway, and others kept alive the struggle that Benjamin Rush and his compatriots began in the late 1700s. In this regard, Francis Cullen and Karen Gilbert comment, "champions of the new penology played a large role in bolstering the legitimacy of rehabilitative ideology at a time when it appeared vulnerable to being discredited and swept aside."[9] The new penologists' support for rehabilitation was grounded in the belief that the "interest of society and the interest of the convicted criminal are really identical." Like schools or other social institutions, criminal justice should focus on molding virtue rather than allocating pain.

This perspective also led the new penologists to condemn contractual penal labor as harming prisoners, free labor, and society at large. Labor organizations pressured state legislatures, Congress, and President Andrew Jackson to restrict contract labor and pay prisoners similar wages to those of free laborers, thereby reducing competition.[10] In the context of post–Civil War optimism (and the reality that northern prisons were filling with Civil War veterans), the combined efforts of the new penologists and workers' groups produced policy changes that reduced the power of businesses to shape the purpose and character of incarceration and led to the introduction of basic reformatory programs in California, Oregon, Massachusetts, New York, Ohio, and Oregon.[11]

Reconstruction also provided opportunities for reformers in southern states. For example, policymakers in Missouri, Georgia, Alabama, North Carolina, South Carolina, Texas, and Louisiana attempted to regulate convict leasing. Some southern states introduced remedial programs to facilitate prisoner reform.[12] Reconstruction governments also sought to eliminate laws that targeted freed slaves; Mississippi and South Carolina ended their "Black Codes," which, as historian Edward Ayers explains, "reserved corporal punishment for blacks and which defined 'vagrancy' in such a broad and ambiguous way as to perpetuate de facto slavery."[13] Although the Freedman's Bureau and its allies in southern states made some positive penal changes, free blacks still experienced extensive repression and brutality at the hands of legal and extralegal actors (e.g., "rifle clubs" and the Ku Klux Klan); the lines separating legal and extralegal were fine and, in some cases, nonexistent.[14]

Despite this burst of postbellum reform, actors in many states (northern and southern alike) faced considerable resistance, and their successes were often short lived.[15] In the years immediately following the Civil War, reformers had curtailed the position of large-scale businesses in state prisons, though smaller businesses continued to operate inside the walls. But with the Financial Panic of 1873 and the ensuing depression (the first in the era of industrial capitalism), many of these small-scale companies failed. Prisons lost sources of revenue and one means of maintaining carceral order. If nothing else, work had kept prisoners occupied and tired them out. The financial disaster, historian Rebecca McLennan writes, "unleashed new forces of resistance and rebellion in the prisons. With whole prison populations left without productive labor of any kind, the daily routines, disciplinary structure, and financial arrangements of prison life were severely disrupted."[16]

Faced with dwindling resources and widespread unrest, many prison administrators and state officials put their hopes behind a revitalized contract labor system. Rather than the smattering of smaller prison industries that had become typical, many states consolidated their contracts to a small number of large manufacturing companies.[17] The "prison factory system" became common during this period. Under this arrangement, businesses literally set up shop behind prison walls and secured captive workforces. Business interests (and the economic imperative) became so dominant in the field of imprisonment that they gained control "in matters of prison governance, institutional discipline, and the political and legal spheres, as well."[18] As the profit motive swamped all other institutional concerns, prisoners experienced extreme exploitation and very dangerous working conditions. Talk of "reformation" would have struck prisoners (or even state officials, for that matter) in this period as ludicrous.

Big business and the state also joined forces in the South to transform punishment. As previously noted, governments in the former Confederacy had begun leasing convicts to private interests at the close of the Civil War. However, the practice did not become fully entrenched until after Reconstruction in the late-1870s. When federal troops returned north and landowning white Democrats (the "Redeemers") seized control of southern governments, southern states expanded and entrenched convict leasing.[19] Ayers describes this penal form as "a sort of mutual aid society for the new breed of capitalists and politics of the white Democratic regimes of the New South."[20] Leasing enriched business owners and contributed greatly to the development of the former Confederacy—convict-laborers rebuilt much of the region's shattered infrastructure and states brought in tax revenue from the businesses that profited from leasing. In turn, states used that tax money to provide services (e.g., schooling and transportation) and low taxes to white voters. According to W. E. B. Du Bois, only southern states turned a profit through imprisonment in this period, while states in other regions of the country lost money.[21]

Although some poor white convicts got caught up in the system, leasing was designed for the poor black laborers who filled southern jails after the war.[22] Leasing effectively reenslaved newly freed blacks, viewed by southern whites as inherently lazy, beholden to "primitive instincts" (including insatiable sexual appetites), and naturally fit for physically demanding manual labor. Employers claimed that repression of and even violence against black convicts was necessary to overcome the workers' alleged vices.[23]

This system was just as (if not more) brutal than slavery.[24] Whereas slave owners had an interest in maintaining their "property," employers did not have to care for convicts. If the prisoners died, the state would lease them new bodies. Along with backbreaking work, convict-laborers were victims of beatings, neglect, and disease. This exploitation and brutality was gendered, with black female prisoners facing unique harms. Historian Talitha LeFlouria explains: "Not only were they overworked (often doing the same jobs as men), they were also subjected to fiendish acts of cruelty, often sexualized in nature, and raped with impunity."[25] Many convicts died laboring in mines, on railroads, and in turpentine camps;[26] in 1882, 126 of 735 (17%) black convict laborers died in Mississippi (of 83 white convict workers, 2 died that year).[27]

Given the entrenchment of contractual penal servitude, it would make sense to view the criminal justice landscape of the Gilded Age as settled. However, during the last couple decades of the 1800s, diverse actors vigorously—and, at times, violently—contested punishment. Convicts in the industrial prisons of the North, Midwest, and Far West (many of whom were Civil War veterans who expected to be treated with dignity) fought against the exploitative conditions. As employers and prison staff sped up production, cut rations, and used harsh disciplinary techniques (lashing, punching, and isolation in a dark cell), prisoners responded with riots, work slowdowns, strikes, self-mutilation, and sabotage (including breaking tools). Consolidation and coordination of the labor process made it possible for prisoners to upset manufacturing by disrupting any of the steps in the process. Large-scale production fueled both convicts' desire and ability to stall or halt production.

Rebellion and subversion did not produce immediate changes in policy or practice; however, it inspired the press, government officials, and social reformers to examine and critique contractual penal servitude. Labor groups spearheaded local and national efforts to end industrial incarceration, demanded legislative investigations, petitioned to curtail and (in some cases) end the contract system, organized boycotts of prison-made goods, and sponsored legislation that would shut down markets for products made behind bars. These actions helped galvanize the budding labor movement around a common cause. In the 1870s, workers' organizations effectively pressured one state legislature (in California) to abolish the contract system.[28] Bigger victories came in the 1880s—including agreement in the US Congress to curtail the contract system, and, in 1884, the outlawing of large-scale, industrial imprisonment in its birthplace, New York (to which we will return later in the chapter).[29]

Labor did not limit its opposition to convict industry in the North and the West; workers also took radical, disruptive actions in the South. They fumed because companies used convicts to break strikes, undercut the wages of free workers, and limit employment opportunities (though companies would have been hard-pressed to hire and retain free laborers in much of the incredibly dangerous and degrading work that convicts were forced to do). Between 1881 and 1900, coal miners in the South organized at minimum 20 strikes to protest convict labor.[30] In at least two states, Kentucky and Tennessee, *armed* miners successfully demanded the release of convicts from labor camps.[31] As historian Karin Shapiro explains, these rebellions and pressure on politicians would prove pivotal in bringing down the lease in the southern states.[32]

Along with unions and small farmers, editorialists and moral reformers also strongly critiqued convict leasing, focusing especially on humanitarian concerns regarding the cruelties endured by prisoners.[33] The print media drummed up public concern by reporting on escapes from leasing camps; lest we paint critics as universally progressive (in a twenty-first-century sense of the word), note that images of black convicts wandering the countryside were widely used, even by "liberal" reformers, to strike fear in the hearts of white readers.[34] Media criticism of the lease led to legislative investigations, which further highlighted brutality in the camps.[35]

Convict leasing ultimately met its demise because of opposition from political actors who claimed to represent poor whites. In the mid-1880s, representatives of the Farmers Alliance and Populist Party advocated abolishment.[36] They argued that leasing unfairly enriched elites at the expense of small farmers and common laborers. Politicians and their supporters wanted penal farms to replace convict leasing; farms would decrease competition for white workers, contain and control blacks, and benefit the state by submitting convicts (primarily) to hard agricultural labor (a situation we take up in more detail in the next chapter). Mississippi became the first state to officially end the lease in 1894, but the practice would persist another decade until replaced by the notorious Parchman Farm prison.[37] Other states followed suit, with the penal farm replacing convict leasing throughout the South.

As a collage of actors stridently opposed contractual penal servitude, new penologists struggled to keep their vision of reformative criminal justice alive. This vision was arguably most fully implemented at the Reformatory at Elmira, New York. Opened in 1877 under the direction of superintendent Zebulon Brockway (one of the key participants in the Cincinnati Congress of 1870), Elmira sought to reform its charges. Offenders sent to the institution, first-time felons between the ages of 16 and 30, received a modified indeterminate sentence: a maximum term was set, but prisoners could earn shorter sentences by showing progress toward reformation.[38] In Elmira's "mark" system, prisoners worked their way up or down three levels, with the ultimate goal of conditional release.[39] True to Brockway's vision, Elmira boasted an impressive array of educational, work, and religious programs; had a well-stocked library; brought in lecturers from local colleges; and instituted an extensive sports program.[40]

Deemed a roaring success, Elmira gained almost mythical status among penologists, notwithstanding evidence that Brockway and his staff enforced their benevolent vision with harsh tactics, including whipping and solitary confinement.[41] Historian Alexander Pisciotta argues that the reformatories for young offenders (20 opened between 1876 and 1920) "promised benevolent reform: humane, constructive, and charitable treatment. In fact, they delivered benevolent oppression."[42] He continues: "The kindly rhetoric of

Elmira's highly successful public relations and marketing campaign masked a repressive class control agenda."[43] Rather than admit that their promises of "reforming" all their charges were quixotic, Brockway and his colleagues invented a new category of criminal: the "degenerate." This label justified the long-term incapacitation of allegedly hopeless cases.[44] Even though reality did not match the image of Elmira (broadcast far and wide by the institution's public-relations operation), Brockway was enormously influential and Elmira was, according to Pisciotta, "the world's model correctional institution" in the last decade of the nineteenth century.[45]

In sum, contestation was ubiquitous throughout the Gilded Age. Even though contractual penal servitude was widespread, there was no consensus over criminal justice. Prisoners with little formal capital worked to disrupt exploitative conditions, as actors with more (and various types of) power—journalists, moral reformers, politicians, and labor organizations—organized outside the walls to demand reforms. Because the dominant players in the field (businessmen, politicians, and state administrators) had extensive economic, political, and bureaucratic resources, the challengers were able to force change only because of their collective efforts on various fronts. At the same time, the new penologists, armed with extensive cultural and social capital, engaged in symbolic struggle, continually advocating for *correctional* criminal justice. They still believed that penal institutions could correct wayward individuals, rather than simply contain and exploit criminals. The pervasive, multisided contestation produced deep fissures in the penal landscape that would help reshape punishment in the Progressive Era.

## The Progressive Opening

At the turn of the twentieth century, "signs of friction" were ubiquitous in the United States, especially in northern cities filled with European immigrants and, increasingly, black families escaping the racial terror and exploitation of the former slave states.[46] White middle-class Americans were anxious about the effects of industrialization, immigration, urbanization, the rise of big business, and the specter of socialism. They fretted about labor unrest, large-scale business mergers, incredible economic inequality, rampant exploitation of workers (including children), and the concentration of vice in urban centers.[47] The middle class felt caught between the ostentatious, rigidly individualistic super-rich and the mutualistic, but rabble-rousing, lower class. They "could no longer abide the alien cultures, class conflict, and violence of a divided industrial nation," in the words of historian Michael McGerr. "By the turn of the century, middle-class men and women, radicalized and resolute, were ready to sweep aside the upper ten [percent] and build a new, progressive America."[48]

The white, middle-class, predominantly Protestant reformers at the forefront of the Progressive movement broke with the individualist ideology that marked upper-class society.[49] Drawing inspiration from the social sciences, the Progressives developed an environmental (or social-ecological) worldview, which posited that social context, rather than simple individual failure, produced ills such as poverty, insanity, crime, and delinquency. At the same time, many believed that particular people were hereditarily hopeless. Taking their cues from the popular eugenics movement, they sought to identify, classify, isolate, and reproductively sterilize individuals deemed "feeble minded," criminal, and generally "unfit" and undeserving. Progressive Era eugenics lent scientific heft to popular prejudices and discriminatory treatment of racial and ethnic minorities, immigrants, the poor, and women (especially "sexual deviants").[50]

The Progressives undertook a "bold effort to remake Americans, to create a new people living by new codes of conduct."[51] Practically, this meant urging the super-rich to spread their wealth and live more righteously, while forcing immigrants and the native poor to live according to white middle-class cultural values. Progressives such as Jane Addams sought to culturally assimilate the disadvantaged through settlement house activities—through *association* with Progressives, immigrants and poor native city dwellers were meant to develop dispositions and practices that, theoretically, would improve their social station. Because many working-class people (especially men, for whom vices were a way to perform masculinity) would not voluntarily give up habits that ostensibly undermined domestic life (such as hard drinking, gambling, and soliciting prostitutes), the Progressives lobbied the state to outlaw these behaviors.[52]

Their benevolent view of the state meant Progressives routinely turned to government to achieve other goals, too: regulating big business, instituting labor standards, and spreading wealth through redistributive taxation.[53] State intervention (in concert with community action and philanthropy) would reform the political and economic systems, quelling unrest between blacks and whites, men and women, workers and owners, and natives and immigrants. The Progressives' campaigns would, in tandem, improve and reinforce existing economic and political orders, making revolutionary transformations unnecessary and unwelcome. The Progressives sought to save the United States from itself.[54]

Their vision materialized in diverse areas of punishment. With the birth of the juvenile court in the late 1800s, states embraced an individualized, rehabilitative approach to curbing youth delinquency and dependency. Reformers pushed through major reforms to professionalize (and depoliticize) policing. Changes included the centralization of police administration, introduction of scientific methods of crime detection, institution of training and education (including the first college-level policing programs), creation of specialized units, and restrictions on discretion (especially related to use of force).[55] On the heels of the new penologists, the Progressives lobbied states for indeterminate sentencing and the creation of parole boards to approve the release of prisoners. Inside prisons, they introduced classification systems to individualize treatment of prisoners, began to classify types of prisons (including reformatories for juveniles and women) to meet the needs of different types of criminals, and worked to transform penal institutions into "therapeutic communities" that drew on a "medical model" of rehabilitation to transform "antisocial" malcontents into "prosocial" contributing members of society.

These changes in criminal and juvenile justice—like many Progressive Era reforms in other policy areas—melded reformation and coercive social control.[56] For example, the juvenile court routinely incarcerated girls for "status offenses" such as drinking, smoking, going to dance halls, or experimenting with sex.[57] In this case, "child saving" and imposed conformity to white, middle-class, Protestant ideals of femininity[58] were part of what political scientist Marie Gottschalk argues was a larger strategy to "expand the surveillance and control of young women by policing their sexuality."[59]

The juvenile court also tried to "normalize" working-class families (that is, make them more like "normal," middle-class white families) by forcing them to adhere to particular cultural standards in regard to diet, child discipline, alcohol consumption, and other private matters.[60] The juvenile court used coercive social control (characterized as reformation) to remake the working class into the middle class (at least culturally) and make European immigrants *white*.[61] It also reinforced the "color line," severely limiting African Americans' opportunities and perpetuating their status as semicitizens.[62] This was especially true in the North; in the South, where the vast majority of African Americans continued to reside, the juvenile justice system was underdeveloped. Those youth penal institutions that did exist were reserved almost exclusively for whites. Black youth in the Jim Crow South were subjected to "severe and violent punishments, including executions, whippings, commitment to adult prisons, and continued ordeals of convict-labor exploitations."[63]

Even in northern cities, black youth were treated far worse than whites. In Chicago, the birthplace of the juvenile court, African American delinquents were typically incarcerated rather than placed on probation because they were seen as disposed to bad behavior and less amendable to rehabilitation via the helping hand of probation officers.[64] The courts assigned black children to black probation officers exclusively; since the courts hired so few African American agents, of course, only a small minority of black youths could receive this sanction.[65] This was especially true for girls, criminologist Geoff Ward details: "Barred from private institutions, and accepted only in small numbers at the state run-institution, they remained in detention longest. Thus, dependent black girls had virtually no access to rehabilitative services through Chicago's early juvenile court."[66]

Segregation within the juvenile justice system (as well as the adult system) was consistent with the Progressives' approach to racial segregation in general. McGerr explains:

> Unlike some other Americans, progressives did not support segregation out of anger, hatred, and a desire to unify whites; but they certainly displayed plenty of condescension and indifference as well as compassion. . . . Progressives fairly readily accepted the inequitable arrangement of segregation. They did so because usually there were worse alternatives. Most of the progressives told themselves that separation allowed reform to continue. Protected by the shield of segregation, the fundamental project of transforming people could go on in safety.[67]

The reformers' acceptance of segregation and unwillingness to challenge structural inequality and violence contributed to the growth of African American activism around the issues of crime and punishment in this period. Ward asserts, for example, that the "relations of oppression and domination, which defined Jim Crow juvenile justice systems, became the main target of oppositional movements to transform the racial structure of American juvenile justice."[68]

The creation of the juvenile court and subsequent expansion of youth justice is one example among many that demonstrates the Progressives' predilection for using the state to police and coercively transform people into their own image. A second prominent example is the campaign against prostitution.[69] Led by women reformers, the campaign both generated and fed off hysteria about the "social evil" of "commercialized vice," as

John D. Rockefeller Jr. called sex work. Concerns about immigration infused this moral panic.[70]

The campaign led to the passage of two major laws, the Immigration Act of 1910 and the White Slave Traffic Act (also called the Mann Act), which expanded regulations of prostitution and "extended federal policing powers by permitting Washington to prosecute anyone suspected of transporting women across state lines for any 'immoral purpose.'"[71] These laws and the larger campaign against prostitution were emblematic of progressive reform, increasing the state's capacity to regulate behavior that offended reformers' sensibilities. Moreover, these legal changes show how the Progressives sought to ameliorate a "social problem" rather than deal with structural inequalities. As Gottschalk explains, the campaign against prostitution, like the efforts to police sexuality through juvenile justice, "legitimized an uncritical acceptance of the state in the area of social control and the greater use of various state-sponsored institutions to reform women and, by extension, men who strayed from traditional norms."[72]

Beyond prostitution, Progressives advocated for a general expansion of policing powers. Indeed, the professionalization of policing is often viewed as a major Progressive Era achievement.[73] In key respects, the changes to police organization, training, and education made during this era *were* remarkable; they went a long way toward depoliticizing police forces (at least in terms of administrative control, hiring, and promotion). Yet, professionalized police forces remained political in that they helped govern and reinforce dominant racial, class, sexuality, and gender orders. In northern cities, the police fortified the walls of urban ghettos, broke strikes, and terrorized dissidents.[74] Policing practices reflected and reaffirmed the tight coupling of blackness with criminality, which, as Khalil Gibran Muhammad demonstrates, grew even tighter in the Progressive Era. This historical reality lends support to one of our core arguments: reform can and often does perpetuate coercive social control, punishment, and oppression. Therefore, it is often incorrect to juxtapose reform *against* other purposes and outcomes—especially in the Progressive Era.

Despite the fact that many individual reformers (Addams[75] is the paradigmatic example) no doubt had great compassion and good intentions, the Progressives' privileged social position led many to hold romantic ideals about the state as an unqualified force for the collective good. They failed to consider (or considered, but did not act accordingly) that social peace for some meant oppression for others. And their paternalistic project of social uplift entailed imposing—often by force—particular cultural ideals, many of which remained stuck in the Victorian era, onto European immigrants, gender and sexual "deviants," ethnic and racial minorities, and rebellious workers. Many of the limitations and exclusions we describe were not unintended consequences. They were purposefully built into the progressive reform agenda by those who led the struggle to implement it.

---

TEXT BOX

## Community Corrections and Net Widening

Along with the creation of the juvenile court, the institutionalization of probation and parole were among the crowning achievements of Progressive Era penal reform. In the case of probation, individuals convicted of a crime—ideally those who would otherwise be incarcerated—would be released directly to the community with supervision. With parole, convicts would be released after a variable term of imprisonment, then receive post-release supervision in the community.

In his influential account of this period, historian David Rothman explains that criminal justice reforms unfolded as a dialectical process of "conscience and convenience." Progressive reforms developed out of *conscience*—or reformers' righteous intentions to better society. Yet they were implemented by government officials and legal actors who favored their *convenience*—adopting new penal practices to achieve practical goals (such as reducing workloads), typically subverting the spirit of the reformers. Thus, reforms predictably failed to live up to their promise. Rothman concludes, "In the end, when conscience and convenience met, convenience won."[76]

Prosecutors, judges, wardens, and state bureaucrats all gained extensive leverage when penal "alternatives" were introduced. For example, probation increased judges' discretionary power, gave prosecutors more ammunition for getting guilty pleas, and provided defense attorneys a way to appease clients (in "saving" them from prison by getting them probation sentences).[77] In cities, especially where probation became common, plea-bargaining rates shot up in the 1920s and 1930s, and defendants who pled guilty were much more likely to receive a suspended sentence with probation.[78] Parole was equally beneficial to criminal justice system actors, particularly wardens, who were responsible for managing prison populations. Given the power to effectively "veto" individual parole cases, wardens gained substantial leverage over prisoners and could manage their institutions' population size. Administrators could then curry favor with politicians, increasing releases during overcrowding without changing the perception that courts meted out tough sentences.[79]

Although reformers considered probation and parole alternatives to imprisonment (or, in the case of parole, an alternative to convicts serving their full sentences behind bars), these institutions effectively expanded social control. Since serious cases were usually sent to state-financed prisons, there was little judicial or prosecutorial incentive to divert "tough" cases to probation. Rather, court actors used probation to lessen the load on local penal systems (primarily county and city jails) while increasing control of those who otherwise might have received nonsupervisory sanctions, such as suspended sentences.[80] Further, the introduction of parole coincided with a *lengthening* in prison terms.[81] Together, probation and parole expanded the number of people subject to state control, the length of that control, and the scope and forms of that control. The Progressives' impulse to provide noninstitutional forms of supervision was co-opted by efforts to manage and discipline ever-broader swaths of the population.

Tellingly, there is little evidence that Progressives viewed this "net widening" as a problem. After all, their benevolent view of the state and their project of social uplift would have led many to see an expansion in the criminal justice system as an *opportunity*: bringing more people under governmental supervision would facilitate resocialization, the process of remaking people to fit the cultural and moral standards Progressives deemed "normal."[82] From a critical perspective, however, net widening represented growth in coercive social control couched in the language of reformation.[83]

## Participatory Imprisonment in the Empire State

As in the Jacksonian Era and Gilded Age, New York was a—if not *the*—leader in criminal justice innovation in the Progressive Era.[84] It experimented extensively with probation and parole and attempted to radically transform prisons into "treatment communities."[85] Whereas the Jacksonians believed that uniform prison routines (often completed in near silence and sometimes in total isolation) would produce disciplined subjects, the Progressives believed that individualized treatment would transform the prisoner (rhetorically presumed to be male) into a masculine citizen-worker. In this vein, Progressives wanted to model prison on free society, believing that practice as responsible, productive citizens would lead convicts to develop the dispositions and skills necessary for post-release success.[86] Thus, reformers strove to replicate the structure of society inside prisons, creating "communities" to generate reformation.

As McLennan argues, New York's penal reforms were in large part fueled by a management problem: prisoner idleness. As previously discussed, struggle by a range of actors culminated in legal changes that all but eliminated the practice of contracting out convicts to private companies (most notably, the 1894 McDonough amendment made illegal both the hiring out of prisoners to private companies and selling prison goods to the public). The abolition of contractual penal servitude generated a series of political, financial, and practical problems for prison administrators. Above all else, it meant prisoners who previously worked 10-hour shifts were now idle.[87]

Thus the New York State Prison Commission spearheaded the task of developing an alternative to the private contract system, a project that came to fundamentally reorganize the prison system. The model centered on the "state-use" system, in which prisoners produced goods for other state departments. In 1986, the state charged its prison commission with integrating New York's penal institutions into one centralized, bureaucratic system of production. All prisoners would be put to labor. Advocates believed this system would pay for the costs of imprisonment, but it faced many challenges in becoming profitable, including the costs of training the labor, organizing prisons around specific production needs, and finding state customers for the stigmatized (and non-discounted) prison-made goods.[88]

The prison labor problem provided an opening for major reforms as the state prison commission began to consolidate multiple independent institutions into a centralized, hierarchical penal *system*. For example, the prison commission instituted an assessment process for sorting prisoners into classes on the basis of their potential for productive labor. In order to track prisoners through assessment and transfers across prisons, the state began to develop records for identifying and tracking individuals as they entered and left the prison system (adopting the Bertillon method, measuring different bodily dimensions and noting any unique features).[89] In lieu of full employment, especially among those deemed unfit for productive labor, officials experimented with other ways to occupy prisoners' time, including education. These classes focused heavily on expanding literacy, with wardens investing in libraries and literacy rates soaring.[90] Officials also expanded religious services and, as McLennan writes, eliminated relics considered "counter to the restoration of manhood," including "shaving prisoners' heads, dressing prisoners in striped uniforms, and forcing prisoners to march in lock-step."[91]

The early progressive reforms produced demonstrable changes in New York prisons. Still, reformers faced stiff opposition from wardens, guards, and prisoners. Wardens resented the increasing bureaucratization of the prison system, which narrowed their managerial control. They particularly disliked the classification system that assigned jobs to prisoners, since that task formerly fell to the warden, giving him plum positions to dole out. Wardens also fought against the loss of control over prison contracts (for such things as prisoners' food) and hiring and firing of prison guards.[92] For their part, guards opposed reforms that increased their workload by letting prisoners have more out-of-cell time or reduced their disciplinary arsenal by outlawing certain forms of corporal punishment and time in the "dark cell." Along with vocal protest, guards and wardens responded to new limitations with creativity. Guards (sometimes with warden cooperation) covered up misbehavior and imposed a code of silence to protect malfeasant coworkers who violated the rules around physical punishment.[93] Wardens undermined administrative authority by subverting prisoner classification procedures and relying on the old patronage model in hiring and firing staff as well as selecting prison supply vendors.[94]

Prisoners protested, in part, because the promise of meaningful employment was never realized. The state-use system struggled to find stable industries, opening up shops only to close them almost immediately under protest from free workers and companies. There was rarely enough semiskilled work for all able prisoners, and prison industries were periodically shut down. For much of this period, the most common form of labor was construction work on building and renovating the prisons. Starting in the 1910s, there was also a somewhat steady stream of hard labor repairing state roads.[95]

In the meantime, the emerging discourse of state "responsibility" for prisoners, alongside increased support for prisoner literacy, had opened up new avenues for protest. For example, prisoners used the newly established inmate newsletter (the *Star of Hope*) to voice concerns around inadequate food, corporal punishment, and limits on prisoners' freedom of movement. Prisoner writers encouraged convicts to think of themselves as a class with common predicaments, needs, and interests.[96] Ironically, progressive reforms—such as the introduction of the *Star of Hope* and educational programs—empowered prisoners to act collectively, often in opposition to the administrators who had initiated such changes.[97]

Prisoner dissatisfaction escalated into a 1913 revolt at Sing Sing. Prisoners threw stale bread through the cellblock windows to protest the quality of the food and began burning areas of the prison. Local and national reporters jumped on the story, exposing the limitations of early progressive prison reform.[98] Reformers struggled to capitalize on the disruption, claiming that the incident highlighted the failures of patchwork solutions to the prison labor question. Searching for a solution to these political challenges, Governor William Sulzer appointed Thomas Mott Osborne, an eclectic and charismatic Progressive leader, to the New York State Prison Reform Commission.[99]

Osborne, together with his progressive coalition, the National Committee on Prisons and Prison Labor (NCPPL), began a bold campaign to transform New York prisons. He began with a publicity stunt: in August 1913, Osborne entered Auburn as a "regular" prisoner for a weeklong sentence, including a night in a dark cell. Despite special privileges (such as being allowed reading and writing materials and a private cell), Osborne wrote that his time in prison was "terrifying" and enlivened his work with a religious zeal. With the publication of his book *Within Prison Walls*, Osborne rose to national prominence and, with the NCPPL, championed a distinctly progressive, three-pronged model of imprisonment: (1) ending forced labor, (2) motivating prisoners to work through a wage system, and (3) embracing alternative modes of producing disciplined citizen-workers. Osborne rallied his supporters (including former president Theodore Roosevelt) with British politician W. E. Gladstone's motto: "It is liberty alone that fits men for liberty."[100]

Osborne tested some of his key reform ideas at Auburn. After getting his close friend and political ally Charles Rattigan appointed warden,[101] the prison introduced prisoner self-governance. At Osborne's request, prisoners elected a governing body to develop the terms of the new model. Although Osborne publicly credited the convicts for deciding how to govern, he had carefully steered the decision-making process.[102] In fact, the system that emerged mirrored that of the George Junior Republic, a New York reform school with which Osborne had been involved for more than a decade.[103]

At Auburn, the new Mutual Welfare League consisted of elected members from each company of the prison. Its central responsibilities included setting wage scales, procuring goods that prisoners could purchase with their earnings, and organizing sports leagues and recreational activities.[104] The League had authority to sanction fellow prisoners; it could even suspend or expel convicts from the governance system. Theoretically, this disciplinary function was an alternative to punishment from prison staff. Practically, it operated as a supplement to official discipline—oftentimes, prisoners received discipline from both.[105] The organization also became a mechanism for enforcing the administration's rules. So while the League was a rather radical experiment, it functioned at least in part as a conventional tool for controlling the general population. Soon, prisoners and guards alike resented the League—the former did not approve of inmates doing the staff's dirty work under the pretense of reform and the latter disliked prisoners usurping any of their disciplinary duties.[106]

In 1914, Osborne became warden of Sing Sing. He worked to turn it into an institution that would exemplify the Progressives' desire to bridge the community and prison, preparing inmates for participation in modern society. He implemented an organization of prisoner self-governance, transforming the prior warden's "Golden Rule Brotherhood" into an Auburn-style Mutual Welfare League.[107] The warden also welcomed an impressive roster of philanthropists, artists, educators, and health professionals into the institution. One of his greatest achievements was convincing Henry Ford to hire ex-prisoners in his car factories.[108] Osborne also created a banking system in which prisoners used their "income" to buy necessities; upon release, former prisoners could convert their savings into real dollars to aid their transition back into the community.[109]

As part of Sing Sing's makeover, Osborne launched a public campaign to eliminate sexual relations between prisoners. The warden maintained that same-sex relations were anathema to the production of manly citizens. As part of the crackdown, prison staff sought to identify, isolate, and punish prisoners involved in sexual behavior. The introduction of health professionals and regular screenings for sexually transmitted diseases were explicitly motivated by a desire to reduce sexual misconduct by identifying "psychopaths" and those with infectious diseases.[110] This campaign was a clear-cut example of coercive social control wrapped in the language of "reform," similar to contemporaneous efforts to use eugenics to identify and contain "feeble minded" youths who allegedly threatened national well-being (not least with their purported fecundity).[111]

The breadth and boldness of Osborne's reforms generated strong resistance from within and beyond the prison system. Custodial staff resented reductions in power and the expansions of prisoners' privileges. Conscious of the importance of winning over guards, the Mutual Welfare Leagues at Auburn and Sing Sing established a fund for officers' widows. Yet, guards argued that the prisons' administrations were more sympathetic to the prisoners than to their employees. Guards were particularly reticent to give convicts the right to punish rule breakers, but when officers spoke out, Osborne found ways to maneuver around the Civil Service Law and dismiss them—further infuriating the guards.[112]

Osborne also faced resistance from outside the prisons, especially from New York's influential political machines, which had long opposed Progressives' "good government" initiatives and efforts to reshape state institutions.[113] Unsurprisingly, the entrenched politicians were particularly hostile toward Osborne (both a shining symbol and an instrument of the larger Progressive movement). They aided the warden's detractors as hostile forces moved to take him down.[114]

The turning point came in 1915, when the superintendent of New York's prison system, John Riley, who resented that Osborne circumvented his control over Sing Sing, learned that Osborne had made secret deals with a group of prisoners who had violated the sexual-conduct rules.[115] Osborne had punished the men informally and kept them at Sing Sing rather than notifying Riley, who likely would have exiled the prisoners to the facility in Clinton (known as the harshest men's prison in New York).[116] The scandal led to a grand jury trial, and Osborne was charged with perjury and neglect of duty. Twenty-one prisoners were charged with sodomy. The district attorney also charged Osborne with "various unnatural and immoral acts" (implying that Osborne himself had engaged in sodomy).[117] Osborne's allies successfully maneuvered to get the charges dropped, but the damage was done. National reform leaders increasingly distanced themselves from Osborne, and the penal bureaucracy clamped down at Sing Sing. After just two years in office, Osborne resigned his wardenship.[118]

William H. Moyer, a former federal prison warden with a penchant for strict discipline, took the helm but was replaced shortly thereafter (in 1920) by Lewis E. Lawes, a former prison guard. Lawes's appointment symbolized a renewed focus on "law and order" inside the walls. Although some of Osborne's reforms remained in place through these two transitions, prison administrators viewed them as a means for managing (not reforming) the incarcerated. For example, guards embraced recreation, but as a tenet of good prison management rather than a way to produce ideal worker-citizens. Prison officials also reduced the power and independence of inmates. Embracing cold practicality, the administration now believed that the "best prison was one in which the prisoners were well-fed, well-exercised, and frequently entertained."[119] Like Osborne, the progressive ideal had lost credibility and the power to shape penal policy in the Empire State.

In all, the case study of New York shows that extensive contestation within and beyond the growing penal field shaped reforms. On the pervasiveness and importance of struggle, McLennan writes:

> At times demonstrative and violent and, at other times, subtle and discursive, the response of convicts and guards to administrators' innovations forged a new prison order that both drew on and undermined,

the sanitized, "civilized," reformatory penal system provided for in law and policy. Outside the prison, meanwhile, workers, the political machines, voters, and, to some degree, industry exercised various degrees of influence over the implementation of the reforms.[120]

McLennan deftly demonstrates that struggle produced a braided form of punishment in New York, the crucible of Progressive Era criminal justice reform. The system was as much managerial and punitive as it was rehabilitative. Fierce, persistent resistance from a range of actors ultimately generated a major shift in the penal terrain—a shift away from Osborne and his colleagues' ideal of reformatory justice and toward a vision of no-frills order maintenance (especially within the prisons).[121]

BEFORE LEAVING NEW YORK, it is important to note that even within the state—and within individual prisons—there was extensive variation. Progressives sought to unify the prison system by differentiating and specializing each facility under the command of a centralized authority. The prisons were graded, first, according to types and extent of labor. Sing Sing housed first-grade (or most-skilled) laborers, Auburn held the second grade, and Clinton—the most remote facility, known for its brutality and nicknamed "Siberia" and the "Dark Hole of Calcutta"—confined the third. Convicts deemed insane or "defective" were sent to the new Dannemore State Hospital.[122] Prisoner transfers gave administrators a powerful disciplinary technique and sorting mechanism, and the official grading of prisons and prisoners was paired with a hierarchy of privileges, with the first-grade prisoners benefiting earlier and more consistently from progressive reforms.

Variation within the prisons also existed along racial lines. Many of the educational programs focused explicitly on socializing European immigrants, and none focused on African Americans. Some black prisoners did benefit from the reforms at Auburn and Sing Sing, but they were concentrated in the idle and unskilled companies, which segregated races across and within prisons.[123] Indeed, new penological reform in general seems to have formalized race segregation and widened racial inequality at Sing Sing.[124]

Gender was another source of variation. In the early 1900s, states built the first reformatories for women. Nicole Rafter defines the reformatories as "separate and independent prison(s) for women, established through efforts of agitators outside the penal bureaucracy with the aim of rehabilitation." By the 1930s, there were 17 in the United States, sharing a vision of "rescue and reform."[125] Female reformers—Rafter's "agitators"—wanted to rescue disadvantaged women from local jails, state prisons, and vice-ridden cities. They believed that women required "specialized treatment" (what is now called "gender-responsive treatment") owing to a "domestic and sensitive nature."[126]

These reformatories were concentrated in the Northeast and Midwest. Once again, New York was at the forefront of penal innovation, and its reformatory for women at Bedford Hills was a trailblazer. Under the leadership of Katherine B. Davis, an exceptionally influential reformer who studied with renowned economist and sociologist Thorstein Veblen while earning her doctoral degree at the University of Chicago, Bedford came closer than any other to a "treatment community." Located in a rural swath of Westchester County, Bedford's design departed from men's prisons: it did not have a wall or fence, and "residents" were housed in cottages rather than cellblocks. The relatively open design reflected the Progressives' anti-institutionalism, and its site, well outside New York City, reflected the reformers' belief that urban environments generated crime and other social ills, while the country purified the body and soul. (Juvenile reformatories were located primarily in rural locations for the same reason.)[127]

Programming at Bedford was distinctly progressive. For example, prisoners participated in limited self-governance; they elected leaders and held responsibility for sanctioning rule violators. Along with academic classes, the facility provided vocational training beyond domestic chores, though according to Rafter, this emphasis on nontraditional vocational training was short lived: "By 1909 Davis was recommending outdoor work for reformatory inmates on the ground [*sic*] that they were intellectually and emotionally capable of little else."[128] Davis also refocused educational training on domestic service because of labor market demands—as white women increasingly landed jobs in manufacturing, retail, and administrative services, there was a high demand for domestic servants. Parolees trained in domestic service, then, could find jobs. "Given that a significant proportion of inmates had worked as domestics prior to incarceration," Anne Bowler, Chrysanthi Leon, and Terry Lilley explain, "reform thus largely functioned to return them to the same degraded economic status they had without the benefit of training and confinement."[129]

Bedford Hills fully embraced "the medical model," assuming that both heredity *and* environmental factors produced crime.[130] With funding from John D. Rockefeller Jr., Bedford established the "Laboratory of Social Hygiene." Staffed by experts such as psychologists and criminologists, the laboratory employed current scientific methods to understand and treat "deviant" women (the primary focus was sexual deviance, such as prostitution). Influenced by the eugenics movement, Davis and her staff implemented procedures for detecting and classifying hopeless cases (that is, "moral imbeciles" who were "resistant to treatment") who required indefinite incarceration.[131] Thus, the leading reformatory for women in the United States employed well-financed technologies for controlling women's sexuality and sorting and incapacitating prisoners deemed "feeble minded" in the name of "reform." For Progressives such as Davis, this was no contradiction: the "reformatory" practices were deemed necessary for the "social defense" of the country.

As was true at Sing Sing, the progressive experiment at Bedford Hills did not last long. In 1914 (13 years after the facility opened), Superintendent Davis left to begin work as the commissioner of corrections for New York City. Shortly thereafter, an investigation into the prison revealed extensive overcrowding and scandalous accounts of sexual deviance—including interracial relations. Historian Estelle Freedman explains that African American and white women had long shared cottages because Davis had opposed residential segregation. However, investigators claimed the living arrangements created institutional disorder. Rather than racial conflict, however, "it was the revelation of homosexual attachments between black and white inmates that proved a source of embarrassment for the administration."[132] As Cheryl Hicks argues, racial segregation would not end "harmful intimacy" (as officials called interracial same-sex relationships), "but it would address institutional and national anxieties about interracial sex."[133]

Bedford moved to segregate the housing units and increasingly turned to brutal, physical punishment to control prisoners. A 1920 investigation showed that Davis's innovations had all but vanished: "while serving in a very limited degree its original purpose, [Bedford] is in the main not a reformatory at all."[134] As the experiments at Bedford Hills and Sing Sing were all but pronounced dead, reformers sought opportunities beyond New York to establish—and maintain—genuine treatment communities.

As actors such as Osbourne and Davis gained power within the Progressive Era penal field, they developed institutions and implemented policies that drew on culturally dominant assumptions and beliefs about race, gender, class, and sexuality. It is a stark reminder that criminal justice is always embedded in larger cultural contexts (such as the influence of eugenics in Progressive Era criminal justice), and that prevailing ideas constrain what is considered possible inside the institutions—as the negative response to interracial housing and relationships in Bedford demonstrated. Race, gender, and sexuality were central to the struggles over imprisonment in New York then and in many penal contests since—perhaps nowhere more pivotal than in the penal battles of the American South.

## An Unlikely Place: Reform in the Lone Star State

In 1927, progressive advocates moved to implement their vision of reformative incarceration in an improbable state: Texas. The NCPPL dreamed of opening a "penal colony" in Austin, building on Osborne's New York innovations and creating a new national model. Texas had proven resistant to progressive penal reform, in part due to a long tradition of austere prisons exploiting the labor of poor Texans. Recall that the most significant improvement in twentieth-century imprisonment upto this point had been the elimination of convict leasing and development of plantation-style penal farms—reforms that spread throughout the South during the Progressive Era.[135] Yet in Texas (and elsewhere), penal farms remained brutal and repressive. Black and Latino convicts suffered more than whites, though prisoners of all races performed backbreaking physical labor.[136]

Local actors who spearheaded the late 1920s campaign to realize the Progressives' dream in Texas had been struggling for reform for years. Elizabeth Speer, a social worker with a background in criminology and penology, and her fellow reformers had developed a coalition of women's organizations and teamed up with the NCPPL in 1923 to conduct a systematic survey of Texas's carceral facilities. They hoped to recommend (and then lobby for) progressive reforms. The *Texas Prison Survey* "brimmed with indignation" at horrendous prison conditions and recommended a complete overhaul of the system, including the implementation of indeterminate sentencing, academic education, professionalization of guards, diagnostic centers, mental hospitals, and a separate reformatory for women.[137]

Governor Pat Neff proved the biggest obstacle, if only one among many in state government. Historian Robert Perkinson explains that Neff "was the first Texas governor to make hard-fisted, no-nonsense crime fighting a central part of his political identity."[138] While rejecting calls for prison reform, he supported policies that expanded the incarcerated population. Meanwhile, a newly energized Ku Klux Klan was gaining extensive political power; in fact, the organization "became a more potent political force than the Democratic Party, which it largely controlled." With regard to crime and punishment, the Klansmen and Governor Neff found few disagreements,[139] leaving the Progressives little chance to generate meaningful reforms.

Speer and her colleagues continued their uphill battle under the governorship of Neff's successor, Miriam "Ma" Ferguson. However, their fortunes changed when Daniel Moody, a prosecutor who campaigned on "prison reform, higher education, and graft-free government," was elected.[140] With Moody in power, NCPPL reformers gained the institutional authority they needed to produce reforms. Speer, for example, became executive secretary to the state's prison board (Robert Holmes Baker, another Progressive, was its chair).[141] And though they failed to convince the legislature to implement their vision for an Austin-based penal colony, the reformers (with Moody's backing) introduced important reforms to existing prisons. They oversaw limitations to work hours, classification of prisoners on the basis of rehabilitative potential rather than physical capacity, expansion of educational and recreational programs, and improvements in post-release employment opportunities. Drawing from Osborne's model, the reformers implemented a Prison Welfare League, led by white trustees at the Texas State Penitentiary at Huntsville (nicknamed "The Walls"), to coordinate recreational and educational programs, run an inmate newsletter, and advocate for prisoner-led reforms (such as an "honor farm" staffed primarily by prisoners).[142]

As in New York, the Texas Progressives faced intense resistance even as they gained influence. Perkinson wryly observes, "With progressives controlling the Prison Board, a feminist social worker setting top-level policy, and a Jewish convict plotting prisoner self-government, Texas's prison administration was fast getting ahead of the political establishment."[143] The new administrators weathered an avalanche of bad publicity, much of it aimed at the "menace" Speer. Demoralized and marginalized, prison guards became less effective, and mutinies and prison escapes increased. By 1928, a record-breaking 17% of the prison population successfully escaped Texas prison farms. When, in 1929, the president of the Prison Welfare League and two other prisoners (both of whom wrote for the newspaper) absconded, public scorn for the system reached a new high.[144] Making matters even worse, politicians and state bureaucrats lambasted the prison system for failing to support itself financially.[145]

By 1930, Governor Moody had to make a change. He curtailed funding from the legislature and recommended that the prison system consolidate its properties in the old sugarcane belt to increase revenues. Board members continued to argue for modernization and centralization, but the legislature was unwilling to shift from the plantation-based agricultural model that had once been so profitable. Further, legislators staunchly opposed the idea—even the possibility—of "reforming" black and Latino convicts. In response to this conflict, Moody officially ousted the progressive leadership, appointing a conservative former sheriff, Colonel Lee Simmons, to lead the prison system. Simmons was the Progressives' loudest critic. His tenure tilted the department back to the "business model," with profitability topping the list of penal priorities.[146] Educational programs and work limits were slashed, and brutal corporeal punishments returned. Simmons kept the inmate newspaper in place, but it was no longer prisoner-directed. Instead, it reflected managerial interests.

Tellingly, recreation was expanded, but as a mechanism for control rather than rehabilitation. Simmons proved a much savvier leader than his Progressive counterparts. In perhaps his most famous move, Simmons started the "Fastest and Wildest Rodeo," which featured white male prisoners competing as "cowboys"; black and Latino males engaging in "farcical free-for-alls like 'Convict Poker,'" in which they played cards while an angry bull ran loose in the arena; white females singing patriotic tunes; and black females participating in "greased pig sacking" contests (trying to catch pigs in a mud pit). By the late 1930s, the prisoner rodeo was one of the state's biggest tourist attractions, a deadly and profitable morality play every Sunday.[147]

The dramatic end to progressive prison reform in Texas reaffirms the importance of local culture, politics, and intergroup relations in shaping policy outcomes.[148] Reformers such as Elizabeth Sheer briefly gained power because of her ties to Governor Moody (and his extensive bureaucratic and political resources), support from the national NCPPL, and ongoing crises within the prison system, but they remained marginal players in the larger political field. Still, their limited reforms were radical in a state that used criminal justice as a blunt-force object to dominate racial minorities and where political culture emphasized small government, low taxes, and self-sustaining state institutions. In retrospect, it is astounding that the Progressives enjoyed even a brief moment of control in Texas's prison system.

The decline of progressive penal reform in Texas and beyond was due to fierce opposition from powerful actors who kept the penal landscape unsteady. But macro-level trends facilitated the opposition's efforts to cripple the progressive agenda. Perkinson summarizes:

Although Progressivism expanded in Texas in the years surrounding World War I, a variety of social dislocations—among them, increased immigration, the Great Migration of African Americans northward,

as well as the rise of the New Woman, the New Negro, and the
Bolsheviks—enervated the movement in the Northeast and Midwest.
Anxiety eclipsed state-building idealism, while conservatism, both
moral and corporate, enjoyed a resurgence. Although many progres-
sive ideas would reappear in the New Deal, they lost oxygen in the
Roaring Twenties.[149]

Thus, the political opening that the Progressives leveraged to produce changes
in juvenile and criminal justice had all but closed by the dawn of the 1920s.

## Conclusion

Against the pendulum view of penal development, which posits a sudden
rupture (or swing) propelled by a burst of reform ideology, this chapter
has shown that progressive criminal justice at the turn of the twentieth
century was born of struggle. During the Gilded Age, a range of actors
(including prisoners, free laborers, journalists, humanitarians, and populist politicians) fought bitterly against incredibly exploitative and often
deadly forms of punishment—namely, industrial imprisonment and convict leasing—that enriched a small number of capitalists and, especially
in the South, produced revenue for state governments. At the same time,
"new penologists" such as Zebulon Brockway continued to advocate for a
reformative vision of penal transformation. Prolonged contestation *against*
contractual penal servitude and *for* correctional criminal justice during
the Gilded Age produced fissures in the penal landscape that spread and
expanded as reformers took advantage of growing political opportunities
in the first decades of the 1900s to implement changes that would "uplift"
downtrodden lawbreakers.

As they gained power in the penal field, the Progressives and their allies
laid the foundation for the modern penal state.[150] They created the juvenile
court, institutionalized probation and parole, and altered aspects of incarceration, especially in the Midwest and Northeast. But as we have demonstrated, progressive criminal justice reform was far less extensive, far more
repressive, and certainly more contested than most accounts indicate. The
cases of New York and Texas showed that strident opposition and changing social-structural conditions eventually weakened progressive reformers
and threatened their gains. In a development that should offer little surprise,
this resistance did not eliminate their resolve. Just as the penologists who
opened this chapter struggled even after the erosion of the penitentiary ideal,

progressive-oriented reformers continued to fight up through the Second World War, advocating for such practices as indeterminate sentencing, prison-based treatment, and expansions of community corrections. These proponents of rehabilitative punishment would find their new political opening in the postwar years.

## 4

# Rehabilitation—All Things to All People

DESPITE INFLUENTIAL ACTORS' Progressive Era efforts to improve American punishment and reform prisoners, the 1920s, 1930s, and some or all of the 1940s and 1950s (depending on the state) have gone down in American penal history mostly as yet another bleak period. In 1931, for example, the federal Wickersham Commission published its ninth volume, dryly titled *Report on Penal Institutions, Probation, and Parole*. Like E. C. Wines and Theodore Dwight more than half a century earlier, the commission lamented—often scathingly—that the American punishment system "does not reform the criminal. It fails to protect society. There is reason to believe that it contributes to the increase of crime by hardening the prisoner."[1] Modern scholars of criminal justice sourly associate the decades between the First and Second World Wars with (among other things) an increase of capital punishment, expansion and militarization of federal law enforcement, ascension of organized crime, and transformation of prisons into warehouses that used prisoners for industrial profit rather than working to reform them through individualized treatment.[2] These decades also are recognized as a period in which punishment intensified class, gender, and racial divisions and hierarchies.[3]

As was the case after the Civil War, criminal justice during the 1920s and '30s was especially bleak in the South. Since the turn of the twentieth century, convict leasing was on the wane, but it was commonly replaced with other brutal, exploitative practices, including chain gangs and plantation-style prisons that were understood, even by contemporaries, as extensions of slavery. Infamous prison farms such as Parchman in Mississippi, Angola in Louisiana, and Tucker in Arkansas put prisoners (disproportionately African American) to work in the fields under the watchful eye of armed convict trustees and white guards.[4]

Although penal actors in western and midwestern states during the early decades of the twentieth century were more likely than their southern compatriots to profess a desire to "reform" the convicts under their supervision, they also often put prisoners to work in deplorable conditions. California, for example, had only two prisons until 1941, and both had notorious worksites, including the dreaded rock quarry at Folsom and the sickness-inducing jute bag[5] factory at San Quentin.[6] Even midwestern prisons, celebrated by their boosters for their modern industrial plants allegedly training prisoners in useful vocational skills, had their share of detested, punitive worksites. All new prisoners at Stateville Penitentiary in Illinois, for instance, were assigned to the quarry or coal piles; more seasoned prisoners were sent there as a form of punishment. Despite the reality of conditions, many politicians, wardens, and guards discussed the vaunted industrial labor shops at newly constructed prisons as useful for putting convicted criminals to work, teaching them "habits of industry" and keeping them busy to maintain order.[7]

But just as criminologists depict the Progressive Era as a period during which the spirit of punishment was transformed from hopeless to hopeful, many scholars of criminal justice portray the two decades or so following the end of the Second World War as the "rehabilitative era" (ca. 1945 to 1965).[8] This period is often romanticized as being wholly dissimilar from the folly and destructiveness of the harsh punishment that grew during the last third of the twentieth century. As Ian Loader and Richard Sparks write:

> There is a standing temptation for the sociology of punishment, dazzled and alarmed in equal measure by the extraordinary growth of prison populations internationally, to treat the 1950s and 1960s as little more than a foil, a screen against which to project the real object of enquiry—criminal and penal policy in the period since the 1970s. Aside from setting up some rather unhelpful binary oppositions . . . such histories of the present run the risk of doing violence to the past, of underplaying its tensions and conflicts, of inadvertently re/producing one-dimensional—implicitly rose-tinted—accounts of both the history of politics of penal modernism, and the reasons for its (apparent) demise.[9]

Thus, the "rehabilitative era" said to have dominated during the mid-twentieth century has become a sort of touchstone against which one can judge much of what came before and unfolded afterwards.

Drawing on and diverging from the dominant narrative of criminal justice in the decades following World War II, this chapter makes four principal arguments. The first section argues that during the 1920s through '40s there was constant contestation, as reformers struggled against what they viewed as the lamentable erosion of Progressive Era goals of using good governance tactics, as well as science and medicine, to prevent crime and "cure" criminals. Just because there may not have been all that much for political liberals and penal progressives to celebrate during this period does not mean they quit struggling. Instead, they critiqued the status quo and planted seeds for reform, some of which would bear fruit after the war.

The second section argues that the rise of the rehabilitative ideal was not a rupture, but the culmination of a long struggle by correctionalists to shape criminal justice in their image. Critical macro-level developments in the economy, education, politics, and "helping professions" (such as psychology, psychiatry, and social work) converged after the war, producing opportunities for actors to obtain dominant positions within penal institutions and the larger field in which key players tussled to decide policy visions and programs. As they gained status and influence, actors (many of them reformers) spread the discourse of rehabilitation and, to a lesser extent, reshaped criminal justice to become more correctional—hence the creation, in the 1940s and '50s, of neologisms such as "correctional institution," "community corrections," "correctional officer," and "correctional counselor."

The third section turns to California, widely considered a bellwether in the realm of criminal justice. Some scholars argue that after the Second World War, California fully embraced and implemented the rehabilitative ideal. Our own view is that it is better characterized as a time and place replete with conflict over punishment in which rehabilitation was implemented in partial and limited ways, intertwined from the start with expressly punitive and managerial logics and practices.

The fourth section travels to Florida. Here we counter the common view that southern states were wholesale exceptions to the rehabilitative movement in the North, Midwest, and West. Instead, we argue that influential actors strategically employed the *rhetoric* of rehabilitation in order to bureaucratize and professionalize criminal justice. While criminal justice leaders may have wanted to implement elements of the socio-medical model of rehabilitation, local culture, politics, and race relations limited their freedom to do so. So although we see little concurrent California-style rehabilitation in Florida, actors in that state deployed correctional language and justifications to usher in important changes to prisons and community sanctions.

We conclude that scholars, policymakers, and journalists look back at the decades following World War II as the rehabilitative era because the correctional ethos spread widely among "correctional experts" and penal practitioners. By the 1950s, "rehabilitation" was effectively common sense among the leaders of national organizations such as the American Prison Association. In fact, the term took on an almost religious quality among criminological and penological elites. Hence, this chapter's title, which comes from Corinthians (9:19–23): in this epistle, Paul says, "I have become all things to all people so that by all possible means I might save some." Rehabilitation, true believers insisted, would save lost souls and revive the progressive project that began decades earlier. And because of rehabilitation's symbolic power, penal actors used the correctional discourse to gain advantage in penal contests and legitimate all sorts of practices, many of which had nothing to do with "correcting" social or psychological maladies. That is, by the middle of the twentieth century, rehabilitation had become the *language* of criminal justice.

## Struggles in the Interwar Years

In the decades between the First and Second World Wars, penal farms in the South and "Big House" prisons in the North expanded. These penal innovations are commonly understood as sites of expansive, relatively uncontested domination. The prison farm came to symbolize southern punishment, with Parchman, located in northwestern Mississippi, exemplifying this penal form.[10] From its inception, Parchman was very profitable: by 1905, only a few years after the arrival of the first state convicts to the former slave plantation in the Yazoo-Mississippi delta, Parchman had funneled nearly $200,000 into state coffers—a veritable fortune in those years.[11] In part, this profitability was due to the fact that politicians and Parchman administrators copied a model they knew well: the slave plantation. Historian David Oshinsky summarizes: "Both systems used captive labor to grow the same crops in identical ways. Both relied on a small staff of rural, lower-class whites to supervise the black labor gangs. And both staffs mixed physical punishment with paternalistic rewards in order to motivate their workers."[12]

Despite how they are described in some scholarly overviews, Parchman and other plantation prisons were not principally the handiwork of elite business interests seeking a return to antebellum slavery. Rather, they were primarily the result of struggle by Populists *against* politically connected elites who held contracts to lease prisoners.[13] In Mississippi, for example, the charge to end the lease and to open Parchman was led by James Vardaman, elected governor in a highly contentious 1904 election during which southern whites repressed many of the modest gains that blacks had eked out during the Reconstruction period.

Known as the "White Chief," Vardaman railed against the immense fortunes planters and nascent southern industrialists gained from convict leasing. While he campaigned on (and later espoused, as governor) violence-inducing vitriol that described black citizens as dangerous, inferior humans who threatened whites' safety and prosperity, Vardaman also believed that black convicts ought to be treated humanely and put to work for the benefit of the white masses, not an elite few. While the conditions at Parchman were horrid and Vardaman (and his contemporaries) espoused blatantly racist demagoguery, this commitment to a modicum of human conditions—and having the state (rather than private interests) responsible for prisons and punishment—represented an amalgamation of both progressive and populist impulses.[14]

Having become governor with support from lower-class whites (and against opposition from elites who profited from convict leasing), Vardaman personally oversaw the draining of swamplands in the Yazoo-Mississippi delta for the opening of a series of prison farms, including the flagship institution at Parchman. The farms represented a Populist victory over well-heeled elites, many of whom shared Vardaman's racist beliefs but disagreed over which (and how many) whites ought to benefit from blacks' forced labor. In short, the struggle between Populist and elite whites was at the heart of the creation of Parchman.

Contestation over punishment in the South persisted throughout the 1920s, '30s, and '40s, as northern criminologists, penal administrators, and politicians condemned punishment south of the Mason-Dixon line as "backward." The American Correctional Association, for instance, "regularly assailed [Texas's] plantation [prisons] as anachronistic and criminogenic"; in 1935 William Cox, the executive secretary of the American Prison Association, flatly called southern prisons "a disgrace."[15] Critiques of southern punishment became more public with the blockbuster success of the 1932 film *I Am a Fugitive from a Chain Gang*. The movie and the book on which it was based told the story of a white northerner subject to the brutalities of Georgia's chain gangs.[16] Southern punishment in academic *and* popular critique was pictured as a lamentable throwback to slavery that caught unfortunate whites in its net.

As administrators at Parchman and their political allies struggled with critiques from within and beyond Mississippi, they sometimes simply refuted the basic allegation that conditions were deplorable. Prison officials insisted that "convicts were fed more, disciplined better, and driven no harder than field workers at other plantations in the state."[17] They also tried to beat southern critics and northern progressives at their own game by selectively incorporating penal innovations. For example, Parchman was the first American prison to adopt conjugal visitation, which gave the institution a progressive gloss—according to administrators, the practice helped keep marriages together and reduced sexual relations (e.g., intercourse) in the prison. Oshinsky argues, though, that conjugal visits had more to do with generating profits than helping prisoners; believing that blacks had animalistic sexual appetites, prison officials figured that African American prisoners would work harder once relieved of pent-up libidinal energy.[18]

Parchman's defenders also evidenced their forward thinking by allowing experimentation on convicts, a practice then seen as modern and progressive. In one particularly alarming instance, a doctor, seeking to confirm his theory about the sources of pellagra, induced the disease in a dozen prisoners (some of whom begged the governor to be let out of the experiment; one noted that "there were moments when he would have welcomed a bullet to the head"[19]). Prison administrators, doctors, and politicians agreed that using prisoners as "test subjects" benefited prisoners and society alike.[20]

Other progressive innovations included Christmas furloughs, the institution of a formal parole board (replacing the old system of politically driven gubernatorial pardons), and the introduction of limited education and vocational programs.[21] By the 1940s, state officials claimed to have a relatively modern, highly effective prison system. Although prisoners told a very different story (those at Parchman described austere, sometimes barbaric conditions, as well as guards' tolerance for contraband, violence, and sex[22]), this official narrative reveals much about the struggle and context in which southern penal change unfolded during the first half of the twentieth century.

IN THE NORTH, Northeast, Midwest, and West, Big House prisons such as San Quentin (California), Florence (Arizona), Stateville (Illinois), Jackson (Michigan), and Sing Sing (New York) were austere places with large tiers of cells (sometimes mixed in with open dormitories) in which prisoner reformation was not a central goal—despite many penal administrators proudly touting their educational and vocational programs. Capturing this bleakness, sociologist John Irwin writes: "This granite, steel, cement, and asphalt monstrosity stood as the state's most extreme form of punishment, short of the death penalty. . . . It was the place of banishment and punishment to which convicts were 'sent up.' Its major characteristics were isolation, routine, and monotony. Its mood was mean and grim, perforated here and there by ragged-edged vitality and humor."[23] As more black families from former slave states moved north, they were increasingly confined in northern prisons (in part due to aggressive policing set off by racialized fear of the influx of migrants).[24] Thus, the face of prisoners in the 1930s in the North was increasingly black and southern.

Those who had struggled during the Progressive Era for a correctional version of criminal justice were rather gloomy about these prisons, which functioned more like warehouses than treatment communities. A New York investigator in 1924, for instance, lamented the nature of punishment at Sing Sing: "The emphasis today is laid on the gaining of privileges as a reward for conduct rather than in stimulating the sense of individual responsibility for the common welfare, which is the basis of good citizenship. In one case the privileges are used as a[n] end in themselves; in the other, merely as the means to a very different, and far greater end."[25]

To make sense of this bleakness we must recognize the nature and role of ongoing struggle. A particularly useful case study can be found in historian Charles Bright's examination of Jackson State Prison—and Michigan politics—during the 1920s and '30s.[26] Like Parchman, Jackson emerged out of a particularly turbulent period. Prohibition, first passed into law in Michigan in May 1918 (nearly two years before the ratification of the Eighteenth Amendment to the Constitution banning the production and sale of alcohol across the country), contributed to a crime wave of alcohol-related arrests surrounding the illegal importation, production, and distribution of beer, wine, and spirits.[27] Given that Prohibition (like many earlier Progressive Era proposals) can be understood at least in part as an effort to monitor and control a perceived threat from "aliens" and "foreigners" (principally poor and working-class ethnic minorities from Europe), it follows that many politicians espoused a "get-tough" attitude on crime, designed to appeal to the supporters of Prohibition (supporters who, tellingly, defy simple categorizations such as "progressive" or "conservative").[28] In Michigan, the growing prison population and punitive political climate made it increasingly difficult for the governor to use parole releases to quietly control the state prison population, as had been customary in earlier decades.[29]

As the state's incarceration rate ballooned (from 70 per 100,000 in 1916 to 149 in 1929[30]), wardens complained of overcrowding, and the state legislature approved several waves of money to build a new prison that, by 1925, would hold an unprecedented 5,000 men.[31] Contestation continued throughout the nearly 10 years of construction, in part due to strife within the state Republican political machine over the spoils of state patronage (in this instance, getting rich and politically powerful by securing contracts to help build a massive new penitentiary).[32] Like criminal justice projects across the country during this period, the building of the prison at Jackson can be understood as part of what Lisa McGirr (looking at Prohibition on a national scale) terms "the first incarnation of the twentieth-century religious right" engaged in a "broad assault on the 'enemies' of white Protestant nationalism."[33]

In this sense, the opening of a massive new prison at Jackson—and the proliferation of Big House prisons across the North and the Midwest (and, to a lesser extent, the West)—can be read as part of a morally conservative effort to police, criminalize, and mold immigrants and the poor. Yet it is also important to recognize that some wardens, prison staff, and politicians continued, even at prisons such as Jackson, to focus on the power of punishment to reform criminals. Adapting and repackaging existing ideas about the restorative value of hard labor, most of the northern and western Big House prisons put prisoners to work in industrial shops meant to mimic blue-collar jobs "on the outside." Jackson's inaugural warden, Harry Hulbert, was borderline obsessed about prisoners' work inside and outside the prison's walls.[34] Jackson's prison industries included a binder twine plant, a brush shop, aluminum stamping, a cannery, and a license plate–manufacturing plant.[35] Few were unaware of the same benefits that appealed to nineteenth-century penal administrators: work "behind the walls" meant convicts were kept busy, created a stable prison social hierarchy, and provided managers and administrators a convenient set of carrots and sticks. They could reward pliable prisoners with attractive work assignments and punish recalcitrant ones with enervating physical labor widely seen as punitive. To make these shops seem valuable beyond the obvious income they produced for the state, Hulbert emphasized how industrial labor taught prisoners marketable skills that improved their chances upon release. In this sense, Hulbert (and wardens such as Joseph Ragen at Illinois's Stateville prison) explicitly framed prison industries as progressive; with his political allies—penal administrators and politicians throughout much of the country—Hulbert creatively adapted long-standing practices in order to proclaim progressive bona fides. These actors signaled that progressive discourses remained important—especially as a form of legitimization—right through the 1930s and early '40s.[36]

The story of Jackson State Prison highlights the main argument of this section: although criminal justice was undeniably bleak in the first few decades of the twentieth century, progressives, now *challengers* in the penal arena, did not give up. Instead, they advocated for their modernist, correctional vision of justice, pushing state leaders and penal administrators to at least use progressive rhetoric to describe practices. The struggles during this bleak period contributed to the braiding together of various impulses, adapting (and sometimes co-opting) the progressive vision of using penal institutions to produce well-adjusted, "good" citizens.

## *The Rise of the Rehabilitative Ideal*

According to the dominant criminological narrative, correctionalists became very powerful in the years following World War II. As their influence grew, we have been told, correctionalists swung the penal pendulum toward the treatment side of the ledger, making the "rehabilitative ideal" the dominant orientation of American criminal justice. As renowned legal scholar Francis Allen explains, the rehabilitative ideal

> . . . assumed, first, that human behavior is the product of antecedent causes. . . . Knowledge of the antecedents of human behavior makes possible an approach to the scientific control of human behavior. Finally, and of primary significance for the purposes at hand, it is assumed that measures employed to treat the convicted offender should serve a therapeutic function, that such measures should be designed to effect changes in the behavior of the convicted person in the interests of his own happiness, health, and satisfactions and in the interest of social defense.[37]

The ideal boiled down to "the view that corrections should be about using the scientific study of crime to save the wayward."[38]

As this view of crime, criminals, and justice spread, rehabilitation ostensibly became a (if not the) primary penal orientation in numerous states.[39] Irwin argues that in this period, penologists created a whole new category of prison: "After World War II, many states replaced Big Houses with *correctional institutions*, which, when they were newly constructed, looked different, were organized differently, housed different types of prisoners, and nurtured different prison social worlds" (emphasis added).[40] Irwin is careful to point out, however, that "correctional institutions were never totally, or even mainly, organized to rehabilitate prisoners" (something we take up later in this chapter).[41]

Yet, the rehabilitative ideal was not cut from whole cloth; the ideas it championed dated back at least to the Progressive Era (and, in some cases, right back to the early nineteenth century, as discussed in chapter 2). In key respects, it was a *continuation* and *adaptation* of the Progressives' efforts to reshape punishment.[42] On this point, Jonathan Simon writes: "The elements of the new model which emerged in California and other states in the 1950s were strikingly similar to the correctional vision of the Progressive era reformers, with stress on classification, training, and treatment."[43]

Macro-level developments in the 1940s and '50s provided opportunities for correctionalists to become influential at the national and state levels. Economic growth and educational expansion (the latter due, in part, to the G.I. Bill) were critical developments. As David Garland explains. "The availability of work, even for unskilled and unreliable individuals, facilitated the resettlement work of probation and parole and gave purpose to the 'treatment and training' programmes [*sic*] of prisons."[44] In this sense, the postwar years were a good time for correctionalists; just as employers were encouraged to welcome returning soldiers into their ranks, many suggested that the social tent was big enough to incorporate at least some criminals. Inspired by the Allies' defeat of the Axis powers, politicians, government administrators, and other elites were willing to spread the wealth in the name of reform and social progress. Prisoners' contributions to the war effort likely added to this willingness: incarcerated people donated blood, fought forest fires, purchased war bonds with their canteen money, and made clothing for the forces and hammocks for submarines. During the war, First Lady Eleanor Roosevelt visited San Quentin to express her gratitude and offer encouragement to the prisoners.[45]

The growth of the social sciences and professional associations also contributed to the expansion and solidification of correctionalist criminal justice.[46] Allen argues that the rehabilitative ideal stemmed from "the development of scientific disciplines concerned with human behavior, a development not remotely approximated in earlier periods when notions of reform of the offender were advanced."[47] Criminologists and other social scientists believed that they possessed knowledge and technologies to diagnose, treat, and cure criminals, and their use of medical metaphors was deliberate. Researchers claimed that criminological sciences would one day match the

medical sciences in identifying and curing ailments.[48] Politicians and government administrators shared this belief in scientific advancement and put their
faith in "experts" and expert knowledge, helping to legitimate and empower
criminologists, penologists, and other specialists who sought to eradicate
crime and fix criminals.

Taking advantage of the favorable conditions, correctionalists obtained
dominant positions in the penal arena and spread the rehabilitation gospel.
Austin MacCormick's career provides an illustrative example. Having worked
during and after World War I under his mentor, Thomas Mott Osborne (at
the Portsmouth Naval Prison in New Hampshire), MacCormick was a successful academic for much of the 1920s at Bowdoin, a small liberal arts college
in Maine. Later in his career, he worked as a professor of criminology at the
University of California, Berkeley (1951–1960), then served as the executive
director of the Osborne Association (founded by his mentor) until his death
in 1979.[49]

MacCormick parlayed his progressive beliefs about crime and punishment
into an active and influential career. To name but a few accomplishments, he
was the first assistant director of the newly formed Federal Bureau of Prisons
in 1930, he was commissioner of the New York Department of Corrections
from 1934 to 1940, and in 1939 he was elected president of the American
Prison Association (renamed the American Correctional Association in
1954). Additionally, MacCormick's book *The Education of Adult Prisoners*
(first published in 1931) became a classic in the field of penology (correctional
education in particular), and he became a successful advocate for prison
libraries, prison education, and prison treatment programs more generally.[50]

Without discounting his personal talents and professional commitment, MacCormick's storied career owes no small part of its success to
the fact that politicians wanted to listen to him—and, in some cases, hire
him—*because* of his status as a correctional expert.[51] Additionally, throughout his career, but especially during the 1940s and '50s, he was commis-
sioned to study prisons across the country. His smooth movement into and
out of penal bureaucracies—serving variously as critic, advocate, and penal
administrator—characterized other key progressive actors' careers during the
decades after the Second World War, including Richard McGee (California)
and James Bennett (Federal Bureau of Prisons).[52] Both at the federal and state
levels, correctional experts became powerful players in the penal field. This
sometimes meant moderating calls for reforms with politicians in socially
conservative states, but the end result was that correctionalists helped to
legitimate and diffuse the discourse of rehabilitation, greatly affecting how

penal practitioners talked about and crafted criminal justice from California to Florida.

## *California: If Not Here, Where?*

Scholars typically consider California[53] the epicenter of postwar rehabilitation, with a "correctional consensus" among most Golden State actors. According to this perspective, while people may have disagreed over how to implement rehabilitation (and how far to take it), there was general agreement that the principal aim of criminal justice was to correct lawbreakers.[54] However, when we look carefully at the actual practices of punishment in this era, a much more knotty—and analytically interesting—reality appears. The rehabilitative ideal was the dominant orientation of California's penal field, but it was not universally accepted. In fact, a wide range of actors fiercely contested the ideal and practices implemented in its name. This contestation generated and, in some cases, intensified variegation and helped undercut the rehabilitative ideal and the correctionalists who championed it.

The signal event of mid-twentieth century prisons and criminal punishment in California was Governor Earl Warren's signing of the 1944 "Prison Reorganization Act." The law affirmed the theory of crime as a byproduct of offenders' psychological and social impairments.[55] To put this theory into practice, California implemented one of the country's most developed systems of indeterminate criminal sentences. The principle was that open-ended prison terms would make parole depend on participation in various programs, not on past criminal actions (as had been a major focus of determinate, or fixed, sentencing regimes). Although no state implemented *total* indeterminate sentencing, California came closest, with sentences such as one to fifteen years for forgery or second-degree burglary, and five years to life for first-degree robbery.[56] Drawing on the medical model that viewed prisoners as "sick" and in need of treatment, the parole board (in California, the "Adult Authority") would, in theory, release prisoners only after they were cured of their criminogenic ailments (and, presumably, had become better citizens).[57]

Richard McGee—appointed by Governor Warren as the first director of the newly minted California Department of Corrections in 1944—worked with a team of correctional administrators, wardens, and penal bureaucrats to institute extensive programs and innovative practices to facilitate prisoners' transformation. And prison officials welcomed researchers and treatment staff into their facilities. Some of these newcomers were responsible for prisoner classification—a favorite practice of Progressive Era reformers, now implemented during the late 1940s and through the '50s and '60s on a scale not seen before. In California, as part of reception into the prison system, prisoners went through a battery of tests and lengthy interviews, after which prison staff evaluated and diagnosed the convict and devised his or her treatment plan. This ongoing process of evaluation and planning ideally continued throughout the person's time in prison.[58] Staff and other experts recommended programs in the form of group counseling, religious instruction, and self-help groups such as Alcoholics Anonymous and Narcotics Anonymous.[59]

Other developments included the expansion of education programs, from remedial and vocational schooling to postsecondary studies.[60] Even putting prisoners to work took on a new flavor, as administrators one-upped their Big House–era compatriots in placing a stronger-than-ever emphasis on using work to transform prisoners into citizens who were more mentally and physically healthy. State officials took particular pride in California's renowned forestry camp program: by the mid-1960s, more than 2,000 prisoners lived in relatively small, minimum-security prison camps scattered across the state, charged with conservation projects and, when needed, fighting the state's many wildfires.[61] Politicians and penal administrators eagerly promoted the forestry program; in 1960, Governor Pat Brown said, for example: "It is a fine, a noble, an essential thing to save our forests. It is an even nobler thing to conserve the greatest of all resources—human beings. By this program, we are doing both."[62] Inside the state's walled prisons, administrators mandated work for all capable prisoners and formally evaluated work records when determining release decisions.[63]

As it sought to transform its prisons into "correctional institutions," California also looked to parole and probation. With a new focus on "individual treatment" and "interpersonal relationships," parole agents were supposed to behave more like social workers, using "objective methodologies such as interviews, residential inspections, and medical histories" to build a trusting relationship with the parolee and help "manage his [or her] relationship to the community."[64] Parole agents were able to provide more intensive supervision with smaller caseloads, treatment-oriented programs for drug addicts, and outpatient clinics for parolees to receive psychological counseling.[65] Similar changes took place with respect to probation (particularly juvenile probation), including reduced caseload sizes and more individualized programs.[66]

Taken together, there is ample evidence that reform-minded managers and bureaucrats in California were able to orient the Golden State's criminal

justice system—from sentencing to parole supervision—toward rehabilitation. Nevertheless, it was not an unadulterated rehabilitative regime; programs invariably blended or braided the impulses to transform, manage, and
punish prisoners. For instance, as during the Progressive Era (see chapter 3),
classification was used to assign prisoners to programs, but it was also a form
of social control; many prison officials used "a pattern of privilege gradation,
[with] the threat of withdrawing privileges [and programs as] one of the primary techniques of control within the prison."[67] Even the most progressive
programs in California during the 1950s and '60s, "the honor blocks, the conjugal visiting programs, the gradation of prisons from minimum to maximum
security," functioned as control mechanisms; staff meted out "progressively
harsher punishments for resistance to the prison regime, and progressively
great[er] privileges for compliance."[68] Ultimately, prisoners who refused to
participate in programs could be denied parole.[69]

The intertwining of rehabilitation with social control was particularly
clear at the California Institution for Women (CIW) in Chino, the state's
celebrated (if only) women's prison from 1952 to 1987. As was the case at many
nineteenth-and early-twentieth-century women's "reformatories," female
prisoners lived in cottages. Group living was supposed to mimic life on the
outside and better prepare women for release, and they had access to group
counseling and myriad educational and vocational programs. As part of the
correctional project, staff and administrators sought to coerce women prisoners to adopt white, middle-class ideals, including a particular feminine pre-
sentation of self and the discipline believed to go along with it.[70]

Along with blending rehabilitation with social control, prison officials
used correctional rhetoric to redefine and justify old punitive practices. For
example, prison officials created "adjustment centers," framed as a progressive version of segregation that offered "programs so that segregated inmates
could demonstrate a positive attitude and earn their return to the general
population housing."[71] Irwin argues that, in reality, the adjustment centers
"were segregation units where prisoners were held for indefinite periods with
reduced privileges and virtually no mobility. . . . No intensive therapy was
ever delivered."[72] Behind the lofty rhetoric of treatment, these units were, for
many prisoners, just another form of punitive isolation. Similar gaps between
the rhetoric and reality of treatment programs were evident for other categories of prisoners as well, including those convicted of sexual offences.[73]

Deficiencies plagued community corrections, too. Just as treatment
staff had no proven way to "cure" criminals, the Adult Authority lacked
reliable and scientific methods to determine whether prisoners had been

"rehabilitated."[74] Parole board members typically had backgrounds in law enforcement rather than social work or social science (as had been intended), and the board relied primarily on the same indicators that had always determined release decisions—especially criminal records and in-prison behavior.[75] Once released, ex-prisoners received far less assistance or therapy than the social work image of parole suggested. Likewise, despite the fact that officials sought to deemphasize the police-work aspects of supervision, the threat of arrest remained a central means of motivating parolees and protecting public safety.[76]

Against this backdrop of competing, and often-contradictory, penal goals,[77] conflict inside California's prisons was organized primarily between two perspectives: that of officers and old-school administrators (hereafter, "Custody") and that of the professional counselors, psychiatrists, social workers, and new-school administrators (hereafter, "Treatment").[78] On balance, Treatment staff worked to "cure" inmates, while Custody focused on confining and punishing prisoners believed to be morally deficient and untrustworthy.[79] Neither group offered the other much support.

Custody-oriented staff tended to disparage what they saw as Treatment's permissive, "soft," feminine vision, claiming it denied personal responsibility and created opportunities for security breaches; Treatment-oriented staff argued that Custody was callous and unnecessarily erected hurdles that obstructed their work and compromised the prison system's rehabilitative mission.[80] The conflict was particularly intense at older, higher-security prisons such as Folsom, where veteran officers and local administrators strongly embraced the custodial orientation and deeply resented the intrusion of "outsiders" into their institutions.[81]

Despite the dominance of the rehabilitative ideology, it was actually security forces that kept the upper hand inside California's prisons during the 1940s, '50s, and '60s. Certainly, prison officials at the California Department of Corrections headquarters and some wardens were overtly pro-Treatment. Nonetheless, Custody staff were the most numerous and powerful actors in most prisons. According to one contemporaneous account, "in practice, all activities [were] subordinate to the decisions of Custody." Looking specifically at psychiatry: "It is hardly surprising that psychiatry in prison consists primarily in therapeutic practices which can have punitive or disciplinary implications: electric shock, insulin shock, fever treatment, hydrotherapy, amytal and pentothal interviews, cisternals and spinals, and so on—that is everything except psychotherapy."[82] Treatment staff unable or unwilling to adapt to the conflict quit; many of those who remained scaled back their therapeutic ambitions and aligned their practices more closely with Custody's interests.[83]

Custody workers, for their part, knew that Treatment staff depended on their cooperation, especially given that they were, in some cases, supposed to lead (not just facilitate) rehabilitation activities such as group counseling. In many cases, officers ignored recommendations made by Treatment-oriented staff by classifying convicts and assigning them to programs according to security risks and convenience factors, rather than rehabilitative "needs."[84] They also punished prisoners who had "too many applications for medical or psychiatric aid."[85] No matter how stridently administrators such as McGee preached rehabilitation as a "new" way of performing punishment, programs varied and incorporated disparate logics due to struggles among those who had the power to translate goals into everyday practices.[86]

In the mid-to late 1960s, conflict among staff and prisoners reached a fever pitch in California. A new generation of Treatment staff entered the prisons; many viewed themselves as social activists and explicitly sought to empower prisoners. Prisoners, for their part, became more politically active and more critical of the rehabilitation regime—many rejected the view that they were "sick" and argued instead that they lacked opportunities for advancement enjoyed by those in the middle and upper classes. They were, in short, victims of the "system," not of their bad choices or pro-criminal thinking.[87] Many were also hostile to indeterminate sentencing, which they believed kept them in a stressful state of "suspended animation," and they were convinced that the parole board was racist and punished prisoners for political activity.[88]

Race and racial antagonism pervaded the conflict between prisoners and staff, especially between line officers, who were mainly white, and prisoners, who were disproportionately black and Latino. Politically radical African American prisoners such as George Jackson organized their fellow convicts to fight back against their captors, calling for a grassroots revolution to force elites to dismantle the penal system. Prisoners, backed by activist lawyers, began to demand "rights" and better confinement conditions, filing numerous lawsuits; interracial strikes broke out at Folsom and San Quentin, and a group of convicts, with outside aid, attempted to start a "prisoners union." Disruption was widespread, and in some prisons there was open warfare.[89]

Custody reacted to the radicalization of Treatment staff and prisoners (as well as the involvement of activist lawyers and federal judges in prison affairs) by condemning rehabilitation in favor of "law and order" behind the walls.[90] Custody won media and political attention to their position, arguing that rehabilitation was dangerous and that the "liberal" approach to punishment

coddled convicts, enabled agitators (especially black and Chicano radi-
cals), and compromised security.[91] In some instances, Custody and its allies
won legal victories; in one such ruling, *In re Ferguson* (1961), the California
Supreme Court ruled that administrators could discriminate against Muslim
prisoners on the basis that their religious ties (and, by extension, political
organizing) threatened institutional order.[92]

Events inside prisons provided considerable fodder for the critics outside
them. Even during the late 1940s, '50s, and early '60s—while the state's leading correctional administrator Richard McGee enjoyed unprecedented support from Governors Earl Warren and Pat Brown (and some support from
Governor Goodwin Knight between them)—there was significant pushback
from law enforcement. McGee explains, for example, that local police chiefs
often called meetings with state leaders when parolees committed crimes,
decrying the "leniency" of the courts and the state parole board. Los Angeles
Police Department (LAPD) chief William Parker would "demand that the
governor and those present listen to some cases," and "then he would pull out
half a dozen summaries of the worst cases his staff had been able to find in
the police files. With a flair for the dramatic, he was able to make the facts of
any case sound even worse and dismissed as irrelevant the fact that his sample
may be in the ratio of one in twenty-five thousand."[93] According to McGee,
political pushback from law enforcement facilitated punitive action on
everything from sentencing bills to prison governance and parole releases.[94]
Nonetheless, during the 1950s and early '60s, the individuals and organizations that opposed rehabilitation and supported tougher penal approaches
were, at best, loosely organized and enjoyed few policy victories. They were
*challengers* in the penal field and had limited success in shaping the general
trajectory of criminal justice policy. But advocates of "law and order" would
soon gain power in California and throughout the country, undercutting the
conceptual underpinnings of the rehabilitative ideal and implementing policies that would spur rapid growth of the carceral state (a topic we take up in
the next chapter).

## Florida: Rehabilitation as Modernization

Florida, like other states in the South and the Sunbelt, is generally viewed as
having missed the postwar turn toward correctionalist criminal justice. This
view is generally accurate, *if* we equate rehabilitation with the socio-medical
model of treatment popularized in such places as California. However, Florida
did implement a variation of rehabilitation that emphasized modernization,

professionalization, and relatively humane treatment. As we will see, this iteration of "corrections" was forged within a particular set of political, racial, and gender relations.

To understand the particular form that rehabilitation took in Florida, we need to briefly discuss the situation at Florida State Prison at Raiford in the 1930s and '40s. Located about 25 miles north of Gainesville, Raiford was the target of significant contestation. Organized labor contested the use of convict labor to manufacture goods, arguing that unfree penal labor was unfair competition. Labor's victories restricted prison industries at Raiford, and, as a result, fewer prisoners worked in the prison industrial shops than on its various farming operations or basic facility upkeep. By the late 1940s, prison industry at Raiford was so small and unprofitable that it arguably existed for the purposes of public relations (newspapers continued to run positive stories about prisoners hard at work at the facility) rather than because it held any penological or pecuniary value.[95]

Raiford also faced criticism over its trustee system. During the 1910s, Superintendent James "Sam" Blitch fired half the guards and replaced them with trustee prisoners, some of whom were armed with guns. The system was cheaper than retaining a paid guard staff, and it provided a way to reward prisoners who were willing and able to keep their brethren in line. It was not until half a century later, as part of court litigation during the 1960s, that the state finally acknowledged what must have been known to prisoners, guards, and administrators all along: the trustee system (or "honor system," as it was euphemistically known) led to rampant abuses and prisoner-on-prisoner violence.[96]

Prison administrators and state officials also received criticism because of poor management and unsavory conditions. For example, in 1935, a prisoner named Paul Hunter sent a letter to the New York City headquarters of the NAACP, alleging terrible conditions and rampant racial abuses of black prisoners at the Florida State Prison hospital in Chattahoochee. After serving a short sentence at Raiford, Willie James sent a similar letter to the NAACP in 1936. Each letter sparked investigations, as a variety of actors inside and outside the state turned their attention to Florida prison conditions, especially for African American prisoners.[97]

Hunter's and James's respective letters did not directly lead to changes in prison policy or practice. Rather, they provided justifications for critics of the prison system—the NAACP, the Southern Committee for People's Rights, and criminologists at Rollins College (in Winter Park, Florida, just outside Orlando)—to demand investigations and reforms.[98] The critics pointedly reminded prison administrators and state politicians that outsiders had a vested interest in punishment in the Sunshine State. In the James case, for example, the NAACP had partnered with Florida newspapers to publish the allegations.[99] Unfortunately, however, the investigations led to few, if any, substantive changes in the lives of black prisoners; Vivien Miller concludes: "an in-house investigation yielded little more than official promise to monitor conditions at Raiford, which did not change."[100]

Under the leadership of Leonard Chapman, Raiford attempted to establish "modern" forms of prison management, which would assuage critics, help maintain discipline and order now that prison labor had been curtailed (recall that work both produced income for the state and contributed to the maintenance of order), and produce moral reform among the convicted. Consistent with the shifting orientation of professional penology, Chapman, the son of a preacher who had a "Christian regard for the oppressed and downtrodden," described his efforts as "rehabilitation."[101]

For Chapman, personal reform would occur through demanding physical labor, a strict prison social order, a judicious use of "wholesome" recreation, and vocational education. In other words, he did not adhere to the "treatment" view of rehabilitation popular in California. Even if he had wanted to implement the socio-medical model, there was little to no political support in the state to provide prisoners counseling or psychological treatment, or even for placing probation and parole fully under the control of penal administrators.[102] Chapman's major accomplishments included improving medical care and housing, expanding vocational training and recreational opportunities, and enhancing education.[103] During his tenure, Raiford established its first permanent school, lauded as a shining symbol of progress—even though it was racially segregated, used convicts to teach classes, and served but a small fraction of the prison population.[104]

Chapman's achievements generated positive responses from the penological community. For instance, the federal Prison Industries Reorganization Administration concluded that Florida's penal system "has been soundly planned in its provision for diversified work opportunities and in its sensible adjustment to the social and economic background of its inmates and of the State."[105] Similarly, the influential American Prison Association judged "the 'curriculum, teaching staff, recreational, and vocational facilities' at Raiford third in the nation, behind San Quentin and Connecticut State Prison."[106] This external affirmation helped Chapman and his political allies fend off criticisms from the media and politicians, and until the last few years of his tenure, Warden Chapman (and "his" prison at Raiford) seemed almost entirely above reproach.

Florida also continued to operate dozens of prison road camps in which men built and repaired roads for long hours under oftentimes excruciating conditions. By the end of 1954, there were 4,340 people incarcerated in Florida's prison system and 1,591 (36.7%) were housed in a prison road camp.[107] State officials praised the camps with similar rhetoric used when describing Raiford; one official, in 1951, declared, "assignment of prisoners to road camps is one of our best means of rehabilitation, as inmates have advantage of outdoor work in the fresh air and plenty [of] sunshine."[108]

This praise is notable given what amounted to a fairly steady flow of evidence that many (perhaps even the vast majority) of prisoners sent to road camps witnessed or were subject to jaw-dropping abuses. Miller's book *Hard Labor and Hard Time* includes chapters titled "Good Roads, Bad Men, and the Ugliest of Conditions," "Cruel and Unusual Punishments," and "Florida's Hard Road During the Depression and War Years." In them, she describes extraordinary brutality, including murder of prisoners by camp staff, punctuated by periodic efforts to reform the camps in response to governmental investigations and media reports about brutality and prisoner deaths.[109] During the 1950s, Florida implemented new regulations that reduced prisoners' workdays, improved housing (e.g., barracks replaced cages in portable units), and created some limited educational programs in the road prisons.[110] In 1958, the infamous "sweatbox"—a crude wooden isolation chamber used to punish prisoners—was finally retired.[111]

Although Florida made modest improvements to the road camps during the 1940s and '50s, prisoners and their advocates took advantage of the more favorable political climate of the 1960s to push for substantial changes. Prisoners went to great lengths to protest conditions at the camps and to earn release from them, including slashing their Achilles tendons or hands.[112] They were aided by the 1965 novel *Cool Hand Luke* and the 1967 film of the same name (see Text Box below). The movie reached a wide, national audience and popularized the view that the road prison camps were truly horrendous places that ruined people's lives.

In this context of prisoner resistance and bad publicity, penal administrators in Florida continued a process already underway by the late 1950s, scaling back the road camp program and improving conditions in the camps that did remain.[113] As sociologist Heather Schoenfeld explains, these developments also came under pressure from the federal government. Because of the country's federalist structure, neither Congress nor the president can directly dictate state-level criminal justice policy. But they *can* strongly encourage states to make changes by (among other techniques) offering funds in exchange for reforms. In 1968, Congress passed the Safe Streets Act, creating the Law Enforcement Assistance Administration (LEAA), which encouraged state-level criminal justice innovation through providing funding and consulta-tion.[114] The LEAA provided funds to Florida to transform its road camps into "progressive," community-based facilities. "This new model of confinement," Schoenfeld explains, "helped [Florida's] Division of Corrections phase out road prisons without completely shutting them down. Instead, remaining structurally sound road prisons were slowly converted into community cor-rections centers."[115]

JUST AS THE Progressive vision of reform—and the Penitentiary ideal before it—were focused on *white men*, the rhetoric of rehabilitation in Florida was not applied evenly. The walled prisons and road camps were racially segregated, and black prisoners received inferior work and housing assignments along with less access to privileges than whites right through the end of the 1950s (and perhaps beyond).[116] Penal administrators in Florida openly boasted of the racial segregation in order to settle public fears that the justice system was "enslaving" white men and forcing them to work alongside black prisoners.[117] Even Chapman, during his reign at Raiford, openly encouraged racial discrimination. For example, Miller writes, "When jewel thief Albie Baker [a white man] arrived at Raiford in the early 1940s, he encountered a Jim Crow prison and was instructed by Chapman, 'You white men remember that you are white. Don't fraternize with the niggahs.'" To the black prisoners, Chapman said, "'When you address a white man, whether he be a free man or convict, you be respectful to him. Take your cap off when you speak to him and call him Mistah or Mistah White Folks.'"[118]

   Gender inequality, too, shaped the scope and character of rehabilitation at this time. Prior to the 1950s, female prisoners were housed at Raiford in a separate unit enclosed by a simple wooden fence (a few were also housed at the state hospital in Chattahoochee).[119] Chapman claimed that the presence of women made running Raiford more difficult and less effective in its reform mission. The eventual opening of a separate women's prison in Lowell had as much to do with administrators' and politicians' desires to get women out of Raiford as it did with any commitment to address the rehabilitative needs of women prisoners. Women (like black men) simply did not figure into discus-sions of prison modernization (described as "rehabilitation") in this period. Where they did enter deliberations, it was as obstacles the state needed to remove or work around.

It is tempting to write off Florida officials' use of rehabilitative rhetoric post–World War II as a mere gloss. But it would be a mistake—"rehabilitation" has no single, static meaning. As one of us (Goodman) has argued previously, the term is a "conceptual shell" that gets filled in specific ways at particular times and places.[120] As a result, "rehabilitation," as a concept, flourishes in particular climates, such as California in the decades after the Second World War. But its constructed nature also means that it often survives in what seem like inimical contexts. In Florida in particular, rehabilitation essentially meant modernization and personal development. Given the concrete political and cultural realities in Florida in the 1940s through the '60s (including rigid racial and gender inequality), it is hard to imagine that rehabilitation could have lived up to the ideal so popular among penological and criminological elites who had their eyes trained on places such as California during the 1950s. Still, it did lead to important changes in penal policy and carceral institutions.

---

TEXT BOX

## Cool Hand Luke

In 1965, Don Pearce published his novel *Cool Hand Luke*, a semi-autobiographical account of a group of prisoners' experiences at a Florida prison road camp during the late 1940s. Pearce drew loosely on his own experiences—he had done time, first at Raiford and then in one of the state's many road camps.[121] Although critically well received, *Cool Hand Luke* did not enjoy commercial success.[122] But when the book was adapted in 1967 for the big screen, things changed.

Starring Paul Newman and George Kennedy (who won the Academy Award for Best Supporting Actor for his role as "Dragline"), the film was a blockbuster. Several lines of dialogue—most famously "sometimes nothing can be a real cool hand" and "What we've got here is failure to communicate"—have penetrated popular culture; the latter shows up today on everything from trendy t-shirts to the American Film Institute's list of the top-100 movie quotes.[123]

To understand the effects of *Cool Hand Luke* on crime and punishment in Florida, we need to recognize that it was but one in a series of novels and films that advanced a nearly constant critique of southern criminal justice as forever and hopelessly "backwards." As historian Heather Ann Thompson writes: "Crime and punishment in the South has long been the subject of public fascination. Like gawkers who just can't seem to avert their eyes from a bloody roadside wreck, Americans have flocked to prison movies in the popular genre of southern Gothic. . . . While the most sadistic aspects of the South's penal system have never ceased to enthrall, they also have never seemed to surprise. After all, the region's economic and political system had formerly revolved around slavery, an institution so barbaric, so heinous, that it assuredly would have tainted southern culture long after it ended."[124]

When trying to stake out a claim that criminal justice in Florida during the 1960s and '70s was progressive, modern, and focused on prisoners' rehabilitation, penal administrators and politicians were arguing against this steady critique of "their" prisons and "their" state. While state legislators and penal administrators rarely explicitly articulated a desire for their prisons to be seen as on par with those in the North, their actions suggest both an acute awareness of the critique and a keenness to join what were perceived as national trends to dodge those attacks. Not unlike the reasoning behind the development of California's prison forestry camps, penal administrators in Florida believed that being perceived as progressive and treatment focused offered them a ticket to respectability (at least among their professional peers), legitimacy, and organizational stability. Popular culture (in this case, a major film) provided external pressure on criminal justice actors, encouraging them to embrace the rhetoric of rehabilitation and to implement reforms that signaled modernization.

# Conclusion

The two decades after the Second World War are widely regarded as a sort of halcyon period in American punishment—a time in which criminal justice eschewed strict punishment in order to rehabilitate women and men convicted of crime. After decades of struggle dating back at least to the Progressive Era, actors allegedly succeeded in making the curing of criminality the dominant orientation of the entire criminal justice apparatus, from law enforcement to parole.

In this chapter we have argued that progressive actors throughout much of the country were indeed successful in seizing opportunities to push criminal justice toward rehabilitation. And yet, rather than constituting a single breakthrough moment, these victories ought to be understood as the result of long contestation over punishment. Significant victories were won not because

1940s-era penal administrators, politicians, and criminologists invented new ways of thinking about crime and punishment, but because those actors seized opportunities to make substantial progress against their foes. The result, as in previous periods, was substantial variegation. Criminal justice shifted in considerable ways, but remained a patchwork of sometimes contradictory (and virtually always competing) impulses, visions, and practices.

This is especially true when we couple an examination of punishment rhetoric with the *practice* of punishment. As we have shown, even in California, rehabilitation was intertwined with and inseparable from social control and retribution. Friction between actors within and outside the criminal justice system intensified the already heated managerial and punitive elements of rehabilitation. Contrary to popular and some academic accounts, there was not a penal consensus in California in the decades following World War II. That was an illusion supported by academics, practitioners, and journalists. Instead, as always, actors wrestled over the orientation of the penal field, with struggle operating at the practical level of organizational priorities and practices and at the levels of ideology and rhetoric (e.g., debates over whom and how to punish). In short, contestation was the rule, not the exception—and it had critical consequences for the development of penal practice.

Likewise, while Florida politicians and prison administrators never meaningfully incorporated the hallmarks of the socio-medical model, there was substantial talk about "rehabilitation" in the Sunshine State. This talk led to important changes in criminal justice. So Florida did not so much miss the "rehabilitative ideal," but rather, actors used the rhetoric of rehabilitation to enact *old* goals of modernization, bureaucracy building, and humane treatment. Because of Florida's political culture (with its emphasis on "small government," fiscal austerity, and strict punishment) and deeply unequal race and gender relations, actors such as Leonard Chapman likely could not have successfully implemented the socio-medical model of rehabilitation even if they had wanted to. In other words, state-level cultural and political constraints shaped the form rehabilitation adopted in Florida, California, and beyond.

So many of us look back as this period as the "rehabilitative era" because we see experts (academics, policymakers, and penal professionals) asserting the importance of correcting offenders and defining a wide range of practices as "rehabilitation." As the correctional discourse spread among the penological and criminological elite, it became a means of legitimation; calling a practice or program "correctional," "therapeutic," or "rehabilitative" made it seem necessary and desirable. In this way, the rhetoric of rehabilitation became a tool in penal struggle—actors used it to defend or promote practices in the face of opposition, as when critics charged that solitary confinement in "adjustment centers" was simply punitive, not correctional. Actors could achieve their bureaucratic and political goals using the language of "helping" offenders (and, by extension, society) for cover.[125]

We do not mean to imply that actors who used the language of rehabilitation did so for purely instrumental reasons. As Garland argues, correctionalism (what he terms "penal welfarism") was a conceptual framework that provided meaning and structure to criminal justice work.[126] For many mid-twentieth-century academics and criminal justice practitioners, rehabilitation was central to their professional self-understandings. They could take pride in being part of an enlightened professional movement that, from their perspective, greatly benefited convicted criminals *and* society (hence their umbrage when prisoners and activists in the 1960s claimed that rehabilitation was just a fancy word for social control).

But as we have seen, competitors within and beyond the penal field did not share penologists' and criminologists' faith in the rehabilitative ideal— nor did they support the policies and practices implemented in its name. They struggled mightily to limit the breadth and depth of correctional criminal justice. This contestation, hidden in pendulum views of this period, helps explain the gap between the rehabilitative ideal and penal practice in the period after World War II. And, as we will see in the next chapter, the ongoing fights among criminal justice actors, from academics to politicians, prisoners, and lawmakers, helps us understand major penal changes that occurred at the close of the twentieth century.

# 5

# *Deconstructing the Carceral State*

THE LAST THIRD or so of the twentieth century was a period of massive penal change. Exhibit A: the rise of a pernicious "carceral state," a uniquely bloated and punitive system of penal control.[1] The national incarceration rate for state and federal prisons more than doubled between 1973 (96 per 100,000 residents) and 1985 (202 per 100,000 residents), then doubled again a decade later (reaching 411 by 1995). That rate began to level off only in the mid-2000s.[2] Add in non-custodial populations, and by 2009 a staggering one in thirty-one American adults was on parole or probation or incarcerated in jail or prison.[3]

Along with the *quantitative* changes, the *character* of criminal justice changed significantly. Examples of the "new punitiveness" include the "war on drugs," the militarization of police forces, and the resurgence of the death penalty.[4] Scholars have also argued that the latter twentieth century was characterized by "expressive justice" and "penal populism," which included the increasing role of crime victims (and *potential* victims) in criminal justice policymaking and the expansion of punishments meant to signal that "offenders" were dirty, evil, dangerous, or all three.[5] David Garland, for instance, cites "laws on public notification of sex offenders' identities, the wearing of the convict striped uniform, [and] work on a chain gang" as examples of late twentieth century criminal justice reforms meant to stigmatize, identify as other, and shame.[6]

This widening carceral net developed in the context of rapid social changes. After the Vietnam War and the civil rights movement came substantial economic insecurity, falling standards of living for the middle and working classes, and a precipitous and well-publicized rise in violent street crime. American politics of "law and order" intensified, with both

Republicans and Democrats vying to be "tougher" by enacting legislation that increased penal severity.[7] With this in mind, it is easy to understand why some leading scholars describe the buildup of the carceral state with pendular logic; a system that had been relatively progressive and moderately sized had become massive and designed to harm and exclude wrongdoers.[8]

In much the same spirit, journalists and academics have declared that around the turn of the twenty-first century, the pendulum began to reverse course and swing back toward penal moderation.[9] In the context of the Great Recession and historically low crime rates, the politics of punishment have again shifted: rather than fighting to be the "toughest" on crime, prominent state and national leaders on both sides of the aisle now strive to be the "smartest" on crime, advocating for penal policies that reduce imprisonment and increase certain forms of treatment (particularly in drug-related cases). Perplexing coalitions of "usually bitter adversaries" such as Koch Industries and the American Civil Liberties Union (ACLU) have banded together to propel penal change.[10] By 2010, the national prison population had finally begun a (tepid) descent.[11]

In this chapter, we analyze the rise of mass incarceration and related phenomena during the "get tough" era (ca. 1970s to the mid-2000s) as well as the current and ongoing movement to roll back these developments (ca. mid-2000s to 2015). Scholars are increasingly treating the two periods as distinct eras, but we see an admixture of change and continuity across them. We do, however, agree with the standard narrative in a crucial respect: there *was* a radical increase and intensification of punishment in the last third of the twentieth century, which produced tragic harms that were especially pronounced in urban minority communities. Furthermore, while the extent and longevity of many current reforms are up for debate, important transformations are certainly afoot. As such, our argument should not be misconstrued as a denial of mass incarceration or of recent, important (if piecemeal and precarious) reform victories.

We begin the chapter with what scholars often call the "punitive turn" in American punishment, taking a national view before zooming in on the state level with brief case studies of California and Arizona. In keeping with our third axiom, we show how actors from the late 1960s through the 1990s seized opportunities related to economic, political, and social changes to transform punishment. These actors, whose ideas had been influential but largely subordinate in the post–World War II period, successfully promoted new laws, policies, and practices that furnished the material for a larger, more intrusive carceral state. The long struggle of actors, rather than some mechanical swing of the pendulum, propelled penal change.

The second section counters the popular claim that "rehabilitation" died during the "punitive era." Unlike many accounts that assert the abrupt end of correctional discourses and programs, we argue that those backing treatment-oriented visions of criminal justice continued to struggle throughout the 1980s and '90s; these actors remained active, if subordinate, players in the penal field. Academics, policy advocates, and criminal justice personnel reconceptualized and repackaged rehabilitation as politically neutral, scientific, and cost-effective, focusing attention on "evidence-based practices" meant to reduce criminals' "risks" and address their "needs." They also focused attention and resources on prisoner "reentry," arguing that helping ex-prisoners promoted "public safety." These efforts to align the correctionalist vision with dominant logics of punishment reconfigured rehabilitation and kept it alive, setting the stage for current reform efforts that seek to downsize the carceral state and mitigate its harms.

The third section builds on the argument that current reform efforts are due in large part to long-term struggle *for* correctionalist criminal justice and *against* the harsh policing and prosecution practices, sentencing laws, and dehumanizing discourses and institutional policies that expanded and intensified punishment. As during earlier historical periods, structural developments (most importantly, the Great Recession and continued crime declines) provided opportunities for activists, politicians, policy organizations, and criminal justice practitioners to shift the penal terrain and erode at least some aspects of the carceral state.

The chapter ends with a case study of New York's Rockefeller Drug Laws from their enactment in the early 1970s to their eventual reform in the 2000s. We argue that the implementation of major criminal justice policy always produces opposition; however, since opponents are typically subordinate actors in the penal, political, and legal fields, they often toil for long periods before seizing political opportunities (if they find any success at all). The campaign to "Drop the Rock" laws did not begin with the Great Recession—rather, reformers started to fight even before the bill took effect and kept struggling right through the thick of the carceral buildup. These agonists got a boost when, among other things, the economy faltered during the first decade of the twenty-first century. Such subterranean work is easily overlooked by scholars and the popular press, who may also then mischaracterize major reforms as sudden ruptures or evidence of the latest penal swing, rather than recognizing reforms as the result of persistent and long-standing resistance.

## Building the Carceral State

The three decades surrounding the relatively recent expansion of the carceral state were by many measures a tumultuous period. In part due to the oil crisis, there was a significant economic recession during the early 1970s. Following a period of sustained economic growth and a comparatively strong welfare state during the 1950s and '60s, much of the 1970s and '80s were marred by "wage and price inflation," declining trade and domestic production, growing government deficits, and "bitter strife" between employers and unions.[12] With the partial exception of those fortunate enough to earn a university degree or otherwise inherit wealth and privilege, most Americans saw their job security erode and their real income stagnate (or even decrease).[13]

The pain of these economic contractions was not borne evenly; instead, class and racial differentials widened as large numbers of American families fell below the poverty line.[14] At the same time, welfare support contracted and became more punitive as the line between "punishing" and "helping" vulnerable Americans became increasingly blurry.[15] Many people—especially blacks and Latinos in urban centers—found themselves not only unable to attain the "American Dream" of doing better (financially) than their parents, but in dire straits in core areas such as work and housing.[16] This was particularly crushing given the heady promises of the civil rights era.

To make matters worse, victimization rates increased in many states. Between 1965 and 1980, the homicide rate nearly doubled (while the reported overall violent crime rate increased threefold), disproportionately impacting low-income communities of color.[17] Funding for policing in urban neighborhoods increased, driving up arrests and further exaggerating statistical evidence of a "crime wave."[18] Changes in the journalistic field contributed to this volatile mix: incessant coverage of "street" crime by print, television, and (eventually) online outlets stoked fears in the middle-and upper-class neighborhoods *least* likely to experience crime.[19]

This context provided a powerful set of opportunities for actors who had long pushed for more punitive criminal justice policies, especially harsher criminal sentencing laws. This political shift, however, did not emerge out of thin air. Here we draw on political scientist Vesla Weaver's concept of "frontlash," or the "process by which formerly defeated groups may become dominant issue entrepreneurs in light of the development of a new issue campaign."[20] Rather than a "backlash" to civil rights victories, the self-styled "law and order" movement was a product of conservative struggle in the 1950s and '60s. During this earlier period, leaders on the political Right linked crime and civil rights by framing freedom rides, sit-ins, and urban protests as "criminal acts," generating fear that residential and educational integration would increase violent crime.[21] In the context of ongoing economic stagnation and anxiety about the United States' declining power and influence on the world stage in the 1970s, the racially coded politics of law and order (the "Southern Strategy") proved effective for gaining electoral advantage, particularly among southern white Democrats who converted to the Republican Party.[22]

Paradoxically, "tough on crime" efforts were also facilitated by political struggle on the Left. Federal Democrats, in particular, symbolically linked poverty and crime—even as they sought to reduce poverty and increase life chances for urban minorities. As political scientist Naomi Murakawa explains, in fighting for the "first civil right"—protection from violence, especially black Americans' protection from race-based hate crimes—liberals linked the lack of opportunities in minority communities to high crime rates. This discourse banded race and crime in the policy arena and public imagination.[23] In what became known as the "Moynihan Report" (published in 1965), for instance, Daniel Patrick Moynihan—a trained sociologist and assistant secretary of the Department of Labor for president John F. Kennedy—lamented ongoing discrimination against blacks and simultaneously suggested that "delinquency, crime, unemployment, and poverty resulted from unstable black families."[24] Influenced by these sloppy, if not downright racist ideas—or, perhaps, seeing in them a convenient scientific cover—the federal government "blended the opportunity, development, and training programs of the War on Poverty with the surveillance, patrol, and detention programs of Johnson's newly declared 'War on Crime,'" writes historian Elizabeth Hinton.[25] Particularly critical was the establishment of the Law Enforcement Assistance Administration (LEAA), part of the 1968 Omnibus Crime Control and Safe Streets Act, which increased the role of the federal government in criminal justice and law enforcement, especially in providing funding for a massive increase in police forces and their access to surplus military gear.[26]

By the late 1980s and '90s, many influential Democrats resembled Republicans on criminal justice issues as the politics of punishment took on a distinctly purple (rather than red or blue) shade.[27] Democrats embraced "tough on crime," in large part to stop a hemorrhaging of their political base (especially among the white working class).[28] By that point, "soft on crime" accusations could seriously harm candidates. The 1988 presidential race between George H. W. Bush and Michael Dukakis presents a particularly famous example. Dukakis was governor of Massachusetts when a black prisoner on furlough, William Horton, committed an atrocious crime. Bush relentlessly presented this incident (including a fear-mongering campaign ad featuring a mugshot photo of "Willie" Horton) as evidence that Dukakis was "soft on crime." Because *every* state had a furlough program at the time, the Horton incident served as a potent cautionary lesson for politicians across the country.[29]

Within this national context, leaders across the country successfully enacted punitive criminal justice legislation. Proposals that increased both the likelihood and length of prison sentences were most common, increasing severity particularly for those convicted of drug, violent, and sex offenses.[30] These changes were furthered by the increasing coordination and strength of key interest groups, including prison officer unions, prosecutors' and sheriffs' organizations, and crime victims' groups.[31] In addition, this context both reflected and ostensibly encouraged increasingly "tough" decisions by local criminal justice actors, including police, prosecutors, and judges, to ramp-up punishment.[32]

---

TEXT BOX

## Penal Change and Presidential Politics

Although presidents can directly influence only federal criminal justice policy—which represents just 13% of prisoners today[33]—presidential campaigns and policymaking provide indicators about national politics related to crime and punishment. The two Democratic presidencies that sandwich the so-called punitive turn offer a chance to examine changes in the national debate over criminal justice policy.

The nation's forty-second president, William ("Bill") Clinton, began his eight-year term in 1993. Public-opinion polls consistently found widespread concern about crime; in 1994, a record 37% of Americans ranked crime and violence as the number-one problem facing the country.[34] Democrats fought to neutralize the advantages Republicans enjoyed on this hot-button issue by adopting similarly draconian policy positions.[35] After years of "tough on crime" campaigns, Clinton's presidency marked the culmination of this convergence between the Right and the Left on criminal justice issues.

One of Clinton's signature policy victories, the 1994 Violent Crime Control and Law Enforcement Act, increased federal funding for police forces and eliminated prisoners' eligibility for Pell Grants to fund postsecondary education. It increased the severity of federal sentencing, adding a "three-strikes-and-you're-out" provision and expanding the number of death-eligible crimes, and provided fiscal incentives to states that adopted "truth in sentencing" initiatives that limited "good time" credits.[36] Although the crime bill included a number of provisions championed by liberals, most notably a ban on assault weapons and the Violence Against Women Act, it is remembered primarily as entrenching tough-on-crime policies in the 1990s.[37]

Eight years after Clinton left office, fellow Democrat Barack Obama moved into the White House. By this point, panic around street crime had largely subsided, with the majority of Americans (even in southern states) supporting a shift of funding away from prisons and toward community-based programs, especially for nonviolent drug offenders.[38] President Obama's early years were fairly quiet on criminal justice issues, although he did appoint an attorney general (Eric Holder) who publically committed to scaling back the federal drug war in 2013. His last two years in office, however, have been a flurry of activity, with Obama commuting the sentences of 46 federal prisoners (a modest but record-setting figure),[39] banning the "box" (the question about criminal convictions) on federal employment application forms,[40] ending solitary confinement for juvenile federal prisoners,[41] and reinstating prisoners' eligibility for federal Pell Grants.[42] All these reforms advocate for a compassionate stance toward current and former prisoners, but the most symbolic change may have been Obama's visit to a federal prison—the first ever by a sitting president. From inside the walls, he decried the United State's "broken" criminal justice system.[43]

Obama never championed a signature piece of criminal justice legislation like Clinton's 1994 bill, though he supported efforts to scale back federal sentencing. These efforts crystalized in the Sentencing Reform and Corrections Act of 2015, which garnered broad bipartisan support after a protracted negotiation.[44] Yet, after a series of high-profile claims that the bill would increase crime (led in part by federal prosecutors), contestation over sentencing reform for white-collar offenses, and jockeying among potential Republican presidential nominees, the bill stalled—serving as one of many examples of the fragility of present-day reform efforts that we return to in the conclusion.[45]

## *The Long Struggle across States*

As we have seen, macro-level and meso-level developments—including changes
in the economy, class and racial stratification, crime rates, and national-level
politics—created opportunities for actors who had never ceased to struggle for
punitive criminal justice policies and practices.[46] All states experienced growth
in imprisonment rates during the latter decades of the twentieth century, but
the degree of that change varied considerably. For instance, between 1960 and
2000, imprisonment rates grew by about 70% in Maine and West Virginia but
by more than 550% in Louisiana, Mississippi, and Delaware.[47]

Figure 5.1 plots the national imprisonment rate (which includes all state
and federal prisoners relative to the resident population) from 1960 to 2014
alongside the trends for a handful of state examples, including the three states
featured in this chapter. Below, we turn to two Sunbelt states, California and
Arizona, both of which pioneered tough punishment, but in quite different
ways. As seen in figure 5.1, Arizona has maintained above-average incarceration rates after 1980, whereas California's imprisonment rate roughly tracked
the national average from 1980 to 2000 (and then sharply declined). Later in
the chapter we profile the Rockefeller Drug Laws in New York, a state that
maintained average to moderate imprisonment rates in the 1980s and '90s
but today exemplifies one of the most extreme downsizing trends.

WHEN WE LAST saw California in these pages, it was the late 1960s.
Tensions between Treatment and Custody forces inside and outside the
state's prisons had reached what seemed like a breaking point. Recall from
chapter 4 that those pushing for harsher punishment had a decades-old lineage—there was never a time in which they were silent, even in the heyday
of the so-called rehabilitative era. These actors gained leverage in the political and penal fields when Ronald Reagan became governor in 1967. While
campaigning, Reagan had deftly portrayed criminals and protesters as
moral failures in need of strict surveillance and punishment; once in office,
he proclaimed that only "the man with the badge" could hold back "the
jungle."[48] In fusing race, crime, and disorder, Reagan argued that welfare
inside and outside prisons enabled "street thugs" and undercut the security
of "law-abiding citizens" (coded as suburban and white). Rehabilitation
and lenient sentencing, Reagan insisted, were *causes* of—not solutions to—
crime in the streets.

In his first year as governor, Reagan appointed former prison officer
Raymond Procunier to lead the California Department of Corrections.

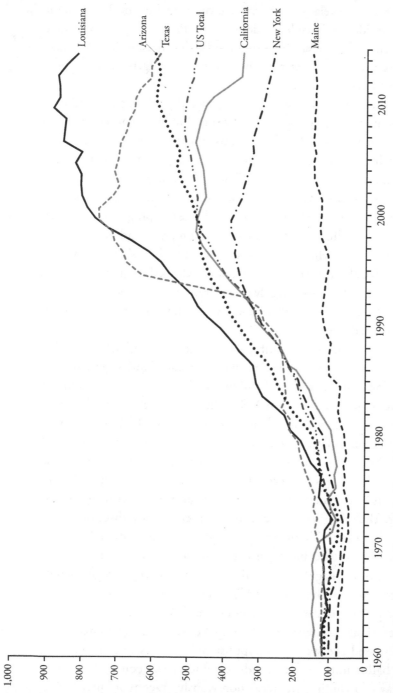

**FIGURE 5.1** Imprisonment Rates in the United States, 1960–2014.

*Notes:* Imprisonment rate is calculated as the number of prisoners in the jurisdiction per 100,000 in the resident population. The total rate includes all state and federal prisoners. State rates include all prisoners under the physical custody of state institutions for the years 1960–1978 and the total under states' jurisdiction serving sentences of more than one year for 1978–2014.

*Sources:* Bureau of Justice Statistics, Historical Statistics on Prisoners in State and Federal Institutions, Yearend 1925-86 [ICPSR 8912] (for the years 1960–1977); Bureau of Justice Statistics, Corrections Statistical Analysis Tool (CSAT) Custom Tables—Imprisonment rates of jurisdiction population—sentences greater than 1 year, Generated May 9, 2016 (for the years 1979–2014). Data for 1978 estimated as the midpoint between estimates to smooth transition.

A mentee of the famed correctionalist Richard McGee, Procunier had worked as warden of a relatively progressive vocational prison.[49] Yet, under new pressures inside and outside the department, Procunier privileged security at the expense of treatment.[50] Abandoning California's position as leader in progressive corrections, the state slashed treatment budgets and hired hundreds of new officers.[51]

Changes in sentencing legislation also signaled the shifting orientation of California's penal field. Governor Reagan teamed up with conservative legislators to implement SB 85-87, which imposed mandatory prison sentences of 15 years to life for certain crimes and framed punishment as necessary to avenge victims, not to rehabilitate offenders.[52] Still, the state's incarceration rate actually *declined* while Reagan was in office, in large part because his administration continued some of its predecessors' progressive criminal justice policies, including a probation subsidy program and early releases through parole.[53] Thus, while Reagan and state Republicans' fiscal conservatism helped keep California's incarceration rate in check during the late 1960s, their policies and rhetoric—especially their carefully timed and worded calls for harsh punishment of black urban residents—solidified the growing power of punitive-oriented actors in the Golden State.

When trying to pinpoint California's "punitive turn," scholars often highlight the passage of SB 42 in 1976, which replaced indeterminate sentencing (the cornerstone of the rehabilitative ideal) with fixed sentencing and substituted "punishment" for "rehabilitation" as the official goal of imprisonment. Signed by Democratic governor Edmund ("Jerry") Brown, SB 42 was the culmination of decades of struggle by "law and order" proponents who distrusted (in some cases, perhaps detested) rehabilitation and wanted convicts to serve long sentences, ideally in austere penal facilities. It was *also* championed by prisoners and their advocates on the political Left. They believed indeterminate sentencing was discriminatory, irrational, and punitive (though they thought, or at least hoped, the legislature would substitute indeterminate sentences with moderate fixed terms). As one of us (Page) traces in detail elsewhere, this struggle would continue right through the 1980s and '90s. Politicians and interest groups (such as the prison officers' union, police and prosecutor associations, and punitive-oriented crime victims' groups) developed a formidable bloc that skillfully used the state's neopopulist political institutions (such as California's ballot initiative) to produce some of the country's harshest sentencing laws (including the state's notoriously draconian Three Strikes law).[54] These laws produced a rapidly expanding imprisonment rate and, together with the growing population of the state, produced an unprecedented prison-building spree.

This long arc of struggle—rather than immediate rupture—can also be seen in Arizona, another "role model" state for tough punishment in the modern era. According to Mona Lynch, penal politics in the Grand Canyon State from the late 1960s to mid-1980s can be best characterized as a comparatively progressive penal-modernization project rather than pure punitive politics.[55] (Arizona during the latter twentieth century thus shares much in common with Florida during the decades immediately after World War II, as discussed in the previous chapter.) Allen Cook, the first director of Arizona's Department of Corrections (appointed in 1968), was a correctionalist from California.[56] Under Cook and his next two successors, the department fought for a vision of modern punishment, expanding progressive hallmarks such as treatment programs and furlough opportunities. Yet, this struggle took place within the broader context of Arizona state politics, with department leaders, for example, justifying treatment programs as more fiscally sound than warehousing prisoners.[57] In addition, as the legislature continued to pass tough sentencing bills that created long mandatory sentences, progressive-oriented directors fought to expand the Department of Corrections' funding to increase prison beds and to stem overcrowding. Ironically, Lynch explains, the administration "most explicitly oriented toward deinstitutionalization and alternatives to incarceration . . . oversaw the beginning of the state's move to mass incarceration."[58]

After the mid-1980s, Arizona strongly embraced a harsh, retributivist approach to crime and punishment. The state's incarceration rate accelerated faster than the national average throughout the 1980s and '90s. But rather than representing a complete reversal, these years are better characterized as *building on* and *reformulating* long-standing struggles over punishment in the Grand Canyon State. Actors who had previously fought against attempts to provide treatment opportunities for prisoners (and, relatedly, maintain low prison costs) increasingly gained dominant positions in the state's penal field. Aided by an economic downturn in Arizona in the late 1980s and increasing anger toward Latino immigrants, calls for austere, tough punishment (and hostility toward welfare and rehabilitative services) were now particularly resonant.[59]

Arizona's penal leaders sought to expand capacity and make the state's prisons more painful places. One of their banner achievements was opening the nation's first super-maximum housing unit at Florence State Prison.[60] As readers will recall from chapter 2, solitary confinement had been essential to the early penitentiary ideal and was realized most fully at Eastern State Penitentiary in Philadelphia. Further, prisoners had been routinely thrown into the "hole" or other crude versions of solitary for as long as prisons have existed,[61] including through the use of "adjustment centers" in such places as California during the heyday of the rehabilitative ideal. To the extent that the discourses justifying solitary confinement shifted, administrators drew on the language that correctionalists developed around risk classification and treatment and argued that mainline prisons would be safer if high-risk prisoners (the "worst of the worst") were further incapacitated in Security Housing Units (SHUs).[62]

In sum, there is no mistaking the fact that the penal landscape changed in significant ways during the late twentieth century; however, this transformation was contested, varied across place, and had deep roots in earlier eras. After a protracted period of pushing against the penal status quo, actors seized opportunities related to changing contexts and conditions to usher in expressly punitive policies and practices. But just as they (and their predecessors) struggled against penal welfarism, a range of actors contested efforts to institute policies based on maximizing "penal harm."

## Rehabilitation's Many Lives

The standard American "punitive turn" narrative often begins in 1974, when Robert Martinson published "What Works?—Questions and Answers about Prison Reform" in the journal *Public Interest*. A systematic review of over 200 studies of correctional rehabilitation, the article concluded: "With few and isolated exceptions, the rehabilitative efforts that have been reported so far have had no appreciable effect on recidivism."[63] Martinson's work was widely framed as definitive evidence that "nothing works" in rehabilitation, a surprising takeaway given that the findings about program success were mixed, and Martinson and his colleagues' methodology was not particularly sophisticated, even by standards at the time.[64]

Still, Martinson appeared on *60 Minutes*,[65] and scholars and pundits seized upon the *Public Interest* piece as an almost subversive tract revealing rehabilitation as a devious waste of taxpayer dollars.[66] Politicians, penal administrators, and even federal judges joined the "nothing works" chorus. In 1984, for example, Congress passed the Sentencing Reform Act, creating a federal sentencing commission, lengthening many federal prison sentences, and officially rejecting rehabilitation as a major justification for punishment, invoking research from Martinson and others to justify the policy change.[67] In a 1989 decision, the Supreme Court wrote: "Rehabilitation as a sound penological theory, came to be questioned and, in any event, was regarded by some as an unattainable goal for most cases."[68]

Martinson's article became a lightning rod because it affirmed widespread opposition to rehabilitation across the political spectrum. It was published amid a growing critique of rehabilitation and penal welfarism, including, notably, the American Friends Service Committee's 1971 scathing report, *Struggle for Justice*. Among other things, the report lambasted indeterminate sentences as unfair, counterproductive, and racist and pointed to myriad ways in which prison "treatment" was coercive, punitive, and ineffective.[69] This progressive critique emerged in tandem with conservative complaints that indeterminate sentencing and rehabilitative services "coddled" criminals.[70] Opponents of rehabilitation (indeterminate sentencing, in particular) used the "nothing works" thesis as a weapon in their symbolic struggle against those who were still committed to the rehabilitative ideal.[71]

Correctionalists fought against Martinson's conclusions from the very start, joining the political ruckus as they argued both over the specifics of the empirical findings and the prospects of penal programming more generally.[72] Criminologists, scholars, activists, and penal administrators struggled to depict prisoners as individuals with potential for reformation, insisting that scientific research could show that rehabilitation "works" when focused on the correct population (i.e., those most likely to benefit from each program) and designed to build individuals' strengths and address their deficiencies. Scholars in Canada, the United States, and the United Kingdom went on to develop an entire body of scholarship on "effective correctional intervention," in part by evaluating effect size across a large number of studies (meta-analyses) and paying careful attention to the methodological rigor of the component evaluations.[73]

As part of this effort, researchers and advocates developed tools for assessing and addressing individuals' "needs" and "risks."[74] Legal scholar Cecelia Klingele explains that "proponents of evidence-based approaches to correctional risk management have argued that statistical prediction methods outperform human intuition in identifying those at greatest risk of reoffense. Moreover, when risk profiles are augmented with information about a defendant's 'criminogenic needs'—that is, the deficiencies most strongly correlated with risk of future criminality—correctional officials can tailor sentencing conditions to target for intervention people most likely to benefit from correctional programming."[75] Despite substantial criticism from critical criminologists,[76] the framework has been hugely influential in the United States, offering language and principles that can be deployed to justify programmatic interventions.[77]

The "what works" approach thus owes at least part of its success to savvy actors who skillfully redefined rehabilitation as politically neutral and grounded in sound, methodologically rigorous "science."[78] It also owes a debt to the myriad ways in which rehabilitation had been defined and practiced in earlier periods; as we argued in chapter 4, the concept of rehabilitation often functioned as an amorphous reference or catch-all category for any attempt to change people. It encompassed goals as diverse as social welfare; the redistribution of power in society; and security, surveillance, and control. During the latter decades of the twentieth century, the reformulated vision of rehabilitation mirrored neoliberal political rationality, emphasizing cost-effectiveness and what some scholars have referred to as "responsibilization"—rhetorically if not literally holding individuals "accountable" for their own rehabilitation.[79] Explaining rehabilitation as giving prisoners the opportunity to fix themselves (rather than a race-coded state "handout") suggests that penal programs are cheap, effective, and make society safer by lowering recidivism.[80] Progressives might prefer explicit talk about rights and the responsibility of the government to level the proverbial playing field, but this reframing has been useful in rehabilitating rehabilitation.[81]

Largely as a result of friction within the penal field, core pieces of the correctional model remained in place throughout the "punitive era." A particularly clear example is the evolution of in-prison rehabilitative (or "treatment") programs. As one of us (Phelps) has documented, between 1979 and 1990, the absolute number of prisoners participating in such programs increased sharply; for instance, the annual number of prisoners participating in psychological counseling doubled from just under 35,000 to more than 70,000 in those 11 years.[82] Even the percentage of prisoners participating in programs declined only modestly during the 1980s. In-prison academic programs—a hallmark of progressive approaches to crime and criminals—saw a doubling in the raw number of prisoners reporting participation since admission, with a modest decline of only four percentage points in the participation rate (from 25% in 1979 to 21% in 1990).[83] Thus, as the nation experienced the first decade of staggering growth in its prison population, administrators in most states were scrambling to meet program demand. To put it mildly, this is not at all what we would expect on the basis of the standard narrative of the death of rehabilitation.

As tough-on-crime rhetoric hit a zenith in the 1990s, prison programs were downsized—yet even here we see transformation rather than disappearance. Education programs were particularly affected, with a drop from 43% of current prisoners in 1991 reporting some form of educational program participation since their admission to just 27% into 2004.[84] In contrast, participation in reentry programs[85] and parenting classes *increased* significantly (from 15% to 25% and from 3% to 8% between 1991 and 2004, respectively). Treatment regimes thus evolved from a primarily education-based system to one that supported "soft-skills" training designed to "habilitate" prisoners for reentry.[86]

Zooming in a bit, consider the case of California's prison fire camps. As one of us (Goodman) has argued elsewhere, the expansion of California's prison fire camp program during the late 1950s and early '60s can be traced directly to penal administrators' and state politicians' efforts to position the Golden State as the national (if not international) leader in modern, progressive penology.[87] Prisoners in the camps were housed in temporary platform tents or permanent army-style barracks, often deep in the wilderness, and spent their time clearing or grading the forest to prevent fire and responding to active wildfires.[88] This work was—and remains—portrayed as deeply rehabilitative. For example, in a 1959 speech calling for prison conservation camp expansion, Governor Pat Brown opined, "It is a fine, a noble, an essential thing to save our forests. It is an even nobler thing to conserve the greatest of all resources—human beings. By this program, we are doing both."[89]

During the 1970s, '80s, and '90s, officials shifted away from using rehabilitation and progressive penology as the definitive justifications for the fire camps. They came to adopt instead a rhetoric that conservation camps provided a steady supply of cheap and carefully managed prisoner-firefighters. In place of earlier, boastful statements about correctional officials' professional knowledge and ability to choose good candidates for forestry camps (and, by extension, rehabilitation), program administrators in the 1980s and '90s soberly focused on the "low risk" classification of the male and (starting in 1983) female "offenders" assigned to a camp. Despite the change in tone, remarkably little changed about the daily reality of life in the camps: the physical work continued,[90] with camp prisoners supervised by a limited number of trained firefighters, rather than prison officers, and receiving rewards (e.g., better food and more freedom than in walled prisons) in exchange for performing hard, dangerous work.[91]

California penal administrators made little attempt to close the camps or otherwise bring daily life inside them more in line with dominant penal logics—namely, that punishment should be painful, cost-effective, and disciplinary. Mid-level bureaucrats and camp managers of the 1980s and '90s simply papered over any differences between seeing prisoners in the camps as cheap, useful, low-risk labor versus humans being "saved" by the rehabilitation of hard work in natural environments. These quiet, rhetorical, and practical shifts avoided changing life in the camps while quelling voices that might have otherwise called for the camps to be shuttered or have their security "upgraded" to more closely match traditional prisons.[92]

To take one last example of how rhetoric often obscures braided practices, one of us (Phelps) develops an account of the rise of *mass probation*.[93] Probation, which allows individuals to remain in local communities under the supervision of a probation officer in lieu of incarceration, initially expanded in the Progressive Era and was championed in many states as an ideal penal form after the Second World War.[94] By staying in the community, individuals could avoid the ravages of institutionalization. Given that prisons are often characterized as punishment for "dangerous" criminals and probation as a progressive alternative for "less-serious" cases, it would be easy to assume that as prison rolls expanded, probation would shrink. And yet, alongside rising imprisonment rates, probation metastasized: between 1980 and its peak in 2007, the state and federal probation population grew from 1 million to nearly 4.3 million. This translated to a supervision rate of 1 in 53 adults and 1 in 12 black men.[95] Probation, framed as an alternative sanction, instead served as a *supplement* to imprisonment—making it relatively cheap and easy to surveil massive numbers of adults.[96] Thus, rather than abandoning probation as inconsistent with the new dominant discourses, probation was instead reformulated and expanded under the banner of public safety.[97]

To recap, at *no time* in the twentieth century was the idea or practice of trying to reform those convicted of crime (including prisoners) ever truly verboten. Major changes occurred in punishment in these decades—changes that mattered very much to those in penal institutions and in the communities that prisoners left behind—but the full story is one of considerable conflict, substantial hybridization, and a mixture of transformation, repackaging, and reformulation, rather than an abject collapse of correctionalist criminal justice.

## A Shifting Terrain

A range of present-day commentators have begun characterizing the late 2000s and early 2010s as the latest swing of the "pendulum," a rupture from the "punitive era" to something new—the contours of which remain hazy.[98]

They point to quantitative and qualitative changes blunting some of the harshest facets of the carceral state. For example, between 2009 and 2012, the national incarceration rate declined slightly and prison admissions hit their lowest rate since 1999.[99] Between 1999 and 2013, two-thirds of states experienced declines in prison populations, with New Jersey and New York reporting drops of more than 25%.[100] Perhaps, some commentators argue, the pendulum is swinging back toward rehabilitation—whether called "neo-rehabilitation," "penal moderation," or "penal optimism"—with states reembracing (certain) diversion pathways, programs and services for supervisees, and more humane and respectful treatment for individuals with a criminal record.[101]

These policy and practice shifts have emerged within a reconfigured political arena. The "tough on crime" mantra has been partially replaced as advocates and policymakers across the political aisle adopt the language of "smart" and "effective" approaches to criminal justice (often retaining the emphasis on "public safety").[102] Early-twenty-first-century reform efforts present a strong contrast with the 1980s and '90s, when calls for judicious use of incarceration and short(er) prison sentences tended to be the sole domain of subordinate penal actors. This shift can be linked to the "purpling" of punishment outlined above, which resulted in a political statement that reduced the benefits of ad nauseam jockeying to be "toughest" on crime and punishment. Political scientists David Dagan and Steven Teles trace how, under the moniker "Right on Crime," a key group of conservative actors helped redefine mass incarceration as a fiscally irresponsible example of "big government" run amok.[103] This framing opened up a new way for Republicans to claim electoral advantage and created more space for Democrats to promote moderate penal policies.

One popular way to understand today's reframing of penal policies is that the pendulum was shoved into motion by the economic collapse that began in late 2007 and continued into the early 2010s. Massive penal systems and their costs were hard to afford, fiscally and *politically*.[104] In one of the most developed accounts, legal scholar Hadar Aviram argues that scarcity generated a new "cheap on crime" ethos that provided political cover for bipartisan compromise on criminal justice reform.[105] Critically, the financial crisis came on the heels of a long decline in crime rates (underway since at least the mid-1990s)—some historically high-crime cities enjoyed lows not seen since the mid-1960s.[106] While crime rates and incarceration rates rarely rise and fall in lockstep, declines in crime (and the public's fear of it) created more political space for considering criminal justice reform.[107] Similarly, as states began to decrease prison populations without crime spikes, actors have been able to use those trends as evidence to support moderate penal reforms.[108]

In addition, these changes have been explained as the result of new dominant actors in the penal field. Reform-oriented politicians were joined by technical assistance providers, such as the Pew Center on the States and the Council on State Government, which provided states with detailed statistical analyses of their penal populations and blueprints for reform.[109] In addition, although the federal judiciary remained involved in the penal field during the prisoners' rights movement of the 1960s and right through the end of the twentieth century,[110] scholars point to judges' renewed importance as a driver of recent shifts. In particular, the 2011 *Brown v. Plata* decision by the United States Supreme Court required California to downsize its prison population (producing a notable decline in the national prison population, given the relative scale of the Golden State's penal system) and served as a warning about the potential fiscal and political risks of overcrowding.[111]

As we have argued throughout the book, we see it differently. Rather than the direct and inevitable product of mechanical structural change or rapid political shifts, we see early twenty-first-century reforms principally as the continuation of a long struggle over whom and how to punish in the United States. Until recently, challengers to the dominant, punitive penal orientation struggled largely without notice, beneath the surface, producing fissures in the penal field but earning few major victories. Recent social, economic, and political developments have opened up space in which actors might shift the penal terrain at the local, state, and national levels.[112] With growing visibility and legitimacy, more (and increasingly ideologically diverse) allies, and expanding political capital, these actors are beginning to blunt the edges of the carceral state.

We can return to Arizona, known for no-nonsense, harsh punishment (emblemized in "America's Toughest Sheriff"), for a good case in point. Throughout the "tough on crime" decades, progressives in Arizona fought what they viewed as destructive penal practices. For example, they launched a series of lawsuits over prison conditions (particularly solitary confinement). With the help of the nonprofit prisoner advocacy group Middle Ground, prisoners sued the Arizona Department of Corrections over various issues, from overcrowding, visitation, and disciplinary procedures to gift packages and racial discrimination.[113]

During much of the 1980s and '90s, the Arizona Department of Corrections pushed back against these efforts, and if anything, the conflict probably aided the state's penal buildup. In particular, key lawmakers and penal administrators used the court decrees as political cover to build more prisons, using "bleeding-heart liberal" judges as a "foil to orate about what was wrong with the justice system and what needed to change."[114] Arizona legislators also helped write the 1996 federal Prisoner Litigation Reform Act, which sharply curtailed prisoners' ability to initiate and fight legal battles against corrections departments.[115]

On the other hand, these legal battles paved the way for some of the positive developments in the field today. For one thing, they kept progressive actors in the game, if only as observers and scouts on the outer boundaries, relaying the austerity Arizona legislators and penal administrators were attempting to institute. Some recent banner successes include a 2014 class-action win by the Arizona ACLU on behalf of solitary prisoners that required the state to overhaul solitary confinement policies, including mental health protections, more out-of-cell time, and restrictions on guards' use of pepper spray on inmates.[116]

This victory was facilitated by a new political climate in Arizona (and beyond), but it was also the product of a very long, multifaceted struggle.[117] As legal scholar Keramet Reiter documents, between the late 1980s and the turn of the century, nearly every state built a "supermax" prison.[118] A decade later, between 89,000 and 120,000 adult prisoners resided in solitary confinement, and 20% of prisoners spent at least part of each year in restrictive housing.[119] However, prisoners and prisoners' rights advocates have fought this development every step of the way, primarily through litigation.[120] In the 1990s and 2000s, researchers and advocates worked to redefine solitary confinement in the public imagination as torture or "social death,"[121] chipping away at the claim that solitary made prisons safer[122] and documenting the many ways it harmed prisoners.[123] Advocacy groups, human rights organizations, and media outlets made explicit links to the experiences of prisoners of war such as Senator John McCain and hostages in the Middle East.[124]

Prisoners themselves also intervened, using disruption to force bureaucrats, politicians, and the media to attend to the deprivations and severe harms of solitary confinement.[125] Back in California, prisoners in the notorious Pelican Bay Secure Housing Unit (SHU) led a hunger strike that rippled through the state's system in 2011.[126] In response to another successful class-action suit, California agreed in 2015 to release many prisoners who had been in long-term solitary (excepting those convicted of the most serious prison infractions). Going forward, the agreement limits the violations for which staff may send prisoners to the SHU, caps prisoners' length of stay, and mandates a modified version of segregation for vulnerable prisoners, including those with mental illness.[127]

Reforms like those seen in Arizona and California are spreading across the country. In just 2014, 10 states adopted new policies for solitary confinement, including limiting the practice (especially for juveniles and mentally ill prisoners), improving conditions in solitary, and transitioning prisoners to general prison units before release back into the community. The federal system is changing as well; in 2016, President Barack Obama restricted the use of solitary in federal prisons.[128]

Or, take the 2007 Second Chance Act—one of the earliest victories of the actors who would eventually start the Right on Crime movement, including Charles Colson (founder of the Prison Fellowship organization) and Pat Nolan.[129] Signed by President George W. Bush, the law funded reentry demonstration projects, substance abuse treatment, housing assistance, educational and vocational training programs, and reentry courts.[130] The legislation was a victory for conservative reform groups (who won a political struggle to allow funding to go to "faith-based" organizations), but it also built on the broader symbolic struggle of various groups to humanize perceptions of prisoners, in part by reframing them as workers, parents, and community citizens.[131]

This reentry movement helped resuscitate rehabilitation by discussing prisoner and ex-prisoner services in the language of "recidivism" and "public safety,"[132] and it hearkened back to the "what works"-in-correctional-intervention movement, which had developed the "risk-need responsivity" assessment tools for release and supervision decisions (discussed earlier in this chapter). In addition, scholars, activists, and others working in the realm of prisoner reentry adapted the framework of "evidence-based" practices that undergirds the recent increase in political optimism around using scientific methods to devise a better criminal justice system.[133] Focusing attention on substantial state-level variation in recidivism rates opened up the possibility that returns to prison were governed more by correctional policy than the individual moral failures of parolees. Therefore, revocation rates could be brought down by smarter policy that improved support for parolees and changed departments' responses to parole violations. This message has helped stabilize prison populations in recent years: between 2006 and 2011, prison admissions for parole violations declined by 31%.[134]

In brief, we agree with the dominant narrative that the penal terrain is shifting. As usual, it is our *characterization* of that change that differs. First, we see considerable continuity even as things shift (e.g., an ongoing "reformulation" of rehabilitation), and second, we attribute the shift not to a *mechanical* result of changing social conditions forcing a pendulum swing, but to continual struggle of dominant and subordinate actors in ever-evolving penal, political, and legal fields.

We turn lastly to a case study of the Rockefeller Drug Laws, which shows the centrality of prolonged contestation in generating one of the most important penal developments in the last half century: the war on drugs and its recent detente. Whereas the examples above focused primarily on prison conditions and community supervision, this history reveals a long fight to moderate the sentencing laws that facilitated and reinforced the carceral state.

## New York's Rockefeller Drug Laws

The Rockefeller Drug Laws are widely understood as emblematic of the nation's war on drugs, among the first in a series of draconian legislative changes that mandated long prison terms for drug offenses.[135] And yet, these harsh drug sanctions did not result from a straightforward law-and-order crusade. The champion of the legislation, Governor Nelson Rockefeller, then considered a moderate Republican, had his sights set on the White House (he contended for the GOP nomination in 1960, 1964, and 1968). Many interpret Rockefeller's push for harsh drug laws as a strategic move to counter the charge that he was "soft on crime," especially in comparison to Richard Nixon.[136] In key respects, however, the drug laws represented an extension (rather than abrupt turn) of Rockefeller's existing preoccupation with chemical dependency.[137] Before 1973, Rockefeller had advocated a mix of strategies for fighting drug distribution and abuse, ranging from federal interdiction to curb the supply of narcotics entering the country to increased drug treatment, including "experimental" approaches such as methadone maintenance and involuntary commitment.[138]

Rockefeller took advantage of the hardening political environment to pivot away from these "weak" interventions toward more punitive drug policies. The nation was experiencing deep panic over drug use (which was particularly acute in New York City) and rapid increases in crime; between 1965 and the early 1970s, the violent crime rate more than doubled (although some of this increase was likely due to better reporting by police agencies).[139] In addition, 1971 brought the nationally televised Attica Prison riot, which ended with Rockefeller's authorization of state troopers to violently retake the prison, killing both prisoners and hostages in the process.[140] People were said (or made) to feel afraid, and punitive approaches to the drug "menace" were framed as the only way to stem the violence and desperation. The Rockefeller Drug Laws, passed in 1973, made prison sentences mandatory for all serious drug-related felonies, with proscribed sentences of 15 years to life for selling or possessing relatively small amounts of LSD, amphetamines, cocaine, and heroin.[141] The laws were widely supported at the time by New York's political elites, passing by large majorities in the senate and assembly.[142]

Another turn against the dominant narrative of a top-down law and order campaign is that the Rockefeller laws had substantial support in Harlem, home to a large concentration of African Americans and the epicenter of New York's drug crisis. Political scientist Michael Fortner argues that the black working-and middle-class residents of Harlem formed a "black silent majority" that had advocated for tough punishment for "pushers" and "junkies" in the two decades before Rockefeller's drug laws. Harlem's black elites and community leaders, including prominent legislators, the NAACP, and other civic advocates, sought increased police presence and stiffer penalties for drug offenses.[143] In 1973, the *Amsterdam News*, a leading black newspaper, declared: "Aggressive state action against narcotics addiction is long overdue."[144] Historians disagree about the extent to which the *majority* of Harlem's residents supported punitive interventions and how much that mattered to Rockefeller, but it is clear at least that there was some support, particularly among religious leaders.[145] There is agreement that many in Harlem also wanted to improve conditions, job opportunities, and treatment for low-level users in the neighborhood, but the state did not respond to these calls with the same gusto.[146]

In short, the Rockefeller Drug Laws are not a simple story of elite-led draconian punishment devised to capture (white) votes and punish poor, minority communities. Instead, the harsh legislation emerged out of—and in tandem with—public health interventions and highly charged concerns about chemical dependency and crime in economically precarious black communities. Further, as criminologist Vanessa Barker argues, the Rockefeller approach was embedded within New York's broader pragmatic and managerial system of governance and its "two tiered approach to penal sanctioning—prison for serious violent offenders [and, later, those convicted of drug crimes], diversion for others."[147] As figure 5.1 documents, this approach allowed New York to maintain an incarceration rate that was equal to or below the national average for most of the late twentieth century.

From the beginning, a range of actors opposed the legislation. Much of the opposition, Fortner argues, came from white progressive reformers who favored an exclusively public health approach to drug abuse.[148] As the law was drafted, the New York chapter of the ACLU argued that the changes represented "a frightening leap toward the imposition of a total police state"; after it passed, they condemned the law as "one of the most ignorant, irresponsible, and inhuman acts in the history of the state."[149] New York City's mayor, John Lindsay, called it "impractical, unworkable, and vindictive."[150] Even some in the Rockefeller administration were skeptical; New York's top drug official correctly predicted that the legislation would fill the state's prisons with young men of color, as an inexhaustible supply of drug couriers in inner-city neighborhoods replaced those who were incarcerated. Rockefeller cynically brushed off the concern, snapping that the African American head of New York's Narcotic Addiction Control Commission was simply "worried about his people."[151]

Law enforcement groups and judges joined in criticizing the Rockefeller laws as an unrealistic waste of limited resources.[152] In the early years after the laws' passage, police and prosecutors subverted full implementation;[153] the total number of felony drug arrests in New York State actually *declined* between 1974 and 1979, as did the percentage of arrests leading to indictment.[154] However, those cases that did make it to court were increasingly brought to trial because the legislation prevented low-level sellers from plea bargaining (this was mitigated in 1975 when the legislature amended the law to allow plea bargaining to reduce incentives to go to trial).[155]

New York's drug war accelerated in the mid-1980s with the emergence of the "crack epidemic." Crack, a new drug formulation that allowed users to smoke cocaine, proliferated in low-income, racially segregated parts of the city. Sellers could peddle smaller, cheaper units of the drug than they could with powder cocaine, effectively lowering the cost to entry for potential users. Sensationalist media coverage produced a moral panic[156] and popular fear of the drug "epidemic" and prejudice against racially coded crack addicts empowered an emergent "law and order" bloc in New York City. In 1978, Ed Koch, a self-described "centrist" who boasted that he would "retake the streets," became mayor.[157] His 1994 successor, Republican Rudolph ("Rudy") Giuliani, was also elected in large part as a "law and order" federal attorney. Throughout their tenures (particularly Giuliani's), the city cracked down on "street crime." Giuliani appointed William Bratton as police commissioner, who began the controversial stop-and-frisk policy that, in the name of "broken windows" or "quality of life" policing, disproportionately targeted poor people of color.[158] Under Bratton's lead, police aggressively ticketed and arrested the homeless, street vendors, sex workers, and graffiti artists, creating a flood of low-level cases.[159]

The numbers tell a stark story. In the 15 years between 1979 and 1994, New York drug felony arrests quintupled (to almost 56,000 per year), and the prison rate per felony drug arrest more than doubled (from 9% to 22%).[160] Throughout the 1990s, drug offenders represented roughly 30% of the state's prison population, up from 11% in 1975 and compared to roughly 20% nationally in state prisons.[161] The state's imprisonment rate peaked at 386 prisoners per 100,000 residents in 1999. From the 1970s to 2000, the raw number of prisoners in the Empire State grew from just over 12,000 prisoners to nearly 70,000.[162] Inner-city minority communities were devastated. By 2002, 94% of prisoners convicted under Rockefeller drug statutes were black or Latino.[163]

In the same period, crime began a steep descent. During the 1990s alone, New York City's crime rate plummeted. Homicide rates went down (73%), as did auto theft (73%), burglary (72%), robbery (70%), larceny (53%), and rape (52%).[164] Midtown Manhattan and its Times Square was reconfigured from a seedy neighborhood overrun with strip joints to a bustling, family-friendly commercial center.[165] To many, it looked as if New York's approach to crime and punishment worked.[166]

For their part, critics of the Rockefeller Drug Laws took rhetorical advantage of the crime drop as well. Given that the "crack epidemic" had abated and residents perceived themselves as relatively safe, critics argued that the Rockefeller Drug Laws were now unnecessary and destructive. Randolph "Randy" Credico, a comedian turned political activist, and famed civil right lawyer William Kunstler worked together to mobilize political opposition, bringing former prisoners, the families of current and former prisoners, and journalists into the fight over New York's drug laws.[167] Drawing on the tactics of the Argentinian "mothers of the disappeared," their campaign highlighted the stories of real prisoners, many with little to no previous criminal history, serving very long drug sentences for relatively minor crimes. Borrowing a favorite tactic of progressives during earlier historical periods, they humanized the men and women who found themselves on the "wrong side" of the law as valuable members of society rather than dangerous "criminals." The campaign launched at Rockefeller Plaza on May 8, 1998—the 25th anniversary of the laws' signing.[168]

In the first few years of the twenty-first century, various developments helped this reform effort. The response to the September 11, 2001 attacks focused concerns on international terrorism and put new fiscal strains on the Big Apple.[169] The economic situation intensified when major financial institutions in New York City imploded with the subprime mortgage crisis, initiating a national recession in 2008. Crime rates continued to decline, as did racial disparities in drug arrest rates (aided by the increasing popularity of drugs such as methamphetamines, which were primarily made, sold, and used by whites),[170] and the oppositional bloc became more organized. Soon they were coordinating actions through the Correctional Association of New York's "Drop the Rock Coalition."[171]

Alternative approaches to sanctioning drug offenses expanded in this period, too. In 1999, the chief judge in New York, Judith S. Kaye, made drug courts a key priority for the state, opening the Office of Court Drug Treatment Programs to facilitate their expansion statewide.[172] Drug courts, popular across the country, blend both criminal justice and public health–oriented approaches to drug abuse, requiring defendants accused of drug offenses to plead guilty to criminal charges in exchange for entering treatment programs. Thus, drug courts provide *coerced treatment*, merging a punitive iteration of chemical-dependency treatment with swift punishments for program infractions.[173] Similarly conceived programs included Brooklyn's Drug Treatment Alternative-to-Prison Program (DTAP)[174] and the Shock Incarceration Program, which provides an intense, prison-based treatment program in exchange for shortened sentences.[175] These programs provided diversion options for bureaucrats and judges looking to reduce the numbers of people sent to prison for drug crimes.

In this context, political leaders in New York increasingly supported reform legislation. The shift began in the first decade of the twenty-first century, with cautious support of drug law reform by Governor George Pataki's administration even as they restricted parole release for violent offenses.[176] These efforts were justified through the "right-sizing" approach, reserving expensive prison beds for violent offenders rather than those convicted of low-level offenses.[177] Between 2003 and 2005, the state legislature passed a series of bills that provided more early-release options for nonviolent drug offenders,[178] eliminated life sentences for drug crimes, reduced mandatory minimums,[179] and increased judicial discretion for drug offense resentencing.[180]

By the late 2000s, moderating the harm (and fiscal costs) of the drug laws was a clear priority among New York State's political elite. In 2007, Governor Eliot Spitzer established a Commission on Sentencing Reform to review the state's "cost-efficient" use of criminal justice resources.[181] Shortly thereafter, Spitzer was embroiled in a prostitution scandal, leading to his resignation and replacement by Lieutenant Governor David Paterson, the state's first African American governor and a vocal opponent of the Rockefeller Drug Laws.[182] In 2009, the New York State Legislature passed the most substantial drug law reform to date, eliminating mandatory minimum sentences, empowering judges to send first-and second-time drug offenders to treatment rather than prison, and allowing some prisoners to petition the courts for resentencing.[183] While not a full reversal of the Rockefeller policies—advocates continue to struggle for more reform[184]—the overhaul was still a major victory for the "Drop the Rock" campaign.

The reforms enacted from 2003 to 2005 and in 2009 translated into real effects. Each time the Rockefeller laws were pared back, there were declines in admission to prison and time served for drug offenses. Racial disparities decreased.[185] But these trends were also driven by the actions of frontline criminal justice agents; as the laws become more unpopular, these actors had increasingly subverted the goals of the Rockefeller Drug Laws. Legal scholar Issa Kohler-Hausmann reports that the raw number of felony drug cases and the percentage of drug cases resulting in a prison sentence actually began their decline well *before* the formal reforms, as police, prosecutors, and judges chose not to aggressively pursue tough arrest, conviction, and sentencing practices.[186]

In sum, we can understand the rise and fall of the Rockefeller Drug Laws as the product of a long struggle that morphed over time. As state and national contexts shifted, contingent events (such as Governor Spitzer's scandal) provided new opportunities. The kind of systemic drug policy reforms witnessed in New York are not unique; similar rollbacks have happened in other states and at the federal level.[187] Declines in admissions to prison for drug offenses have been a substantial contributor to declining prison populations nationwide; between 2006 and 2011, new court commitments for drug offenses declined by 22%.[188] While it remains to be seen how far drug law reforms will extend, it is clear that there has been an important shift in the country's dominant approach to drug offenses. Yet, as we discuss in the final chapter, advocates for punitive punishment continue to struggle, with some politicians fighting today, for example, to make selling certain kinds of opioids a capital offense.[189]

## Conclusion

By almost any definition of "punitiveness," the United States was a decidedly more punitive place in 2000 than it was, say, in 1968; during the last three decades of the twentieth century, penal actors changed the American criminal justice landscape in important ways. But this did not happen overnight, and it was not an all-encompassing, one-dimensional pendulum swing from one ideal form to its opposite. Even in places such as California and Arizona, the frictions and dislocations that preceded these shifts are deep and complex. Picking up the story from chapter 4, in California we saw the long history of actors struggling for tough punishment. They gained strength as "Custody" forces became dominant inside and outside prisons. In Arizona, correctionalist forces controlled the directorship of the Department of Corrections well into the 1980s and implemented a wide variety of reforms, including (ironically) an expansion in the number of prison beds.

Further, throughout this period, rehabilitation was reinvented, not buried. Actors continued to advocate for correctional programs with the potential to facilitate individual transformation and for services to help people involved in the criminal justice system. Moreover, they reframed rehabilitation in the language of "evidence-based practices," cost-effectiveness, and public safety; developed techniques such as risk assessments that gave their projects scientific legitimacy; and, drawing on neoliberal logic, insisted that individual offenders (rather than the state) were responsible for rehabilitation. Correctionalists kept rehabilitation alive by reformulating it, in turn setting the stage for the reform efforts that gained steam in the early years of the twenty-first century.

As correctionalists fought for their vision of treatment-oriented criminal justice, a range of actors struggled against harsh sentencing laws and austere, destructive conditions within penal institutions. This contestation created substantial variegation across time and place and set the stage for the twenty-first-century reforms. Recent changes to sentencing-related laws and criminal justice practices are the result of ongoing struggle aided by macro-level developments (particularly low crime rates and the fiscal crisis). By examining New York State's Rockefeller Drug Laws and the resistance they faced all along, we showed how the earliest acts of resistance laid the groundwork for the eventual victories. Rather than a unique story specific to New York or the war on drugs, we see the case of the Rockefeller Drug Laws as key to understanding a variety of popular reform efforts, including today's renewed focus on reentry and community supervision and "evidence-based" rehabilitative programs.

None of this means the "end" of the carceral state is in sight. In a context where influential politicians from both major parties were concerned with demonstrating that they were *tough on crime*, regardless of punishment's fiscal, social, and human consequences, correctionalist advocates' reliance on frames such as "what works," "public safety," and "low-level offenders" (especially those incarcerated for drug possession) made sense. Yet, as we discuss in the following chapter, the discourses and policy priorities developed to *upend* the penal status quo in the last couple of decades of the twentieth century are now serving to limit the scope and depth of what is possible in penal reform.

# 6

## Beyond the Pendulum

THE PRECEDING CHAPTERS have argued a straightforward though important point: struggle—not the predictable, mechanical swinging of a pendulum—is the source of penal development. Economics matter. Crime trends matter. Racial, ethnic, and gender inequality matter. Wars, depressions, moral panics about gruesome violence—they all matter. But they do not matter in a vacuum. People make them matter. And people make them matter in particular ways (and not others) in the face of opposition from other actors who have competing visions of crime, punishment, justice, rights, freedom, and a host of other ideologically inflected issues.

Rather than summarize versions of this story from earlier chapters, in these concluding pages we revisit the axioms of the agonistic perspective to think through ongoing penal development in the United States—namely, efforts to decrease the size and harmful consequences of the carceral state. Bringing the book full circle, we explore the contradictions, limitations, and possibilities of early twenty-first-century reform efforts. The chapter concludes with several implications (or lessons) of our agonistic perspective for researchers, teachers, advocates, and others aiming to understand and change criminal justice.

### The Agonistic Perspective Revisited

The agonistic perspective provides a lens for understanding the unfolding of penal development. As we explained at the outset, it is not a grand theory that outlines which social-structural factors independently or collectively produce penal change across time and place.[1] Nor does it attempt to predict the future. Instead, the agonistic perspective posits three central axioms focused on how and why criminal justice changes (or does not change) in particular contexts. These axioms are akin to "sensitizing concepts" that instruct us where to look to grasp complex social phenomena. First and foremost, they direct us to struggle.[2]

## Axiom 1: Penal development is the product of struggle between actors with different types and amounts of power

From the champions of the Eastern State and Auburn prison models in the nineteenth century to reformers fighting to end mass incarceration in the twenty-first century, actors including lawmakers, scholars, activists, prisoners, journalists, and penal professionals have shaped the nature and scope of punishment in the United States. This understanding encourages us to examine the struggles that shape the field, producing variegated penal regimes rather than clearly distinguishable epochs of punishment.

As discussed in chapter 5, there has been a long struggle to promote and harden discourses, collective representations, and power relations that prop up the current penal arrangements. At the same time, actors have sought to limit, re-route, and reverse the expansion and toughening of punishment, and these efforts have begun to bear fruit, leading to claims that the pendulum is once again on the move. Yet, change so far is limited, sluggish, and, in some respects, inimical to reducing the size and harshness of the carceral state.

In line with our first axiom, we see contestation at the national, state, and local levels as central to this latest penal development. A host of actors with extensive and wide-ranging resources maintain dominant positions in policy struggles and continue to fight against even moderate reforms. Political scientist Marie Gottschalk argues:

> Vested interests will fight against attempts to dismantle the carceral state. Prison guards' unions, state departments of corrections, law enforcement associations, the private corrections industry, and the financial firms that devise bonds and other mechanisms to fund prison infrastructure all stand in the way of a deep reduction in the incarcerated population.[3]

Marc Mauer, executive director of the Sentencing Project (a nonprofit that advocates for progressive penal policies), highlights still more actors who favor the status quo: "Opposition will come from rural community leaders who see prisons as economic development, legislators who still respond emotionally to the 'crime of the week' and prosecutors who measure success by convictions and incarcerations, rather than by resolving conflict."[4]

We can see this centrality of struggle in recent federal sentencing reform efforts. After drawn-out negotiations between reformers and politicians from both major parties, there was major momentum to pass the Sentencing Reform and Corrections Act of 2015, which would reduce federal mandatory minimums for some offenses and increase "good time" credits to expedite release for non-violent, first-time prisoners deemed "low risk."[5] In response, struggle against the bill intensified, with law enforcement organizations leading the charge.[6] The president of the National Association of Assistant United States Attorneys (federal prosecutors), for example, warned that the legislation would increase murders, rapes, and robberies.[7] A group of Republican senators fanned the flames in a "Dear Colleague" letter that warned of chaos:

> We believe that the possible release of thousands of violent criminals is a risky and possibly devastating social experiment in criminal leniency. If this grand experiment goes awry, how many lives will be ruined? How many lives will be lost? How many families will be torn apart? How much of the anti-crime progress of the last generation will be wiped away for the next?[8]

The senators attached a newspaper article to their letter, featuring a picture of a black man accused of killing his ex-girlfriend and two of her children after receiving "early release" from a federal prison, allegedly because of recent changes to federal sentencing guidelines. The senators raised the specter of "Willie Horton" (see chapter 5), sending an unmistakable warning to candidates running for office in 2016: support this legislation and risk being tarred as "soft on crime."[9] While politicians (especially those in relatively uncontested districts) may be less fearful of this label than they were in earlier years, it remains a liability to be perceived as "pro-criminal" (meaning pro-black and Latino "street" criminals) and insensitive to public safety.

This and many other examples suggest the continued influence of a "law and order" bloc of conservative legislators, law enforcement organizations, crime victims groups, and prosecutors.[10] These actors combine significant political resources and symbolic capital (in part because many of them portray themselves—and are often depicted in the popular press—as disinterested advocates of crime victims and public safety). If some version of the federal sentencing reform legislation passes, its scope and likely consequences have been shaped (critics would say "watered down") through protracted struggle in and out of Congress.

Even as incumbents in the penal field—powerful actors committed to the status quo or a version of it—limit reform efforts, the shape of struggle is changing. Some of the "usual suspects" who supported or facilitated "tough on crime" in earlier decades are now switching sides, working to reform criminal justice and, in some cases, opposing the very policies they pioneered or propped up. And although some individual law enforcement officials, legislators, and others have long opposed expressly punitive policies, their voices are now reaching the mainstream instead of being drowned out by calls to crack down on the "criminal element."

For example, the recently formed "Law Enforcement Leaders to Reduce Crime and Incarceration," which brings together 120 high-profile leaders including former New York Police Chief William Bratton and New York Attorney General Eric Schneiderman, insist that policymakers can simultaneously improve public safety, decrease imprisonment, and enhance trust between communities and police.[11] As explained in the *New York Times*, this group "represents an abrupt public shift in philosophy for dozens of law enforcement officials who have sustained careers based upon tough-on-crime strategies."[12] Along with backing important legislation, this campaign is redefining public perceptions about the sources of crime, effectiveness of law enforcement strategies, and consequences of "tough on crime" politics.

We see a similar shift in the area of crime victims' rights. Throughout the 1990s and into the early twenty-first century, punitive-oriented crime victims' organizations such as Crime Victims United of California (CVUC) occupied privileged positions in national and state penal fields. Equipped with extensive moral capital, these advocates (primarily white, middle-class mothers of abducted or murdered children) combined forces with law enforcement organizations, prison officer unions, and leading politicians, becoming major political players and, in key respects, the public face of the "tough on crime" movement.[13] While some advocates argued that groups such as CVUC did not represent all victims, these oganizations maintained a near monopoly on the public discourse around victims' rights.

Today, alternative victims' coalitions are developing and gaining political influence. For example, in 2012, Californians for Safety and Justice (CSJ) organized victims and victims' families who do not support the policies and priorities of the older victims' rights groups. CSJ is part of an evolving network of new advocacy groups that share a "vision of a justice system focused more on prevention than overreaction" and emphasize public welfare–oriented interventions such as education and job–training programs, physical and mental healthcare, substance-use treatment, and services for crime victims.[14] They are also working to alter public and political understandings of crime victimization—showing, for example, that the vast majority of crime victims are young people of color in low-income, high-crime communities.[15] Importantly, some of these groups (such as CSJ) have substantial financial backing and are engaged in political struggle, providing a counterweight to punitive organizations such as CVUC.[16]

Changes in the media have also reflected and facilitated recent efforts to reform criminal justice. New media outlets—most prominently the *Marshall Project*—that focus specifically on criminal justice have systematically high-lighted penal problems and potential reforms. Traditional news sources also increased attention to criminal justice matters. Rather than simply reporting on unfolding events, media organizations in many cases are actively fighting for reform and pushing back against those seeking to thwart change.

For example, the number of articles in the *New York Times* on imprison-ment per year more than doubled in the last 15 years, growing from around 350 in the first few years of the twenty-first century to 740 in 2015.[17] And that coverage has become increasingly bold; as we mentioned in the pref-ace, the *New York Times* published a hard-hitting Sunday editorial with the declarative title "End Mass Incarceration Now," concluding: "The American experiment in mass incarceration has been a moral, legal, social, and eco-nomic disaster."[18] When electoral candidates recently ran advertisements in 2016 designed to stoke fear of crime and racial prejudice (most nota-bly David Vitter, one of the authors of the "Dear Colleague" letter against federal sentencing reform), they were shamed in media outlets, including the *Washington Post, Salon*, and the *New York Times*.[19] Following protests over police killings of black men (and boys) in 2014 and 2015 (including Michael Brown in Ferguson, Missouri; Eric Garner in Staten Island, New York; Freddie Gray in Baltimore, Maryland; and Tamir Rice in Cleveland, Ohio), calls for policing reform intensified across old and new media out-lets as well.[20]

Taken together, these examples show that the shape of struggle over crim-inal justice is changing as actors take on new positions and those favoring more moderate punishment gain increased leverage. These and other changes in the field (more than any particular policy victory or sets of victories) should offer hope for those seeking to change criminal justice regimes. Contestation over the legitimate authority to speak on behalf of law enforcement, crime victims, and other important constituencies is vital to the process of penal development. The fact that this struggle is playing out in the popular media, state legislatures, and Congress is evidence that the penal landscape is indeed shifting, and there are real possibilities that existing fissures may transform into significant seismic activity.

### Axiom 2: Contestation over how (and whom) to punish is constant; consensus over penal orientations is mostly illusory

Periods of apparent consensus typically reveal themselves, upon deeper investigation, to be rife with conflict. As shown in chapter 4, even at the height of the "Rehabilitative Era" of criminal justice (and even in California, the famed epicenter of correctionalism), there was extensive antagonism between players in the state's penal field. Similarly, in chapter 5, we showed that during the "punitive turn" (roughly the 1980s and '90s), actors struggled to maintain versions of rehabilitation and to defeat (or at least soften) draconian penal policies.

Increasingly, commentators declare the 2010s as the arrival of new consensus around liberalizing punishment and shrinking the carceral state. But as discussed above, very influential actors continue to back the status quo, arguing that expansive and intensive policing, prosecution, and sentencing practices drove the United State's crime drop and now protect the country from plummeting into violent chaos.[21] Some even reject the existence of "mass incarceration," arguing that only a small portion of people who commit crime are caught, convicted, and incarcerated.[22] A group of high-profile current and former law enforcement officials (including Rudy Giuliani) recently declared: "Our system of justice isn't broken. . . . Mandatory minimums and proactive law enforcement measures have caused a dramatic reduction in crime over the past 25 years, an achievement we cannot afford to give back."[23]

This lack of consensus makes sense from our perspective; as we showed in earlier chapters, incumbents in one era do not stop fighting once their preferred visions come under sustained critique and lose political valence. Our framework also cautions against mistaking agreement about the *need* for reform for consensus about the *content* of reform. Take, for example, the federal sentencing legislation discussed above. This bill hit a roadblock in 2015 when House Republicans presented their version of it. Due in large part to pressures from Charles and David Koch (of Koch Industries), the legislation included a provision that would make it more difficult to prosecute white-collar crimes. Liberals—including those who had joined together with the Koch brothers in the Coalition for Public Safety—charged that conservatives had "ulterior" motives for supporting reform.[24] This seemingly fundamental disagreement—based in divergent social and ideological positions—stalled the bill.

Or consider the much-publicized Justice Reinvestment Initiative (JRI), which aimed to provide states with "data-driven" blueprints to bring down prison populations (with the ultimate goal of saving money that could be reinvested into disadvantaged communities).[25] JRI efforts have fallen short due in part to disagreement over reforming sentences for "serious," "violent," and "sexual" crimes. Originally, policy advocates emphasized reducing admissions and length of stay for people convicted of these types of crimes; they understood that if every person currently in prison for a "non–violent" drug offense was released immediately, the United State's prison population would shrink by only about 20% and remain the largest in the world.[26] "Violent" offenders continue to make up the greatest proportion of prisoners (54% in 2012), serving sentences that are more than double that of property offenders (averaging 28 months).[27] To date, JRI efforts have instead focused reform efforts on "low-hanging fruit" such as parole violators and first-time, non-violent drug offenders. And even when the efforts have produced cost savings, states have typically put the money back into the penal system instead of investing directly in low-income communities.[28] In short, what was originally heralded as a profound shift has produced very little change—not because of actors' lack of commitment to reform, but because of disagreement about the breadth and depth of change.

More troubling than this lack of action is the fact that in some cases, punishment has become *harsher* for serious, violent, and sex offenses.[29] As Gottschalk explains, current reform rhetoric often pits "low-level" offenders (who deserve leniency) against those deemed "truly" violent or dangerous (who deserve tough punishment).[30] For example, consider the "Realignment" reforms in California, which reduced prison time for only the "non non nons" (those who have been convicted of non-violent, non-serious, and non-sexual felonies) by diverting them to local counties.[31] As we traced in chapter 5, efforts to reform solitary confinement focus explicitly on "special populations," such as juveniles, pregnant women, and the mentally ill (thereby reinforcing the idea that isolation is acceptable for most adult men). Campaigns to limit capital punishment have also increased and helped to legitimate sentences of life without the possibility of parole (presented as a realistic alternative to the death penalty).[32] Or consider legislation that differentiates between "dangerous" sex offenders and those who have been unfairly lumped into the sex offender category and are therefore good candidates for reduced sanctions.[33] These trends could very well harden public attitudes and policy for allegedly dangerous "others," bolstering the carceral state.

These outcomes are clearly in part the consequence of powerful actors who do not support reform (the "holdouts"). But they are also the result of hesitation or opposition from *within* loosely held together reform coalitions. As many have argued, there is little hope of seriously reducing penal populations without shortening the length of prison and community supervision terms—even for serious, violent, and sexual offenses.[34] Yet, for many supporters of reform, changes must not signal lenience toward these pariah groups. This position comes in part because reformers fear losing the support of valorized professional groups, including law enforcement and prosecutors, whose daily actions ultimately shape the carceral state.[35] It is also linked to trends in public opinion; a 2016 poll found that while most adults supported criminal justice reform, the majority of respondents under-estimated the share of the prison population convicted of violent offenses and were *against* reducing prison time for these prisoners (even those violent offenders deemed "low risk" for committing another crime).[36] These constraints sharply bound the possibilities for a radical rethinking of punishment in the United States.

As these examples show, consensus around reform is an illusion, even as more and more Americans believe the country incarcerates too many people.[37] As we would expect from axiom 2, there is deep disagreement over how to define—and solve—the problem. And while many celebrate the unique coalitions supporting reform, distance between group members means that coalition efforts are often ideologically incoherent. In addition to stalling reform, these divisions have the potential to distort reforms in ways that further entrench the carceral state.[38]

Yet, there are growing pressures (yes, more contestation!) on established reformers, policymakers, and criminal justice officials to broaden their visions of transformation. Lacking official political capital, social movement groups and prisoners are engaging in *disruption*, or confrontational politics from below. Activists involved with the Black Lives Matter network, Assata's Daughters, the Dream Defenders, and others are using disruptive tactics to force politicians and other powerful actors (especially liberals and moderates) to link criminal justice reform to related issues, including racial inequality and injustice, immigration, and sexism. They have been particularly effective at forcing reformers to seriously address the problems of police brutality, over-policing of low-level offenses (especially drug and "quality of life" offenses), and under-policing of violence (particularly rape, assault, and homicide) in low-income minority communities.[39] Moreover, social-movement groups are pushing electoral candidates, lawmakers, and legal professionals to address structural issues that contribute to poverty, crime, victimization, and other "social problems" rather than simply tweak individual practices and policies (such as equipping cops with body cameras). Many activists insist that struggles to decrease violence and to reform criminal justice will prove ineffective if disconnected from campaigns to reduce racial and class inequality.[40]

Disruptive pressure is also coming from inside prisons. For example, in the summer of 2016, a group of prisoners in Alabama engaged in a 10-day work strike because, the group maintained, refusing to work was the only way for them to draw attention to their conditions and concerns. Echoing prisoners in California who organized hunger strikes to change policies in that state's security housing units,[41] Kinetik Justice, a leader of the Free Alabama movement (the group of striking prisoners), argued:

> These strikes are our method for challenging mass incarceration. As we understand it, the prison system is a continuation of the slave system, and which in all entities is an economical system. Therefore, for the reform and changes that we've been fighting for in Alabama, we've tried petitioning through the courts. We've tried to get in touch with our legislators and so forth. And we haven't had any recourse.[42]

On September 9, 2016, a work strike organized by this group spread to at least 12 other states. Striking prisoners marked the 45th anniversary of the Attica prison uprising and protested unfair conditions inside prisons. In a surprising turn, Alabama prison officers joined the work strike.[43] Such disruption from collectivities such as the Free Alabama movement and the Black Lives Matter network further highlights the lack of consensus, with radical groups critiquing the dominant reform agenda as too narrow and, in some respects, counterproductive.

These examples demonstrate that various social-movement groups have the potential to change the shape of struggle. However, it is important to acknowledge that disruption can—and often does—produce its own resistance. When groups make radical (or what powerful incumbents deem "radical") demands, they threaten powerful entrenched interests, including dominant political parties, and typically face extensive opposition.[44] Further, the inherent breeching of norms and conventions that come with disruption is easily framed by opponents as dangerous disorder or a sign of a breakdown in "law and order."

We saw this process play out in the late 1960s, when conservatives argued that protests and riots against racism were intimately connected to rising crime rates and justified the need for cracking down on "street crime" in "inner cities." In other words, politicians claimed that disruption "in the streets" justified harsh penal policies and cuts to social programs such as Aid to Families with Dependent Children. Similar efforts are currently underway to discredit radical reformers, as seen in Republican presidential candidate Donald Trump's insistence that disruption in places such as Ferguson and Baltimore requires bolstering law and order, not reforming (and definitely not shrinking) the carceral state. Further, claiming that gangs of "illegal immigrants" are responsible for crime and disruption, Trump has capitalized on unrest in these and other cities (such as Chicago) to justify calls for draconian immigration policies such as mass deportations.[45]

Thus, disruption could conceivably nudge the country closer to larger-scale transformations that would promote dignity, humanitarianism, fairness, and other moral values—rather than small-scale reforms that narrowly focus on "what works" for cutting costs and recidivism rates. Disruptive action may lead elected officials, state bureaucrats, and other policymakers to expand their visions of change so that unruly groups will stop causing trouble and allow the leaders to once again convincingly perform consensus and "get back to the business of governing."[46] But there also is the possibility that disruption may facilitate backlash against reform efforts, as political actors frame it in ways that promote new and defend old "tough on crime" (and more recent "tough on immigration") policies. Either way, it is clear that we are in the midst of a process that is significantly more complex than an uncontested national consensus on "ending" mass incarceration.

*Axiom 3: Large-scale trends in the economy, political arena, social sentiments, intergroup relations, demographics, and crime affect—but do not determine—struggles over punishment and, ultimately, local penal outcomes*

Our third axiom pairs our focus on actors and struggle with attention to macro-level developments and contingent events. We contend that changes in, for instance, crime rates or economic conditions do not generate "swings" of the pendulum. Instead, large-scale trends create opportunities and roadblocks for agonists, while also influencing how actors think and talk about crime, criminal responsibility, punishment, justice, and the like. For example, scholars have demonstrated that neoliberal political and economic discourses help shaped twentieth and twenty-first century penal practices, rhetoric, and policies.[47] More broadly, American punishment has developed in relation to a long history of ethnic and racial division and domination, resulting in what some scholars describe as a lineage from slavery to today's drug war and hyper-incarceration.[48] Thus, while criminal justice outcomes result from struggles within the penal field, those contests are situated within broader political, economic, and social trends.

Within this framework, we argue that large-scale trends unfolding in the 2010s condition the sorts of penal reforms now seen as possible. This is reflected in activists' and scholars' anxieties about the potential for backlash if and when macro-level contexts shift. Perhaps most saliently, increases of serious crime (especially "street" crime typically associated with poor blacks and Latinos) could be used to forestall or roll back reforms. Indeed, actors recently took advantage of episodes of violent crime by parolees to effectively fight against reform efforts in Michigan,[49] Pennsylvania,[50] and Illinois[51]—and competitors in and beyond California assert that efforts to reduce the Golden State's prison population (through "realignment" and Proposition 47) have produced crime and, therefore, should cease.[52]

We can also see these fears at least partially realized in the battle over what some refer to as the "Ferguson Effect." In August 2014, a black teen-ager, Michael Brown, was shot and killed by a white officer, Darren Wilson, during a police stop in Ferguson, Missouri. The teen's death (and later, the non-indictment of Wilson) sparked protests in Ferguson that spread across the country, bringing concerns about police brutality and disproportional police contact in minority communities to the fore.[53] As this conversation developed—facilitated by several other high-profile cases—violent crime (and particularly homicide) did increase sharply in some cities in 2015, gener-ating news reports of a "homicide surge."[54] Conservative critics charged that "disrespect for the law" and a "war on cops" caused the crime spikes, while criminal justice researchers argued that incidents of police brutality could lead to declining trust in the police, which in turn would fuel violent crime.[55] Media attention to upticks in violence—along with public-opinion data showing growth in concern about crime—has provided critical openings for those who support punitive penal policies.[56]

In these contexts, politicians may double down on "law and order" in order to gain political leverage. The Ferguson debates—and, more broadly, the con-versation around violent crime—played a key role in Senate Republicans' mobilization against federal sentencing reform, and Donald Trump has used it to show that he is "tough on crime" (and arguably to fuel racial resentment).[57]

Before backing out of the 2016 Republican primary, Governor Scott Walker and Senator Ted Cruz also sought to parlay fears about "street crime" into political support.[58]

Likewise, politicians, pundits, and electoral candidates have tried to stir up public sentiment about immigration (and about so-called sanctuary cities) in support of stricter security measures targeting crime and undocumented migrants.[59] These efforts tap into and seemingly activate nativist sentiments that blame immigrants for all sorts of problems—from criminal victimization to unemployment and underemployment. As Gottschalk notes, "A century of convincing research findings that influxes of immigrants tend to reduce—not increase—crime rates has been no match against politicians exploiting false stereotypes that equate more immigrants with more crime."[60]

There also is concern that changes in the economy may weaken policymakers' commitment to downsizing criminal justice. Without the intense budget pressures of the Great Recession, politicians might use unexpected budget surpluses to alleviate prison crowding by building new penal institutions rather than backing criminal justice reforms.[61] At the same time, significant downturns in the economy could also hinder efforts as politicians tend to respond to budget crises by reducing funds for programs and policies that prevent crime, help prisoners, and facilitate re-entry.[62]

International developments also are important for recent reform efforts. For example, terrorism and the "War on Terror" seem to have supplanted many politicians' (especially national lawmakers') fixation on domestic "street" crime. Electoral candidates and officeholders currently are more committed to showing they are "tough on terror" than "tough on crime." At the same time, terrorist attacks here and abroad—for example, the 2016 mass shooting at a gay club in Orlando, Florida—provide opportunities for influential actors to demand "law and order," including hardening immigration laws.[63] Because acts of terror generate widespread fear and anxiety, calls by politicians and other influential actors to bolster "law and order" with strict—even draconian—crime measures may appeal to a broad audience.

Activists, policymakers, and academics worry about macro-level trends and critical events because they understand the importance of these factors in the trajectory of struggle. However, these developments do not automatically produce transformations in policy or practice. Rather, as articulated in axiom 3, they are filtered through national, state, and local penal fields. They matter to the extent that actors skillfully use them as political opportunities to achieve their goals.

TAKEN TOGETHER, THIS section has revisited the axioms of the agonistic perspective to explain how ongoing reform efforts are unfolding. In line with our first axiom, continued struggle between incumbents and challengers is molding these contests at local, state, and federal levels. This struggle is producing a gradual reshaping of the field, changing power relations and offering possibilities for more consequential transformations down the road. However, "holdouts" still retain extensive power vis-à-vis reformers, limiting the depth and breadth of reform.

Reforms are also circumscribed, contradictory, and, in some cases, counterproductive because there is not a consensus about what needs to be done. As we highlight in the second axiom, under the rhetoric of consensus is invariably contestation. Today, while there is some agreement emerging around the need for criminal justice reform, the content of that reform remains hazy and conflicted. The narrowness of the limited policy reforms that have succeeded (focusing, for example, only on the "non non nons" or low-level drug offenses) is helping fuel additional contestation from below (or disruption) from social movement groups with more expansive visions of transformation.

Lastly, our third axiom draws attention to social-structural developments and contingent events that condition criminal justice change (or lack thereof). To understand the unfolding of current reform efforts, we must recognize that structural conditions and changes, including racial divisions, economic conditions, and crime trends, infuse and reshape political opportunities for competitors. As we have seen throughout the book, the relative success of a given "side" in penal contests will depend, at least in part, on contextual developments that are beyond agonists' immediate control. In addition, they will depend on whether and how those structural conditions are shaped by the struggles of reformers.

## Lessons from the Break

In this final section, we lay out several principles that guided our analysis in chapters 2 through 5. Although the following discussion (like this book) focuses on prison, probation, and parole in the United States, we believe these lessons may prove useful for comprehending the unfolding of other aspects of criminal justice practices and punishment outside the American context. After all, studies from diverse topics and countries informed our analytical approach throughout.

The first lesson is to *examine the spaces in between*—or the periods in which the penal terrain appears settled. For good reasons, scholars often focus on periods of major transformation—those moments of "rupture"—because we want to know why the earth below us is moving. These hinge points help us distill the dominant discourses, rationalities, and actors generating change. But because of our concentration on pivotal moments, we often pay little attention to factors that set the stage for transformation. This principle encourages us to focus also on the periods between what seems like major seismic activity.[64] It guards against "presentism"—ahistorical analyses that mistake immediate catalysts and contemporaneous events as the *causes* of penal development (for example, mistaking Robert Martinson's suggestion that "nothing works" as the reason for the "decline of the rehabilitative ideal").[65]

Snapshots taken during, or just after, "rupture" moments often mischaracterize the nature (and sometimes the degree) of change. This can result in researchers offering misleading characterizations of how those changes came about, mostly because snapshots miss historical antecedents and overlook the consequential struggle of subordinate actors and institutional transformation. For example, take the snapshots of California we presented in the 1960s and 1980s. While a quick look at each would suggest radical ruptures, instead we see the long-simmering struggle between prison staff affiliated with "Treatment" and those aligned with "Custody" (and prisoners themselves). The result was sometimes a tense detente, sometimes near-warfare, limiting the scope of "rehabilitation" in practice and contributing to the next penal shift.

Similarly, we saw long struggle in chapter 5, as correctionalists fought to keep alive rehabilitation during the heyday of "tough on crime" politics. Attention to those contests helps us understand why reformers today frame their efforts in terms of "risks and needs" and insist that in-prison and re-entry programs, drug courts, sentencing proposals, and policing reforms must be "evidence based"—that is, shown through statistical (or better yet, experimental) methods to reduce the targeted problem and, ideally, save money). Attention to struggles in earlier decades also helps us understand the current focus of sentencing reform on the "non non nons"; during the 1990s and into the early twenty-first century, this concentration was a pragmatic strategy that reformers used to get sentencing reform on the agenda. This tactic, which developed within particular political constraints, now limits the changes that reformers view as necessary, realistic, and desirable.

Focusing on the spaces in between leads us to examine the field from multiple angles and over extended periods, making it possible to see when—and understand why—shifts in macro-level contexts create strategic opportunities for actors to improve their positions in and have significant effects within a given field. Moreover, longer-term, multisided analyses can help us understand how actors produce political openings—and create fissures in the penal landscape—even when social structural conditions seem unfavorable to their cause.

This guideline can also help us understand the variegated nature of penal practice. As we and other scholars have shown, the operations of criminal justice often vary considerably from official goals, dominant discourses, and governmental rationalities. To use the language of law and society scholars, the law on the books is often quite different from the law in action. The complicated, braided nature of practice is due primarily to everyday struggles within and beyond criminal justice institutions among penal practitioners (e.g., judges, attorneys, prison officers, police, wardens), political leaders, and others. If we focus solely on periods of transformation, we miss the subterranean struggles that culminate in an uneven landscape during periods of relative calm and precipitate the next reversal.

Our second lesson is to *map it out*. As we have tried to show, penal policies, practices, and priorities depend greatly on local context—the particularities of time and place. It is, therefore, important that we take stock of the central actors involved in struggles over criminal justice outcomes we want to understand. Ian Loader and Richard Sparks write, "A properly historical sociology of the crime control field would ... seek to discern the intentions of the array of actors—politicians, civil servants, practitioners, campaigners, think tanks, editorialists, social scientists—who struggle to shape the contours of crime control and criminal justice."[66] We also attempt to situate the actors in relation to each other, highlighting their respective types and amounts of resources. The structure of any battle is central to its outcome.

For example, in the Jacksonian period, supporters of the congregate system (the Auburn model) did not win the "Great Debate" because the congregate system was demonstrably more effective at producing prisoner reformation than the separate system (the Pennsylvania model). Both forms of imprisonment violated the penitentiary ideal and were quite brutal. However, advocates of the congregate model were much better organized and richer in material, social, and cultural resources than their competitors. They were particularly adept at selling their ideas to state officials and politicians who were uneasy about imprisonment (which was then a novel penal form) and concerned about its costs to the state and opposition from various camps, such as free laborers and religious leaders. Unlike supporters of the Pennsylvania model, they understood that practical matters such as cost-effectiveness were more important than the transformation of prisoners through penitential practices. To understand this struggle, we must recognize that one side had far more (and varied) power than the other—power they skillfully used to convince decisionmakers in many states that the Auburn model "worked" better than the Pennsylvania model.

Mapping it out also encourages us to recognize that the penal field's prevailing orientation—beliefs, norms, values, and sentiments—affects the trajectory and outcome of struggles. These cultural forces help constitute what is thinkable or unthinkable, realistic or unrealistic, shaping both current practices and the potential for transformation. They help us understand, for instance, why criminal justice actors may speak the language of rehabilitation but implement policies that have little to do with treating prisoners' psychological, emotional, or social deficiencies. As shown in chapter 4, such actors may not be disingenuous; instead, they may simply perceive that expansive rehabilitation programming is unrealistic given prevailing sentiments about prisoners' deservedness and the overarching purposes of imprisonment.

We also need to map out the legal and political institutions that affect the character of struggle. For example, rich individuals or groups in California need not go through the legislature or a sentencing commission to change policy; instead, they can use the state's ballot initiative process to pass legislation such as the "Three Strikes" law.[67] In states without the ballot model, these same actors would have to find other means of enacting sentencing laws. For example, in states with sentencing commissions, struggle occurs over appointments to the commissions, development of sentencing guidelines, and legislative approval of those guidelines. Legal and political institutions help determine what types of resources actors need to advance their goals; political capital, for instance, is essential for affecting gubernatorial appointments to sentencing commissions.

Because of the United States' federalist system and the historical development of criminal justice in this country, struggles occur at various levels of government, which have particular institutional makeups. For example, because police forces are funded and managed mostly at the local level, demands for policing reform often focus on city councils, mayors' offices, and, more infrequently, state legislatures. While there are some national-level modes of reform (such as Department of Justice investigations and federal funding incentives), their scope and power are limited. Recall, however, that contestation over sentencing or prison conditions occurs primarily at the state and federal levels. In brief, the character of contestation (and the types of resources needed to achieve success) may differ significantly depending on the location of struggle.[68]

Our third lesson is to *keep criminal justice in society*. A central statement of "punishment and society" scholarship is that economic, intergroup, political, cultural, and other social forces shape penal development. Extracting punishment from society makes it impossible to understand. We have tried to show that developments ostensibly outside the realm of criminal justice provide opportunities for some actors, while closing off or limiting possibilities for others. Moreover, social forces such as race and gender relations, media coverage of crime and punishment, political movements, and migration patterns motivate, infuse, and help determine the outcome of struggle.

For example, as shown in chapter 3, we cannot understand convict leasing outside larger projects to reassert white supremacy and rebuild the South in the wake of the Civil War; likewise, white racism and populism contributed greatly to the rise and proliferation of the southern prison farm during the late nineteenth and early twentieth centuries. Similarly, reform campaigns in the Progressive Era were intertwined with trends in labor, politics, and science (such as the eugenics movement), and efforts to contain and control African Americans, Americanize European immigrants, reinforce patriarchal conceptions of proper womanhood, and solidify hetero-normative views of acceptable sexuality. And correctionalists' successes after World War II were bound up with the growth of the professions, economic growth and optimism, and trust in government and expert knowledge.

Studies in other countries also highlight the importance of this lesson. Gail Super demonstrates, for example, that South Africa's colonial past, history of apartheid, and post-apartheid politics indelibly shape the country's criminal justice policies and practices.[69] Similarly, research shows that Canadian punishment is tied to the country's long history of oppressing Aboriginal Canadians. Although typically considered as having moderate penal policies (especially compared to the United States), Canada incarcerates Aboriginal Canadians at an estimated rate of about ten times that of non-Aboriginal Canadians (in comparison, the incarceration rate of black Americans is about five times higher than that of white Americans).[70] Loïc Wacquant argues that France's colonial history and immigration policies greatly affect its penal practices and prison demographics.[71] By keeping criminal justice *in* society, we see that systemic inequality shapes punishment at the same time as criminal justice contributes to social division and stratification.

Perhaps the most important lesson is to *avoid fatalism*.[72] Legal scholar Pat O'Malley refers to a strand of scholarship as "criminologies of catastrophe," which depict the present as wholly different and worse than the past, and suggests that change is unlikely, if not impossible. Steven Hutchinson agrees,

"There seems then a clear tendency to interpret criminal justice and penality as having undergone a 'catastrophic' transformation. As the argument goes, things are now and will be in the future completely different from the previous era."[73] Focusing on present-day reforms, David Green cautions: "there is the danger that the very success and proliferation of the harshness narrative have produced an orthodoxy about American punitiveness which hinders our ability to notice and appreciate developments in penal thinking and policy that run counter to it."[74]

We would add that pendular thinking contributes greatly to this catastrophic (or fatalistic) thinking. Because the pendulum perspective imagines penal development as mechanical, actors can do little to shift the playing field. The logic of the pendulum posits that ruptures send "the system" to one side or other of the pendulum—and only incredibly strong forces can dislodge the ball and send it back in the other direction. We see this both as pessimistic and disempowering.

As we have shown, activists, academics, journalists, judges, and a host of other actors continually (though often subtly) struggle to alter discourses, collective representations, practices, and institutions. Through political lobbying, symbolic struggle, co-optation, subversion, and disruption, actors generate friction and heat that braids (or assembles[75]) penal practices and periodically fuels major transformations. Yet, we often ignore the past—even the immediate past—and fail to link reforms to preceding struggles. In the process, we erase the important work that happens out of the public eye and sets the stage for future changes. While highlighting the institutional and structural obstacles that frustrate penal change is important, it is equally essential to demonstrate the manifold ways that actors navigate and, at times, push through roadblocks.

Throughout this book we have emphasized the *long struggle*. Often, those advocating for change get frustrated with transformation's slow progress, which is understandable because, from their perspective, existing policies, practices, images, and rhetoric produce major social suffering. Pendular thinking and its vision of rupture contribute to that consternation. We forget that penal earthquakes (such as the rise of mass incarceration) develop over a long period of time—they begin as fissures that splinter and expand before producing shockwaves across the field. *Breaking the Pendulum* encourages us to see the potential of gradual changes to produce instability in the penal landscape (to shake things up!) that can generate major transformations, as long as combatants see those small victories as means to greater ends—rather than ends in themselves—and continue the fight.

# Notes

### PREFACE

1. Scott Horsley, "Obama Visits Federal Prison, A First for a Sitting President," *National Public Radio* (July 16, 2015), http://www.npr.org/sections/itsallpolitics/2015/07/16/423612441/obama-visits-federal-prison-a-first-for-a-sitting-president (accessed May 13, 2016).

2. *New York Times*, "End Mass Incarceration Now" (May 24, 2015), http://www.nytimes.com/2014/05/25/opinion/sunday/end-mass-incarceration-now.html (accessed May 13, 2016).

3. E. Ann Carson, *Prisoners in 2014* (Washington, DC: Bureau of Justice Statistics, 2015).

4. We have two related articles that outline and apply the agonistic perspective. Readers interested in a longer theoretical discussion and empirical analysis of the "rehabilitative era" in California can consult Philip Goodman, Joshua Page, and Michelle Phelps, "The Long Struggle: An Agonistic Perspective on Penal Development," *Theoretical Criminology* 19, no. 3 (2015): 315–35. For more on recent reforms, see Michelle S. Phelps, "Possibilities and Contestation in Twenty-First-Century US Criminal Justice Downsizing," *Annual Review of Law & Social Science* 12 (2017).

5. Each of the authors contributed equally to the final work. Thus, we have listed our names alphabetically.

### CHAPTER I

1. William J. Stuntz, *The Collapse of American Criminal Justice* (Cambridge, MA: Belknap Press of Harvard University Press, 2011), 2–3.

2. Throughout the book, we use the terms "criminal justice," "penal system," and "punishment" interchangeably. All three refer to the practices, discourses, institutions, and actors formally responsible for sanctioning lawbreakers.

3. This concept draws on Vanessa Barker's notion "dominant penal regime," which includes "the discourse on crime, conceptualizations of justice, the rational for punishment, the character and type of sanctions, and imprisonment rates" (Vanessa Barker, *The Politics of Imprisonment: How the Democratic Process Shapes the Way America Punishes Offenders* [New York: Oxford University Press, 2009], 7)).

4. By this term, we mean the social space in which actors struggle to accumulate and employ penal capital—the legitimate authority to determine penal policies and priorities. There is not just one penal field; there are national, state, local, and even international penal fields. The specific qualities of the field depend on scholars' objects and levels of analysis.

5. Harold Garfinkel, *Studies in Ethnomethodology* (Englewood Cliffs, NJ: Prentice-Hall, 1967).

6. Charlie Savage and Erica Goode, "Two Powerful Signals of a Major Shift on Crime," *New York Times* (August 12, 2013), http://www.nytimes.com/2013/08/13/us/two-powerful-signals-of-a-major-shift-on-crime.html?pagewanted=all (accessed March 20, 2014).

7. George F. Cole, Christopher E. Smith, and Christina DeJong, *Criminal Justice in America* (7th ed.) (Independence, KY: Cengage Learning, 2013), 310.

8. Kären Matison Hess and Christine Hess Orthmann, *Introduction to Law Enforcement and Criminal Justice* (10th ed.) (Belmont, CA: Delmar, Cengage Learning, 2012), 68–69.

9. George F. Cole, Christopher E. Smith, and Christina DeJong, *The American System of Criminal Justice* (15th ed.) (Boston: Cengage Learning, 2016), 527.

10. "Evidence Based Community Corrections," *DC Public Safety Radio* (July 31, 2013), http://media.csosa.gov/podcast/transcripts/tag/joan-petersilia (accessed April 12, 2016).

11. Edward E. Rhine, Tina L. Mawhorr, and Evalyn C. Parks, "Implementation: The Bane of Effective Correctional Programs," *Criminology & Public Policy* 5, no. 2 (2006): 347–58, 347.

12. Joshua Page, *The Toughest Beat: Politics, Punishment, and the Prison Officers Union in California* (New York: Oxford University Press, 2011), 4.

13. Jill A. McCorkel, *Breaking Women: Gender, Race, and the New Politics of Imprisonment,* (New York: New York University Press, 2013).

14. Émile Durkheim, *The Division of Labor in Society* (New York: Free Press, 1997).

15. Georg Rusche and Otto Kirchheimer, *Punishment and Social Structure* (New Brunswick, NJ: Transaction, 2003).

16. David J. Rothman, *Conscience and Convenience: The Asylum and Its Alternatives in Progressive America* (rev. ed.) (New York: Aldine de Gruyter, 2002a), 11.

17. David Garland, *The Culture of Control: Crime and Social Order in Contemporary Society* (Chicago: University of Chicago Press, 2001). For another high-profile example, see Michael Tonry, *Thinking about Crime: Sense and Sensibility in American Penal Culture* (New York: Oxford University Press, 2004).

18. David Garland, *Punishment and Welfare: A History of Penal Strategies* (Aldershot, UK: Gower, 1985), 262. We thank Ashley Rubin for bringing this passage to our attention.

19. David Garland, "Beyond the Culture of Control," *Critical Review of International Social and Political Philosophy* 7, no. 2 (2004): 160–89, 167–68.

20. See, e.g., John Pratt, David Brown, Mark Brown, Simon Hallsworth, and Wayne Morrison (eds.), *The New Punitiveness: Trends, Theories, Perspectives* (Cullompton, UK: Willan, 2005).

21. See also Michael C. Campbell and Heather Schoenfeld, "The Transformation of America's Penal Order: A Historicized Political Sociology of Punishment," *American Journal of Sociology* 118, no. 5 (2013): 1375–1423; and Pat O'Malley, "Volatile and Contradictory Punishment," *Theoretical Criminology* 3, no. 2 (1999): 175–96. For a more detailed review of this literature, see Philip Goodman, Joshua Page, and Michelle Phelps, "The Long Struggle: An Agonistic Perspective on Penal Development," *Theoretical Criminology* 19, no. 3 (2015): 315–35.

22. For a similar critique of the rupture narrative in scholarship on punishment and welfare, see Joe Soss, Richard C. Fording, and Sanford F. Schram, *Disciplining the Poor: Neoliberal Paternalism and the Persistent Power of Race* (Chicago: University of Chicago Press, 2011).

23. We borrow these metaphors from an extensive literature. See, e.g., Steven Hutchinson, "Countering Catastrophic Criminology: Reform, Punishment, and the Modern Liberal Compromise," *Punishment & Society* 8, no. 4 (2006): 443–67; Kelly Hannah-Moffat, "Criminogenic Needs and the Transformative Risk Subject: Hybridizations of Risk/Need in Penality," *Punishment & Society* 7, no. 1 (2005): 29–51; and Paula Maurutto and Kelly Hannah-Moffat, "Assembling Risk and the Restructuring of Penal Control," *British Journal of Criminology* 46, no. 3 (2006): 438–54.

24. See, e.g., Philip Goodman, "'Another Second Chance': Rethinking Rehabilitation through the Lens of California's Prison Fire Camps," *Social Problems* 59, no. 4 (2012a): 437–58; Mona Lynch, "Rehabilitation as Rhetoric: The Ideal of Reformation in Contemporary Parole Discourse and Practices," *Punishment & Society* 2, no. 1 (2000): 40–65; Fergus McNeill, Nicola Burns, Simon Halliday, Neil Hutton, and Cyrus Tata, "Risk, Responsibility and Reconfiguration: Penal Adaptation and Misadaptation," *Punishment & Society* 11, no. 4 (2009): 419–42; Michelle S. Phelps, "Rehabilitation in the Punitive Era: The Gap between Rhetoric and Reality in U.S. Prison Programs," *Law & Society Review* 45, no. 1 (2011): 33–68; and Gwen Robinson, "Late-Modern Rehabilitation: The Evolution of a Penal Strategy," *Punishment & Society* 10, no. 4 (2008): 429–45.

25. Franklin E. Zimring and Gordon Hawkins, *The Scale of Imprisonment* (Chicago: University of Chicago Press, 1991); Michelle S. Phelps, "Mass Probation: Toward a More Robust Theory of State Variation in Punishment," *Punishment & Society* OnlineFirst (May 10, 2016); Natasha A. Frost, "The Mismeasure of

Punishment: Alternative Measures of Punitiveness and Their (Substantial) Consequences," *Punishment & Society* 10, no. 3 (2008): 277–300; Michael Jacobson, *Downsizing Prisons: How to Reduce Crime and End Mass Incarceration* (New York: New York University Press, 2005); David Jacobs and Ronald Helms, "Collective Outbursts, Politics, and Punitive Resources: Toward a Political Sociology of Spending on Crime Control," *Social Forces* 77, no. 4 (1999): 1497–1523; and Franklin E. Zimring, Gordon Hawkins, and Sam Kamin, *Punishment and Democracy: Three Strikes and You're Out in California* (New York: Oxford University Press, 2001).

26. Ian Loader and Richard Sparks, "For an Historical Sociology of Crime Policy in England and Wales since 1968," *Critical Review of International Social and Political Philosophy* 7, no. 2 (2004): 5–32, 12.

27. Ibid., 16, emphasis added.

28. Examples include Harry Annison, *Dangerous Politics: Risk, Political Vulnerability, and Penal Policy* (Oxford: Oxford University Press, 2015); Barker, *The Politics of Imprisonment*; Michael Campbell, "Ornery Alligators and Soap on a Rope: Texas Prosecutors and Punishment Reform in the Lone Star State," *Theoretical Criminology* 16, no. 3 (2012): 289–311; Michael Javen Fortner, *Black Silent Majority: The Rockefeller Drug Laws and the Politics of Punishment* (Cambridge, MA: Harvard University Press, 2015); Marie Gottschalk, *The Prison and the Gallows: The Politics of Mass Incarceration in America* (New York: Cambridge University Press, 2006); Mona Lynch, *Sunbelt Justice: Arizona and the Transformation of American Punishment* (Palo Alto, CA: Stanford University Press, 2009); Rebecca McLennan, *The Crisis of Imprisonment: Protest, Politics, and the Making of the American Penal State, 1776–1941* (New York: Cambridge University Press, 2008); Robert Perkinson, *Texas Tough: The Rise of America's Prison Empire* (New York: Metropolitan, 2010); Andrew Rutherford, *Transforming Criminal Policy: Spheres of Influence in the United States, the Netherlands, and England and Wales during the 1980s* (Winchester, UK: Waterside, 1996); Mick Ryan, *Penal Policy and Political Culture in England and Wales: Four Essays on Policy and Process* (Winchester, UK: Waterside, 2003); and Heather Schoenfeld, "The Delayed Emergence of Penal Modernism in Florida," *Punishment & Society* 16, no. 3 (2014): 258–84.

29. Loïc Wacquant, "Pierre Bourdieu," in *Key Sociological Thinkers* (2d ed.), ed. Rob Stones (New York: Palgrave Macmillan, 2008a), 264. Frances Fox Piven similarly argues, "Domination and challenge, and thus conformity and deviance, are the center of history. They are expressions of the basic dialectical movement through which societies change, or perhaps fail to change" (Frances Fox Piven, "Deviant Behavior and the Remaking of the World," *Social Problems* 28, no. 5 [1981]: 489–508, 489).

Our perspective also draws on conflict theorists such as Karl Marx and C. Wright Mills, who view contestation, power imbalances, and social cleavages as characteristic of modern society.

30. Pierre Bourdieu and Loïc J.D. Wacquant, *An Invitation to Reflexive Sociology* (Chicago: University of Chicago Press, 1992); see also Neil Fligstein and Doug McAdam, "Toward a General Theory of Strategic Action Fields," *Sociological Theory* 29, no. 1 (2011): 1–26.

31. Page, *The Toughest Beat.*

32. Gresham M. Sykes, *The Society of Captives: A Study of a Maximum Security Prison* (Princeton, NJ: Princeton University Press, 2007).

33. See, e.g., John Irwin, *The Felon* (Englewood Cliffs, NJ: Prentice-Hall, 1970); and Mary Bosworth, *Engendering Resistance: Agency and Power in Women's Prisons* (Aldershot, UK: Ashgate, 1999).

34. David Garland, *Punishment and Modern Society: A Study in Social Theory* (Chicago: University of Chicago Press, 1990), 182.

35. Lisa L. Miller, *The Perils of Federalism: Race, Poverty, and the Politics of Crime Control* (New York: Oxford University Press, 2008).

36. Garland describes resistance of southern states to Supreme Court decisions regarding the death penalty (Garland, *Peculiar Institution: America's Death Penalty in an Age of Abolition* [Cambridge, MA: Belknap Press of Harvard University Press, 2010]). Similarly, Anjuli Verma shows that some counties in California subvert the intent of California's "realignment" law, which shifts responsibility for incarceration of low-level convicts from the state to counties (Anjuli Verma, "The Law-Before: Legacies and Gaps in Penal Reform," *Law & Society Review* 49, no. 4 [2015]: 847–82).

37. Joachim J. Savelsberg, "Knowledge, Domination, and Criminal Punishment," *American Journal of Sociology* 99, no. 4 (1994): 911–43; James Q. Whitman, *Harsh Justice: Criminal Punishment and the Widening Divide between America and Europe* (New York: Oxford University Press, 2005); Gottschalk, *The Prison and the Gallows*; John R. Sutton, "Imprisonment and Social Classification in Five Common-Law Democracies, 1955–1985," *American Journal of Sociology* 106, no. 2 (2000): 350–86; and Tonry, *Thinking about Crime.*

38. Barker, *The Politics of Punishment*; Lisa Miller, *The Perils of Federalism*; Page, *The Toughest Beat.*

39. Joachim L. Savelsberg, "Law That Does Not Fit Society: Sentencing Guidelines as a Neoclassical Reaction to the Dilemmas of Substantivized Law," *American Journal of Sociology* 97, no. 5 (1992): 1346–81.

40. Rothman, *Conscience and Convenience.*

41. Here we discuss key types of struggle separately for clarity's sake; however, in practice, these forms often overlap, lead into each other (for instance, when conventional politics does not produce desired ends, disruption may follow), and can be difficult to disentangle.

42. Ashley T. Rubin, "Resistance or Friction: Understanding the Significance of Prisoners' Secondary Adjustments," *Theoretical Criminology* 19, no. 1 (2015a): 23–42.

43. Frances Fox Piven, *Challenging Authority: How Ordinary People Change America* (Lanham, MD: Rowman & Littlefield, 2006), 20.

44. Ibid., 21.

45. Bourdieu and Wacquant, *An Invitation to Reflexive Sociology*, 14.

46. Loader and Sparks, "For an Historical Sociology of Crime Policy," 19.

47. We do not mean to imply that material and symbolic struggles are mutually exclusive. Political campaigns that include lobbying, protests, and the like are intensely symbolic (and often purposely attempt to "shape the debate" and "educate the public"). Our intent here is to highlight the importance of cultural struggle because some cultural producers (especially academics and journalists) often present their work as neutral and apolitical. However, we view efforts to shape collective understandings as critical forms of contestation—and therefore political.

48. Fligstein and McAdam, "Toward a General Theory of Strategic Action Fields."

49. On the concept of "policy feedback," see Paul Pierson, "When Effect Becomes Cause: Policy Feedback and Political Change," *World Politics* 45, no. 4 (1993): 595–628. David Dagan and Steven M. Teles further develop this idea in the context of criminal justice reform ("The Social Construction of Policy Feedback: Incarceration, Conservatism, and Ideological Change," *Studies in American Political Development* 29, no. 2 [2015]: 127–53).

50. Rothman, *Conscience and Convenience*. For another example, Page's *The Toughest Beat* shows that hyper-incarceration facilitated the growth of powerful organizations such as the state's prison officers' union. As these groups became influential actors in California's penal field, they helped entrench "punitive segregation" as the field's dominant orientation. The growth of such organizations as the officers' union was a "feedback effect" that helped entrench punitive segregation in California.

51. Elmer Eric Schattschneider, *The Semisovereign People: A Realist's View of Democracy in America* (Boston: Cengage Learning, 1975), 75, emphasis in original.

52. Karl Marx famously argued, "[Wo]men make their own history, but they do not make it as they please; they do not make it under self-selected circumstances, but under circumstances existing already, given and transmitted from the past" (Karl Marx, *The Eighteenth Brumaire of Louis Bonaparte* [1852], https://www.marxists.org/archive/marx/works/1852/18th-brumaire/ch01.htm (accessed May 29, 2016).

53. Joshua Page, "Punishment and the Penal Field," in *The SAGE Handbook of Punishment and Society*, eds. Jonathan Simon and Richard Sparks (London: SAGE, 2013), 152–65.

54. See, e.g., Mustafa Emirbayer and Victoria Johnson, "Bourdieu and Organizational Analysis," *Theoretical Sociology* 37, no. 1 (2008): 1–44; Fligstein and McAdam, "Toward a General Theory of Strategic Action Fields"; and Diane Vaughan, "Bourdieu and Organizations: The Empirical Challenge," *Theory and Society* 37, no. 1 (2008): 65–81.

55. This argument draws on the notion of "political opportunity structure," which scholars use to understand origins and relative success of social movements. See,

e.g., Sydney Tarrow, *Power in Movement: Social Movements, Collective Action and Politics* (New York: Cambridge University Press, 1994).

56. Tonry, *Thinking about Crime*, 93–95.

57. This claim draws on Verta Taylor's concept of "abeyance structures" (Verta Taylor, "Social Movement Continuity: The Women's Movement in Abeyance," *American Sociological Review* 54, no. 5 [1989]: 761–75). Taylor argues that social movement actors and issues typically do not disappear when movements decline. Rather, actors reconfigure repertoires of contention, build new alliances, rework collective identities, and engage in other activities that are critical for future mobilization.

58. We are not the first to use the plate tectonics metaphor to discuss change and stability of public policy. Political scientists Frank Baumgartner, Bryan Jones, and Peter Mortensen employ it while describing the theory of "punctuated equilibrium," which seeks to explain why public policy is typically characterized by long periods of stasis and periodic, sudden transformations. They argue that American political institutions (which were structured to resist change), policy images that bolster the status quo (by, for example, equating existing gun laws with freedom and patriotism), and vested interests limit major shifts in policy regimes. Equilibrium is punctuated when critical changes in government (for example, large shifts in the makeup of the US Congress) or in the broader society (for example, shifts in public opinion about smoking or homosexuality) provide opportunities for marginalized issues to move to the forefront of legislative action. While our perspective focuses more centrally on the role of struggle in precipitating shifts in public policy (and we see far less stasis than do Baumgartner and Jones, at least in the penal realm), it shares with punctuated equilibrium an appreciation of the often long, laborious process of policy change, as well as the importance of macro-level developments and contingent events in facilitating it. See Frank R. Baumgartner, Bryan D. Jones, and Peter B. Mortensen, "Punctuated Equilibrium Theory: Explaining Stability and Change in Public Policymaking," in *Theories of the Policy Process* (3d ed.), eds. Paul A. Sabatier and Christopher M. Weible (Boulder, CO: Westview, 2014), 59–104.

59. See, e.g., David Nelken, *Comparative Criminal Justice: Making Sense of Difference* (Los Angeles: SAGE, 2010).

60. On the latter, see Gottschalk, *The Prison and The Gallows*.

61. We agree with Issa Kohler-Hausmann that "misdemeanor justice—the processing, adjudication, dismissal, plea bargaining, sentencing, and punishment of misdemeanor cases"—is widespread and very important (Issa Kohler-Hausmann, "Misdemeanor Justice: Control without Conviction," *American Journal of Sociology* 119, no. 2 [2013]: 351–93, 353); see also Christopher Uggen, Mike Vuolo, Sarah Lageson, Ebony Ruhland, and Hilary K. Whitham, "The Edge of Stigma: An Experimental Audit of the Effects of Low-Level Criminal Records on Employment," *Criminology* 52, no. 4 (2014): 627–54. A full rendering of criminal justice in the United States definitely would include misdemeanor justice. Our

goal, however, is not to provide a comprehensive overview of American criminal justice. Rather, our much more selective account focuses on some core areas of punishment to demonstrate the value of our agonistic perspective on penal development. Ideally, other scholars will examine the usefulness of our approach to understanding development in other areas of punishment (such as misdemeanor justice).

62. All the chapters draw on the extensive "punishment and society" literature, which encompasses both penetrating analyses of macro-level shifts and in-depth local case studies of punishment in practice. The field of punishment and society is increasingly recognized as a mature field of inquiry. See, e.g., Jonathan Simon and Richard Sparks, "Punishment and Society: The Emergence of an Academic Field," in *The SAGE Handbook of Punishment and Society*, eds. Jonathan Simon and Richard Sparks (London: SAGE, 2013), 1–20. This has meant that scholars are beginning to provide synthetic analyses (like our own) that span existing research (e.g., Campbell and Schoenfeld, "The Transformation of America's Penal Order").

63. These alternative narratives often come from southern states (but are certainly not limited to them). As other scholars have noted, punishment in the South followed a unique trajectory. At the peak of state prison populations in 2008, 46% of state prisoners resided in the South (William J. Sabol, Heather C. West, and Matthew Cooper, *Prisoners in 2008* [Washington, DC: Bureau of Justice Statistics, 2009], Appendix, table 1). Thus, scholars cannot claim to provide a "national" account while excluding this region.

64. Jerome G. Miller, "The Debate on Rehabilitating Criminals: Is It True That Nothing Works?," *Washington Post* (March 1989), http://www.prisonpolicy.org/scans/rehab.html (accessed April 18, 2015).

## CHAPTER 2

1. As discussed below, penitentiaries were meant for men—especially younger white men—and not women.

2. Lawrence Friedman, *Crime and Punishment in American History* (New York: Basic Books, 1993), 76; Rebecca McLennan, *The Crisis of Imprisonment: Protest, Politics, and the Making of the American Penal State, 1776–1941* (New York: Cambridge University Press, 2008), 14–52; and Michael Meranze, *Laboratories of Virtue: Punishment, Revolution, and Authority in Philadelphia, 1760–1835* (Chapel Hill: University of North Carolina Press, 1996), 8. Michel Foucault famously argued that the demise of the public execution was only superficially related to genteel notions of reform, pointing instead to changing technologies of power, especially the spread of the disciplines (Michel Foucault, *Discipline and Punish: The Birth of the Prison* [New York: Vintage, 1995]).

3. McLennan, *The Crisis of Imprisonment*, 20.

4. See also W. David Lewis, *From Newgate to Dannemora: The Rise of the Penitentiary in New York, 1796–1848* (Ithaca, NY: Cornell University Press, 1965), 3–28. At least one state, Pennsylvania, experimented with public hard labor before turning toward imprisonment. While in theory the punishment would reform the "wheel-barrow men" and provide a public service, in practice the work crews were often raucous spectacles and many convicts ran off, leading the state to quickly search for alternatives (McLennan, *The Crisis of Imprisonment*, 34–35). See also Meranze, *Laboratories of Virtue*, 55–86.

5. Edward L. Ayers, *Vengeance and Justice: Crime and Punishment in the 19th-Century American South* (New York: Oxford University Press, 1984), 37.

6. David Garland, *Punishment and Modern Society* (Chicago: University of Chicago Press, 1990), 266–67.

7. Friedman, *Crime and Punishment in American History*, 110.

8. Ashley T. Rubin, "Institutionalizing the Pennsylvania System: Organizational Exceptionalism, Administrative Support, and Eastern State Penitentiary, 1829–1875" (PhD dissertation, University of California, Berkeley, 2013), 26.

9. Philip Smith, *Punishment and Culture* (Chicago: University of Chicago Press, 2008), 68–69. Smith's argument is about Newgate, a proto-prison in London, but his analysis applies equally well to Newgate's counterparts in the United States.

10. Indeed, by 1860 the only states in the South that did *not* have a state penitentiary were the Carolinas and Florida. Rubin, "Institutionalizing the Pennsylvania System," 33.

11. Meranze, *Laboratories of Virtue*, 137.

12. Benjamin Rush, "An Enquiry into the Effects of Public Punishments upon Criminals, and upon Society" (March 9, 1787), 7–8, emphasis in original, http://quod.lib.umich.edu/e/evans/N16141.0001.001/1:1?rgn=div1;view=fulltext (accessed February 11, 2016).

13. Rush, "An Enquiry into the Effects of Public Punishments," 10.

14. Ibid., 9.

15. Ibid., 11.

16. Ibid., 11.

17. Meranze, *Laboratories of Virtue*, 4, emphasis added.

18. Ibid., 43.

19. Negley K. Teeters, *The Cradle of the Penitentiary: The Walnut Street Jail at Philadelphia, 1773–1835* (Philadelphia: Temple University Press, 1955), 32.

20. McLennan, *The Crisis of Imprisonment*, 37.

21. Quoted in Stephen P. Garvey, "Freeing Prisoners' Labor," *Stanford Law Review* 50, no. 2 (1998): 339–98, 348.

22. Meranze, *Laboratories of Virtue*, 16.

23. Ashley T. Rubin, "Penal Change as Penal Layering: A Case Study of Proto-prison Adoption and Capital Punishment Reduction, 1785–1822," *Punishment & Society* 18, no. 4 (2016), 420–41, 427.

24. McLennan, *The Crisis of Imprisonment*, 38.

25. David J. Rothman, *The Discovery of the Asylum: Social Order and Disorder in the New Republic* (rev. ed.) (New York: Aldine de Gruyter, 2002b), 92.

26. Meranze, *Laboratories of Virtue*, 8, 97–127; Rothman, *The Discovery of the Asylum*, 90.

27. Rothman, *The Discovery of the Asylum*, 93.

28. McLennan, *The Crisis of Imprisonment*, 14–52.

29. Rothman, *The Discovery of the Asylum*, 92; McLennan, *The Crisis of Imprisonment*, 48.

30. McLennan, *The Crisis of Imprisonment*, 39–40.

31. Ibid., 43. See also Glen A. Gildemeister, *Prison Labor and Convict Competition with Free Workers in Industrializing America, 1840–1890* (New York: Garland, 1987), 129.

32. McLennan, *The Crisis of Imprisonment*, 50–52.

33. Ibid., 49. See also Meranze, *Laboratories of Virtue*, 222.

34. Meranze, *Laboratories of Virtue*, 224–25.

35. McLennan, *The Crisis of Imprisonment*, 51–52.

36. Meranze, *Laboratories of Virtue*, 222.

37. Ibid., 219–23.

38. Ibid., 224.

39. See especially Rothman, *The Discovery of the Asylum*, 55–76.

40. Quoted in Rothman, *The Discovery of the Asylum*, 76.

41. Rubin, "Institutionalizing the Pennsylvania System," 30.

42. McLennan, *The Crisis of Imprisonment*, 62.

43. Ibid., 56.

44. Lewis, *From Newgate to Dannemora*, 70.

45. McLennan, *The Crisis of Imprisonment*, 54.

46. Rothman, "Perfecting the Prison: United States, 1789–1865," in *The Oxford History of the Prison: The Practice of Punishment in Western Society*, eds. Norval Morris and David J. Rothman (New York: Oxford University Press, 1995), 105–106; see also Lewis, *From Newgate to Dannemora*, 1.

47. Rubin, "Institutionalizing the Pennsylvania System," 11.

48. Ibid., 6.

49. Ibid., especially 40–95.

50. Rothman, *The Discovery of the Asylum*, 87.

51. Rubin, "Institutionalizing the Pennsylvania System," 82–83.

52. Ibid., 6, 38; see also Rubin, "A Neo-institutional Account of Prison Diffusion," *Law & Society Review* 49, no. 2 (2015b): 365–400. The Dickens quotes are from Mary Hawthorne, "Dept. of Amplification: Charles Dickens on Solitary Confinement, *New Yorker* (March 23, 2009), http://www.newyorker.com/books/page-turner/dept-of-amplification-charles-dickens-on-solitary-confinement (accessed June 27, 2016).

53. Rubin, "*Institutionalizing the Pennsylvania System*," 109–10.

54. Ibid., 162.

55. Ibid., 136–59.

56. Ibid., 46.

57. Quoted in Rubin, "Institutionalizing the Pennsylvania System," 90.

58. Rubin, "Institutionalizing the Pennsylvania System," 147.

59. Ibid., 137.

60. Ibid., 191.

61. Ibid., 142.

62. McLennan, *The Crisis of Imprisonment*, 54.

63. New York passed legislation in 1819 making flogging legal (James Q. Whitman, *Harsh Justice: Criminal Punishment and the Widening Divide between America and Europe* [New York: Oxford University Press, 2005], 175).

64. McLennan, *The Crisis of Imprisonment*, 68.

65. Ibid., 70.

66. Ibid., 70–71.

67. Another widely lauded prison was Wethersfield State Prison in Connecticut (in operation from 1827 to 1963). For a nineteenth century account praising Wethersfield, see Dorothea Dix, *Remarks on Prisons and Prison Discipline in the United States* (1845) (Whitefish, MT: Kessinger, 2008).

68. Rothman, *The Discovery of the Asylum*, 100.

69. McLennan, *The Crisis of Imprisonment*, 72.

70. Ibid., 72–76.

71. Ibid., 77.

72. Ibid., 79.

73. Ibid., 79.

74. Ayers, *Vengeance and Justice*, 55.

75. Robert Perkinson, *Texas Tough: The Rise of America's Prison Empire* (New York: Metropolitan, 2010), 74.

76. David M. Oshinsky, *Worse Than Slavery: Parchman Farm and the Ordeal of Jim Crow Justice* (New York: Free Press, 1996), 6–7.

77. See also Robert David Ward and William Warren Rogers, *Alabama's Response to the Penitentiary Movement, 1829–1865* (Gainesville: University Press of Florida, 2003).

78. Dario Melossi and Massimo Pavarini argue that the congregate model provided much needed manufacturing labor and educated prisoners in factory discipline (Dario Melossi and Massimo Pavarini, *The Prison and the Factory: Origins of the Penitentiary System* [New York: Macmillan, 1981], 129). Similarly, Georg Rusche and Otto Kirchheimer argue that imprisonment served the economic needs of capitalism, the new mode of production (Georg Rusche and Otto Kirchheimer, *Punishment and Social Structure* [New Brunswick, NJ: Transaction, 2003]).

79. Rubin, "A Neo-institutional Account," 390.

80. Ibid., 391.

81. Ayers, *Vengeance and Justice*, 53.

82. Ibid., 54.

83. Ward and Rogers, *Alabama's Response to the Penitentiary Movement*, especially 24–28.

84. Ayers, *Vengeance and Justice*, 55. Ayers explains that one group of elites, ministers of evangelical Christian churches, did not support imprisonment or the penitentiary ideal because they believed that only God's law could (and should) set delinquents on the path of righteousness (Ayers, *Vengeance and Justice*, 56–57).

85. Ayers, *Vengeance and Justice*, 55.

86. Marie Gottschalk, *The Prison and the Gallows: The Politics of Mass Incarceration in America* (New York: Cambridge University Press, 2006), 48. See also Michael S. Hindus, *Prison and Plantation: Crime, Justice, and Authority in Massachusetts and South Carolina, 1767–1878* (Chapel Hill: University of North Carolina Press, 2012).

87. Ayers, *Vengeance and Justice*, 65.

88. Ibid., 65.

89. Ibid., 67.

90. Ward and Rogers, *Alabama's Response to the Penitentiary Movement*; 80; Ayers, *Vengeance and Justice*, 61.

91. Hindus, *Prison and Plantation*; Ayers, *Vengeance and Justice*.

92. Ayers, *Vengeance and Justice*, 62.

93. Ibid., 62.

94. Oshinsky, *Worse Than Slavery*, 7; Ward and Rogers, *Alabama's Response to the Penitentiary Movement*, 80–81.

95. Ayers, *Vengeance and Justice*, 63. See also Oshinsky, *Worse Than Slavery*, 77.

96. Ayers, *Vengeance and Justice*, 63.

97. Ward and Rogers, *Alabama's Response to the Penitentiary Movement*, 75.

98. Alex Lichtenstein, *Twice the Work of Free Labor: The Political Economy of Convict Labor in the New South* (New York: Verso, 1996), 22.

99. Martha A. Myers, *Race, Labor, and Punishment in the New South* (Columbus: Ohio State University Press, 1998), 14.

100. Perkinson, *Texas Tough*, 77.

101. Ayers, *Vengeance and Justice*, 70.

102. Lichtenstein, *Twice the Work of Free Labor*, 24.

103. Myers, *Race, Labor, and Punishment*, 14.

104. Gottschalk, *The Prison and the Gallows*, 48.

105. Perkinson, *Texas Tough*, 80 (or, more generally, 78–82).

106. Ibid., 81, emphasis added.

107. Whitman, *Harsh Justice*, 174.

108. Ayers, *Vengeance and Justice*, 70.

109. Even if the elite reformers had desired to include these groups in their visions of reformation, they would not have been able to do so because opposition would

have destroyed any hope of turning these visions into reality; the social structures of racial and gender inequality, in other words, circumscribed what was even "thinkable" in terms of reform.

110. Nicole Hahn Rafter, *Partial Justice: Women, Prisons, and Social Control* (2d ed.) (New Brunswick, NJ: Transaction, 1990), 4.

111. Ibid., 21.

112. See, e.g., Enoch Wines and Theodore Dwight, *Report on the Prisons and the Reformatories of the United States and Canada* (1867) (Ann Arbor: Scholarly Publishing Office, University of Michigan Library, 2005).

113. Gottschalk, *Prison and the Gallows*, 48.

114. McLennan, *The Crisis of Imprisonment*, 85.

115. Rubin, "*Institutionalizing the Pennsylvania System*," 1.

## CHAPTER 3

1. Rebecca M. McLennan, *The Crisis of Imprisonment: Protest, Politics, and the Making of the American Penal State, 1776–1941* (New York: Cambridge University Press, 2008), 84–85.

2. Quoted in Francs T. Cullen and Karen E. Gilbert, *Reaffirming Rehabilitation* (2d ed.) (New York: Routledge, 2013), 40.

3. David M. Oshinsky, *Worse Than Slavery: Parchman Farm and the Ordeal of Jim Crow Justice* (New York: Free Press, 1997), 20–21.

4. Ibid. See also Alex Lichtenstein, *Twice the Work of Free Labor: The Political Economy of Convict Labor in the New South* (New York: Verso, 1996).

5. Samuel Walker, *Popular Justice: A History of American Criminal Justice* (2d ed.) (New York: Oxford University Press, 1998), chaps. 4 and 5.

6. E. C. Wines (ed.), *Transactions of the National Congress on Penitentiary and Reformatory Discipline* (Albany, NY: Weed, Parsons, 1871), 2.

7. Wines, *Transactions of the National Congress,* 541–47. All the quotations in this discussion of the "Declaration of Principles" are from these page numbers.

8. As with the penitentiary ideal, the "new penology" developed, in part, through dialogue between American and European intellectuals.

9. Cullen and Gilbert, *Reaffirming Rehabilitation*, 45.

10. McLennan, *The Crisis of Imprisonment*, 92. McLennan adds, "The presence in Northern prisons of so many citizen-soldiers—who had just risked their lives fighting for the Union—appears to have helped stimulate support for the prison reform movement of the late 1860s" (92, fn. 10).

11. McLennan, *The Crisis of Imprisonment*, 93.

12. Ibid., 95.

13. Edward L. Ayers, *Vengeance and Justice: Crime and Punishment in the 19th-Century American South* (New York: Oxford University Press, 1984).

14. Ibid.; Oshinsky, *Worse Than Slavery.*

15. McLennan, *The Crisis of Imprisonment*, 97; David Garland, "Penal Excess and Surplus Meaning: Public Torture Lynchings in Twentieth-Century America," *Law & Society Review* 39, no. 4 (2005): 793–833.

16. McLennan, *The Crisis of Imprisonment*, 97.

17. Ibid., 100.

18. Ibid., 107.

19. Ibid., 101.

20. Ayers, *Vengeance and Justice*, 195. Oshinsky writes about convict coal miners in Alabama: "Their numbers ebbed and flowed according to the labor needs of the coal companies and the revenue needs of the coal companies and the state. When times were tight, local police would sweep the streets for vagrants, drunks, and thieves. Hundreds of blacks would be arrested, put on trial, found guilty, sentenced to sixty or ninety days plus court costs, and then delivered to a 'hard labor agent,' who leased them to the mines" (Oshinsky, *Worse Than Slavery*, 77).

21. W. E. B. Du Bois, "The Spawn of Slavery: The Convict Lease System in the South," in *African American Classics in Criminology and Criminal Justice*, eds. Shaun L. Gabbidon, Helen Taylor Greene, and Vernetta D. Young (Thousand Oaks, CA: SAGE, 2002), 81–88.

22. Ayers, *Vengeance and Justice*, 197.

23. Oshinsky, *Worse Than Slavery*, 57. Debt peonage and chain gangs also were used in this period to force free blacks into involuntary servitude. Peonage kept black workers tied to private individuals, while the chain gang provided labor for local governments (Douglas A. Blackmon, *Slavery by Another Name: The Re-enslavement of Black Americans from the Civil War to World War II* [New York: Anchor]; Ayers, *Vengeance and Justice*; and Lichtenstein, *Twice the Work of Free Labor*).

24. Blackmon, *Slavery by Another Name*; Talitha L. LeFlouria, *Chained in Silence: Black Women and Convict Labor in the New South* (Chapel Hill: University of North Carolina Press, 2015b); Oshinsky, *Worse Than Slavery*.

25. Talitha L. LeFlouria, "'Under the Sting of the Lash': Gendered Violence, Terror, and Resistance in the South's Convict Camps," *Journal of African American History* 100, no. 3 (2015a): 366–84, 369.

26. LeFlouria, *Chained in Silence: Black Women and Convict Labor in the New South* (Chapel Hill: University of North Carolina Press, 2015b); and Oshinsky, *Worse Than Slavery*.

27. Oshinsky, *Worse Than Slavery*, 46.

28. McLennan, *The Crisis of Imprisonment*, 152, fn. 36.

29. Ibid., 173, 185.

30. Lichtenstein, *Twice the Work of Free Labor*, 96.

31. McLennan, *The Crisis of Imprisonment*, 159.

32. Karin A. Shapiro, *A New South Rebellion: The Battle against Convict Labor in the Tennessee Coalfields, 1871–1896* (Chapel Hill: University of North Carolina Press, 1998).

33. Oshinsky, *Worse Than Slavery*, 49.

34. Ibid., 50–1.

35. Ibid., 48.

36. McLennan, *The Crisis of Imprisonment*, 158.

37. Oshinsky, *Worse Than Slavery*, 52.

38. Cullen and Gilbert, *Reaffirming Rehabilitation*, 44–45.

39. David J. Rothman, *Conscience and Convenience: The Asylum and Its Alternatives in Progressive America* (rev. ed.) (New York: Aldine de Gruyter, 2002a), 33–34.

40. Larry E. Sullivan, *The Prison Reform Movement: Forlorn Hope* (Boston: Twayne, 1990), 20, emphasis added.

41. Pisciotta argues that romantic reflections on Elmira (and the larger reformatory movement) distort reality: in fact, the rhetoric of reform justified and masked extremely harsh treatment (Alexander W. Pisciotta, *Benevolent Repression: Social Control and the American Reformatory-Prison Movement* [New York: New York University Press, 1994]).

42. Pisciotta, *Benevolent Repression*, 4. Nicole Rafter argues that Brockway and his staff made some inmates "defective" (that is, physically and morally damaged) through abusive treatment (Nicole Hahn Rafter, *Creating Born Criminals* [Urbana: University of Illinois Press, 1997], 103–104).

43. Pisciotta, *Benevolent Repression*, 7.

44. Rafter, *Creating Born Criminals*, chap. 5.

45. Pisciotta, *Benevolent Repression*, 102.

46. Michael McGerr, *A Fierce Discontent: The Rise and Fall of the Progressive Movement in America, 1870–1920* (New York: Oxford University Press, 2003), 4.

47. On the incredible exploitation of workers (especially immigrant women) and their efforts to fight back via unionization, see David Von Drehle, *Triangle: The Fire That Changed America* (New York: Grove, 2003).

48. McGerr, *A Fierce Discontent*, 39.

49. David S. Tanenhaus, *Juvenile Justice in the Making* (New York: Oxford University Press, 2004), 5.

50. Thomas C. Leonard, "Retrospectives: Eugenics and Economics in the Progressive Era," *Journal of Economic Perspectives* 19, no. 4 (2005): 207–24. See also Steven Schlossman and Stephanie Wallach, "The Crime of Precocious Sexuality: Female Juvenile Delinquency in the Progressive Era," *Harvard Educational Review* 48, no. 1 (1978): 65–94.

51. McGerr, *A Fierce Discontent*, 79.

52. Ibid., chap. 3.

53. McLennan, *The Crisis of Imprisonment*, 378.

54. Nicole Hahn Rafter, *Partial Justice: Women, Prisons, and Social Control* (2d ed.) (New Brunswick, NJ: Transaction, 1990), 55.

55. Walker, *Popular Justice*, chaps. 4 and 5.

56. See John Whiteclay Chambers II, *The Tyranny of Change: America in the Progressive Era, 1890–1920* (2d ed.) (New Brunswick, NJ: Rutgers University Press, 2000).

57. Status offenses are behaviors for which juveniles can be punished (or rehabilitated) because of the individuals' "status" as minors. Adults cannot be punished for these same behaviors; they must be charged with breaking the law to receive punishment.

58. Schlossman and Wallach, "The Crime of Precocious Sexuality"; Tanenhaus, *Juvenile Justice in the Making*.

59. Marie Gottschalk, *The Prison and the Gallows: The Politics of Mass Incarceration in America* (New York: Cambridge University Press, 2006), 56.

60. Victoria Getis, *The Juvenile Court and Progressives* (Urbana: University of Illinois Press, 2000).

61. Geoff K. Ward, *The Black Child-Savers: Racial Democracy and Juvenile Justice* (Chicago: University of Chicago Press, 2012), 86–87.

62. Ward, *The Black Child-Savers*, 86.

63. Ibid., 98. Pisciotta explains that the adult reformatories also reflected and reinforced existing racial and gender inequality (Pisciotta, *Benevolent Repression*).

64. Ward, *The Black Child-Savers*, 85.

65. Tanenhaus, *Juvenile Justice in the Making*, chap. 2.

66. Ward, *The Black Child-Savers*, 85. Michael Schlossman demonstrates that in Los Angeles in the 1930s and 1940s (though technically after the Progressive Era, juvenile courts held onto progressive ideals), "Mexican-American youth were overrepresented in the Los Angeles Juvenile Court" but were "less likely to be removed from their homes comparable to whites. In a juvenile system in which there was still confidence in using out-of-home placements to accomplish rehabilitation . . . officials were more interested in 'saving' white than minority youths" (Michael B. Schlossman, "Less Interest, Less Treatment: Mexican-American Youth and the Los Angeles Juvenile Court in the Great Depression Era," *Punishment & Society* 14, no. 2 [2012]: 193–216, 195).

67. McGerr, *A Fierce Discontent*, 183–84.

68. Ward, *The Black Child-Savers,* 106.

69. Gottschalk, *The Prison and the Gallows*, 56.

70. Ibid., 57.

71. Ibid., 57.

72. Ibid., 56. See also Janis Appier, *Policing Women: The Sexual Politics of Law Enforcement and the LAPD* (Philadelphia: Temple University Press, 1998).

73. See, e.g., Walker, *Popular Justice*.

74. Khalil Gibran Muhammad, *The Condemnation of Blackness: Race, Crime, and the Making of Modern Urban America* (Cambridge, MA: Harvard University Press, 2010); Gottschalk, *The Prison and the Gallows*; and Shelton Stromquist, *Reinventing "The People": The Progressive Movement, the Class Problem, and the Origins of Modern Liberalism* (Urbana: University of Illinois Press, 2006).

75. Erik Schneiderhan, *The Size of Others' Burdens: Barack Obama, Jane Addams, and the Politics of Helping Others* (Stanford, CA: Stanford University Press, 2015).

76. Rothman, *Conscience and Convenience*, 10.

77. Ibid., 77–78, 98–106.

78. Ibid., 98–100.

79. Ibid., 183–89.

80. Ibid., 109–13.

81. Ibid., 193–201.

82. Tanenhaus, *Juvenile Justice in the Making*, 35.

83. See, e.g., Getis, *The Juvenile Court*.

84. Illinois was the undisputed leader in juvenile justice in the late 1800s and early 1990s (Tanenhaus, *Juvenile Justice in the Making*).

85. On community sanctions in New York during this period, see Rothman, *Conscience and Convenience*.

86. McLennan, *The Crisis of Imprisonment*, 327.

87. Ibid., 194–97.

88. Ibid., 200–15.

89. Ibid., 217–18. See also Simon A. Cole, *Suspect Identities: A History of Fingerprinting and Criminal Identification* (Cambridge, MA: Harvard University Press, 2001), 32–59.

90. McLennan reports that between the 1840s and 1903, the literacy rate of prisoners increased from 10% to 80% (McLennan, *The Crisis of Imprisonment*, 243).

91. Ibid., 226.

92. Ibid., 257–59.

93. Ibid., 255–57.

94. Ibid., 257–62.

95. Ibid., 268–69.

96. Ibid., 247.

97. Ibid., 247–50.

98. As this example suggests, the media were a central player in the struggle to reshape New York's prisons. Popularizing mishaps and scandals undercut the Progressives' efforts to implement and maintain reforms. But the media also aided the reformers by highlighting their innovations and successes. Newspaper reporters and editorialists were becoming influential players within the penal field—and their influence would only grow in subsequent decades.

99. McLennan, *The Crisis of Imprisonment*, 327.

100. Estelle B. Freedman, *Their Sisters' Keepers: Women's Prison Reform in America, 1830–1930* (Ann Arbor: University of Michigan Press, 1981), 130. Efforts to implement progressive reforms in New York were a particularly prominent (and crucial) demonstration of the national progressive movement.

101. An ironic power play, given the Progressives' stated preference for neutrally appointed civil servants.

102. McLennan, *The Crisis of Imprisonment*, 337–55.

103. Ibid., 330–31.

104. Ibid., 356–59.

105. Ibid., 361–69. The League also worked with Warden Rattigan to set up a segregation company for prisoners expelled from the League; these men were provided "rehabilitative" services and could be paroled back into the mainstream units upon good behavior (370–71).

106. McLennan, *The Crisis of Imprisonment*, 367–70.

107. Ibid., 387.

108. Ibid., 387–93.

109. Ibid., 394–96.

110. Ibid., 396–403. On the history of same-sex relations within prisons (and efforts to repress those relations), see Regina G. Kunzel, *Criminal Intimacy: Prison and the Uneven History of Modern American Sexuality* (Chicago: University of Chicago Press, 2008).

111. Schlossman and Wallach, *The Crime of Precocious Sexuality*.

112. Rothman describes the incredible resistance to reform seen in the prison at Norfolk, Massachusetts, during the Progressive Era. Custodial staff intensely resented professionals (such as social workers) who gained status and power in the prison, and they sought to thwart their efforts. Struggle inside the prison, Rothman demonstrates, greatly compromised reformers' efforts and sharpened the punitive and managerial edges of imprisonment (Rothman, *Conscience and Convenience*, 401).

113. McLennan, *The Crisis of Imprisonment*, 278.

114. Ibid., 409.

115. McLennan suggests that Tammany Hall Democrats and Republican political leaders collaborated with Riley to undermine Osborne (McLennan, *The Crisis of Imprisonment*, 409–10).

116. McLennan, *The Crisis of Imprisonment*, 411.

117. Ibid., 412.

118. Ibid., 415.

119. Ibid., 443.

120. Ibid., 239–40.

121. Ibid., 447.

122. Ibid., 271–73.

123. Ibid., 349.

124. Ibid., 404.

125. Rafter, *Partial Justice*, 55.

126. Ibid., 58.

127. Freedman, *Their Sisters' Keepers*, 116–17, 130–32; on the location of juvenile reformatories, see Tanenhaus, *Juvenile Justice in the Making*.

128. Rafter, *Partial Justice*, 66.

129. Anne E. Bowler, Chrysanthi S. Leon, and Terry G. Lilley, "'What Shall We Do with the Young Prostitute? Reform Her or Neglect Her?': Domestication as Reform at the New York State Reformatory for Women at Bedford, 1901–1913," *Journal of Social History* 47, no. 2 (2013), 458–81, 476.

130. Rafter, *Partial Justice*, 66.

131. Ibid., 69–72; Bowler et al., "What Shall We Do with the Young Prostitute?," 468–70.

132. Freedman, *Their Sisters' Keepers*, 140.

133. Cheryl D. Hicks, "'Bright and Good Looking Colored Girl': Black Women's Sexuality and 'Harmful Intimacy' in Early-Twentieth-Century New York," in *The Punitive Turn: New Approaches to Race and Incarceration*, eds. Deborah E. McDowell, Claudrena N. Harold, and Juan Battle (Charlottesville: University of Virginia Press, 2013), 91.

134. Quoted in Freedman, *Their Sisters' Keepers*, 141.

135. Jane Zimmerman, "The Penal Reform Movement in the South during the Progressive Era, 1890–1917," *Journal of Southern History* 17, no. 4 (1951): 462–92.

136. Perkinson, *Texas Tough*, 172.

137. Ibid., 182–83.

138. Ibid., 183.

139. Ibid., 187–88.

140. Ibid., 189.

141. Ibid., 197.

142. Ibid., 198–200.

143. Ibid., 200.

144. Ibid., 200–202.

145. Ibid., 202–203.

146. Ibid., 204.

147. Ibid., 206–207.

148. See also, Michael Campbell, "Ornery Alligators and Soap on a Rope: Texas Prosecutors and Punishment Reform in the Lone Star State," *Theoretical Criminology* 16, no. 3 (2012): 289–311.

149. Perkinson, *Texas Tough*, 196.

150. David Garland, *Punishment and Modern Society: A Study in Social Theory* (Chicago: University of Chicago Press, 1990).

CHAPTER 4

1. Quoted in Robert Perkinson, *Texas Tough: The Rise of America's Prison Empire* (New York: Metropolitan, 2010), 197.

2. Ethan Blue, *Doing Time in the Depression: Everyday Life in Texas and California Prisons* (New York: New York University Press, 2012); Charles Bright, *The Powers That Punish: Prison and Politics in the Era of the "Big House," 1920–1955* (Ann Arbor: University of Michigan Press, 1996); Marie Gottschalk, *The Prison and the Gallows: The Politics of Mass Incarceration in America* (New York: Cambridge University Press, 2006); John Irwin, *Prisons in Turmoil* (Boston: Little, Brown, 1980), especially 1–36; Lisa McGirr, *The War on Alcohol: Prohibition and the*

*Rise of the American State* (New York: W. W. Norton, 2016); and Jonathan Simon, *Poor Discipline: Parole and the Social Control of the Underclass, 1890–1990* (Chicago: University of Chicago Press, 1993), especially 39–67.

3. See especially Bright, *The Powers That Punish*; Anthony M. Platt, *The Child Savers: The Invention of Delinquency* (2d ed.) (Chicago: University of Chicago Press, 1977); and Simon, *Poor Discipline*.

4. Mark T. Carleton, *Politics and Punishment: The History of the Louisiana State Penal System* (Baton Rouge: Louisiana State University Press, 1971); Matthew J. Mancini, *One Dies, Get Another: Convict Leasing in the American South, 1866–1928* (Columbia: University of South Carolina Press, 1996); and David M. Oshinsky, *Worse Than Slavery: Parchman Farm and the Ordeal of Jim Crow Justice* (New York: Free Press, 1996).

5. Made of jute (plant fiber), these bags were used mostly by farmers to store and transport grain and other crops.

6. Blue, *Doing Time in the Depression*, 199; Ward M. McAfee, "A History of Convict Labor in California," *Southern California Quarterly* 72, no. 1 (1990): 19–40; Leo L. Stanley, "Tuberculosis in San Quentin," *California and Western Medicine* 49, no. 6 (1938): 436–39; and Barbara Jeanne Yaley, "Habits of Industry: Labor and Penal Policy in California, 1849–1940" (PhD dissertation, University of California, Santa Cruz, 1980).

7. See especially Bright, *The Powers that Punish*; James B. Jacobs, *Stateville: The Penitentiary in Mass Society* (Chicago: University of Chicago Press, 1977); and Simon, *Poor Discipline*. On the multifaceted nature of prison labor today, see Philip Goodman, "Hero *and* Inmate: Work, Prisons, and Punishment in California's Fire Camps," *Working USA: The Journal of Labor & Society* 15, no. 3 (2012b): 353–76.

8. For one influential description of this period, see Francis A. Allen, "Criminal Justice, Legal Values and the Rehabilitative Ideal," *Journal of Criminal Law, Criminology & Police Science* 50, no. 3 (1959): 226–32.

9. Ian Loader and Richard Sparks, "For an Historical Sociology of Crime Policy in England and Wales since 1968," *Critical Review of International Social and Political Philosophy* 7, no. 2 (2004): 5–32, 14–15.

10. Other classic penal farms included Angola in Louisiana, Tucker in Arkansas, Ramsey in Texas, and Milledgeville in Georgia.

11. Oshinsky, *Worse Than Slavery*, 109. By 1917, annual profits at Parchman were nearly a million dollars, or "almost half of Mississippi's entire budget for public education." Not surprisingly, "politicians and editors were soon calling Parchman the 'best prison' in America, as fertile and productive as the 'Valley of the Nile'" (155).

12. Oshinsky, *Worse Than Slavery*, 138–39.

13. Alex Lichtenstein, *Twice the Work of Free Labor: The Political Economy of Convict Labor in the New South* (New York: Verso, 1996); Mancini, *One Dies, Get Another*, especially pp. 198–232; and Oshinsky, *Worse Than Slavery*.

14. "During the 1903 campaign," Oshinsky notes, "Vardaman blasted Roosevelt for allowing blacks to hold federal appointments in Mississippi. The president, he charged, was a 'coon-flavored miscegenationist' bent on 'filling the head of the nigger' with dangerous ideas" (Oshinsky, *Worse Than Slavery*, 88). The result was support from the governor's mansion in Mississippi for some of the most horrible years for blacks during the postbellum period in the South.

15. Oshinsky, *Worse Than Slavery*, 83; Perkinson, *Texas Tough*, 235.

16. On reaction to that film, and the North's convenient fascination with the barbarity of southern punishment, see Heather Ann Thompson, "Blinded by a 'Barbaric' South: Prison Horrors, Inmate Abuse, and the Ironic History of American Penal Reform." In *The Myth of Southern Exceptionalism*, eds. Matthew D. Lassiter and Joseph Crespino (Oxford: Oxford University Press, 2010), 74.

17. Oshinsky, *Worse Than Slavery*, 224.

18. Ibid., 153.

19. Ibid., 190–93.

20. On the myriad links between scientific experimentation on prisoners and the rhetoric and practice of rehabilitation, see Allen M. Hornblum, *Acres of Skin: Human Experiments at Holmesburg Prison; A True Story of Abuse and Exploitation in the Name of Medical Science* (New York: Routledge, 1999). For a similar argument in the Canadian context, see Geraint B. Osborne, "Scientific Experimentation on Canadian Inmates, 1955 to 1975," *Howard Journal of Criminal Justice* 45, no. 3 (2006), 284–306.

21. Oshinsky, *Worse Than Slavery*, 227–29.

22. Ibid., 226–27.

23. Irwin, *Prisons in Turmoil*, 5. For other vivid descriptions of the "Big House," see Blue, *Doing Time in the Depression*; Bright, *The Powers That Punish*; Donald Clemmer, *The Prison Community* (Boston: Christopher, 1940); R. Theodore Davidson, *Chicano Prisoners: The Key to San Quentin* (New York: Holt, Rinehart and Winston, 1974); Jacobs, *Stateville*; and Gresham M. Sykes, *The Society of Captives: A Study of a Maximum Security Prison* (1958) (Princeton, NJ: Princeton University Press, 2007).

24. Christopher Muller, "Northward Migration and the Rise of Racial Disparity in American Incarceration, 1880–1950," *American Journal of Sociology* 118, no. 2 (2012): 281–326.

25. Quoted in Rebecca McLennan, *The Crisis of Imprisonment: Protest, Politics, and the Making of the American Penal State, 1776–1941* (Cambridge, MA: Cambridge University Press, 2008), 447.

26. Bright, *The Powers That Punish*.

27. Ibid., 35–42; McGirr, *The War on Alcohol*.

28. McGirr, *The War on Alcohol*; see also Joseph R. Gusfield, *Symbolic Crusade: Status Politics and the American Temperance Movement* (Urbana: University of Illinois Press, 1963).

29. Bright, *The Powers That Punish*, 44–45.

30. Ibid., 43.

31. Ibid., 41–46.

32. Ibid., 93–104.

33. McGirr, *The War on Alcohol*, preface.

34. Bright, *The Powers That Punish*, 70–93. According to Bright, "by the mid-1920s Hulbert could boast that 75 percent of the prisoners at Jackson were gainfully employed, half of them on projects outside the prison walls" (84).

35. Bright, *The Powers That Punish*, 84–86.

36. Ibid., 70–93. See also Jacobs, *Stateville*.

37. Allen, "Criminal Justice, Legal Values and the Rehabilitative Ideal," 226.

38. Francis T. Cullen, "Rehabilitation: Beyond Nothing Works," in *Crime and Justice in America, 1975–2025*, ed. Michael Tonry (Chicago: University of Chicago Press, 2013), 313.

39. David Garland, *The Culture of Control: Crime and Social Order in Contemporary Society* (Chicago: University of Chicago Press, 2001); Franklin E. Zimring and Gordon Hawkins, *Incapacitation: Penal Confinement and the Restraint of Crime* (Oxford: Oxford University Press, 1995). One occasionally gets the sense from reading criminal justice textbooks that the shift toward rehabilitation was like a self-propelled boulder set loose in the Progressive Era, crashing down to great clatter around 1950. That's clearly not right.

40. Irwin, *Prisons in Turmoil*, 37.

41. Ibid., 47.

42. Simon, *Poor Discipline*, 69. See also Cullen, "Rehabilitation: Beyond Nothing Works," 312.

43. It is at least in part because of those ties that even today many scholars (including us) refer to interventions designed to "straighten out" wayward offenders or moderate the severity or harshness of punishment, as *progressive*.

44. Garland, *The Culture of Control*, 48–49.

45. Ted Conover, *Newjack: Guarding Sing Sing* (New York: Vintage, 2001), 206; Angela Hill, "Doing Time at the San Quentin Museum," *Oakland Tribune* (January 2, 2015), http://www.mercurynews.com/eat-drink-play/ci_27246254/doing-time-at-san-quentin-museum (accessed April 9, 2016); Lloyd Thorpe, *Men to Match the Mountains* (Seattle, WA: Met, 1972).

46. Garland, *The Culture of Control*, 50.

47. Allen, "Criminal Justice, Legal Values and the Rehabilitative Ideal," 227.

48. Garland, *The Culture of Control*, especially 15–16; 41–44.

49. Trent Shotwell, "Austin H. MacCormick Papers, 1923–1978," Thomason Special Collections, Newton Gresham Library, Sam Houston State University, Huntsville, TX, https://archon.shsu.edu/?p=collections/findingaid&id=6&q= (accessed February 8, 2016). See also Paul W. Keve, *Prisons and the American Conscience: A History of U.S. Federal Corrections* (Carbondale: Southern Illinois

University Press, 1991); and Charles Phillips and Alan Axelrod, *Cops, Crooks, and Criminologists: An International Biographical Dictionary of Law Enforcement* (New York: Checkmark, 2000).

50. Austin H. MacCormick, *The Education of Adult Prisoners: A Survey and a Program* (New York: National Society of Penal Information, 1931); William R. Muth and Thom Gehring, "The Correctional Education / Prison Reform Link: 1913–1940 and Conclusion," *Journal of Correctional Education* 37, no. 1 (1986): 14–17.

51. Mayor Fiorella La Guardia, for instance, worked closely with MacCormick while the latter was commissioner of the New York Department of Corrections to stage a high-profile raid of New York City's most infamous prison in the 1930s, Welfare Island, where mobsters allegedly lived in relative luxury. Prison conditions improved (especially when the city opened a new jail on Riker's Island), as did La Guardia's reputation for attacking corruption (Carl Sifakis, "Welfare Island Prison Scandal," in *The Encyclopedia of American Prisons* [New York: Facts on File, 2003], 281–83).

52. For an introduction to McGee, see Daniel Glaser, *Preparing Convicts for Law-Abiding Lives: The Pioneering Penology of Richard A. McGee* (Albany: State University of New York Press, 1995). For a short introduction to Bennett's career, see Marilyn D. McShane and Frank P. Williams III (eds.), *Encyclopedia of American Prisons* (New York: Garland, 1996), 89–93.

53. Much of the material on California in this section is adapted from an earlier publication. See Philip Goodman, Joshua Page, and Michelle Phelps, "The Long Struggle: An Agonistic Perspective on Penal Development," *Theoretical Criminology* 19, no. 3 (2015): 315–35.

54. See, e.g., Vanessa Barker, *The Politics of Imprisonment: How the Democratic Process Shapes the Way America Punishes Offenders* (New York: Oxford University Press, 2009); Irwin, *Prisons in Turmoil*; Joshua Page, *The Toughest Beat: Politics, Punishment, and the Prison Officers Union in California* (New York: Oxford University Press, 2011); Joan Petersilia, *When Prisoners Come Home: Parole and Prisoner Reentry* (New York: Oxford University Press, 2003); and Simon, *Poor Discipline*.

55. See, e.g., Irwin, *Prisons in Turmoil*; Simon, *Poor Discipline*.

56. Irwin, *Prisons in Turmoil*, 41.

57. On the idea that treatment of felons could make them into better citizens, see especially Volker Janssen, "From the Inside Out: Therapeutic Penology and Political Liberalism in Postwar California," *Osiris* 22, no.1 (2007): 116–34.

58. Norman Holt, "A Brief History of Inmate Classification in California" (unpublished manuscript on file with the authors, 1998); John Irwin, *The Felon* (Englewood Cliffs, NJ: Prentice-Hall, 1970); Irwin, *Prisons in Turmoil*; and Heather Jane McCarty, "From Con-Boss to Gang Lord: The Transformation of Social Relations in California Prisons, 1943–1983" (PhD dissertation, University of California, Berkeley, 2004).

59. McCarty, "From Con-Boss to Gang Lord," 60.

60. Irwin, *Prisons in Turmoil*, 46; McCarty, "From Con-Boss to Gang Lord," 58.

61. Philip Goodman, "Hero or Inmate, Camp or Prison, Rehabilitation or Labor Extraction: A Multi-level Study of California's Prison Fire Camps" (PhD dissertation, University of California, Irvine, 2010); Janssen, "From the Inside Out."

62. A copy of the speech can be found in the California State Archives (F3717: 438).

63. McCarty, "From Con-Boss to Gang Lord," 55. The work programs were also deeply gendered; men participated in manual labor that would restore them to vital, masculine citizenship, while women received work that included "feminized" tasks such as sewing and laundry, building better *female* citizens. Janssen, "From the Inside Out"; Candace Kruttschnitt and Rosemary Gartner, *Marking Time in the Golden State: Women's Imprisonment in California* (Cambridge, UK: Cambridge University Press, 2005), 73.

64. Simon, *Poor Discipline*, 76–77.

65. Mona Lynch, "Rehabilitation as Rhetoric: The Ideal of Reformation in Contemporary Parole Discourse and Practices," *Punishment & Society* 2, no. 1 (2000), 40–65, 42. See also Simon, *Poor Discipline*, 81–88.

66. Paul Lerman, *Community Treatment and Social Control: A Critical Analysis of Juvenile Correctional Policy* (Chicago: University of Chicago Press, 1975).

67. Erik Olin Wright, *The Politics of Punishment: A Critical Analysis of Prisons in America* (New York: Harper & Row, 1973), 49.

68. Ibid., 155.

69. Ibid., 157. See also David Rothman, *Conscience and Convenience: The Asylum and Its Alternatives in Progressive America* (rev. ed.) (New York: Aldine de Gruyter, 2002a).

70. Kruttschnitt and Gartner, *Marking Time in the Golden State*, especially 72–83.

71. Holt, "A Brief History of Inmate Classification in California," 34.

72. Irwin, *Prisons in Turmoil*, 61.

73. The Golden State was renowned for being on the cutting edge of treating, rather than punishing, those convicted of a sexual offences. This included expanding the category of civil commitments, by which people were supposed to be sent to secure treatment facilities, rather than traditional prisons. Despite considerable talk in California of a completely new approach to those convicted of a sexual offence, Chrysanthi S. Leon (*Sex Fiends, Perverts, and Pedophiles: Understanding Sex Crime Policy in America* [New York: New York University Press, 2011]) explains, "It turns out that rather than experimenting with rehabilitation of 'nearly all criminals, no matter how bad,' those offenders who seemed most like 'useful citizens' were diverted from prison, while those who had less in common with the decision makers and whose offences seemed more 'harmful' were sent to prison—and little therapy took place in either location" (p. 77).

74. Simon, *Poor Discipline*.

75. Davidson, *Chicano Prisoners*; Irwin, *The Felon* and *Prisons in Turmoil*; McCarty, "From Con-Boss to Gang Lord"; and Wright, *The Politics of Punishment*.

76. Irwin, *Prisons in Turmoil*; Lerman, *Community Treatment and Social Control*; Simon, *Poor Discipline*.

77. In addition to this braiding, there is the fact that rehabilitation-oriented programs were never fully implemented, even in California. Indeed, even the vaunted classification process—the very hallmark of the treatment model—was only partially implemented, given that ground staff lacked "valid diagnostic methods and effective cures for criminality" (Irwin, *Prisons in Turmoil*, 43). Similarly, programs were chronically understaffed, therapy was often run by prisoners (not trained professionals), and demand for programs (from prisoners) outstripped supply (program slots), among other problems. See especially American Friends Service Committee, *A Struggle for Justice: A Report on Crime and Punishment in America* (New York: Hill & Wang, 1971); Holt, "A Brief History of Inmate Classification in California"; McCarty, "From Con-Boss to Gang Lord"; and Jessica Mitford, *Kind and Usual Punishment: The Prison Business* (New York: Knopf, 1973).

78. We use "Custody" and "Treatment" as umbrella terms for general orientations, with the understanding that diversity existed within these ideal types.

79. Irwin, *Prisons in Turmoil*, 124; Page, *The Toughest Beat*; and Harvey Powelson and Reinhard Bendix, "Psychiatry in Prison," *Psychiatry* 14, no. 1 (1951), 73–86, 78.

80. Irwin, *Prisons in Turmoil*; Page, *The Toughest Beat*; and Powelson and Bendix, "Psychiatry in Prison."

81. McCarty, "From Con-Boss to Gang Lord"; Page, *The Toughest Beat*; and William Richard Wilkinson, *Prison Work: A Tale of Thirty Years in the California Department of Corrections*, eds. John C. Burnham and Joseph F. Spillane (Columbus: Ohio State University Press, 2005).

82. Powelson and Bendix, "Psychiatry in Prison," 78 and 82.

83. Holt, "A Brief History of Inmate Classification in California"; Irwin, *Prisons in Turmoil*; and McCarty, "From Con-Boss to Gang Lord."

84. See, e.g., Irwin, *Prisons in Turmoil*, 130.

85. Powelson and Bendix, "Psychiatry in Prison," 80.

86. See also Elliot Studt, Sheldon L. Messinger, and Thomas P. Wilson, *C-unit: Search for Community in Prison* (New York: Russell Sage Foundation, 1968).

87. Ironically, some of the most strident critics of rehabilitation were those prisoners who became educated on the inside during the early years of the "Treatment era" (Irwin, *Prisons in Turmoil*). See also McCarty, "From Con-Boss to Gang Lord."

88. McCarty, "From Con-Boss to Gang Lord"; Petersilia, *When Prisoners Come Home*, 63.

89. Dan Berger, *Captive Nation: Black Prison Organizing in the Civil Rights Era* (Chapel Hill: University of North Carolina Press, 2014); Eric Cummins, *The Rise and Fall of California's Radical Prison Movement* (Stanford, CA: Stanford University Press, 1994); McCarty, "From Con-Boss to Gang Lord"; and Page, *The Toughest Beat*.

90. Michael C. Campbell, "The Emergence of Penal Extremism in California: A Dynamic View of Institutional Structures and Political Processes," *Law & Society Review* 48, no. 2 (2014): 377–409; Irwin, *Prisons in Turmoil*; and McCarty, "From Con-Boss to Gang Lord"; and Page, *The Toughest Beat*.

91. Irwin, *Prisons in Turmoil*; Mitford, *Kind and Usual Punishment*.

92. Volker Janssen, "Sunbelt Lock-Up: Where the Suburbs Met the Super-Max," in *Sunbelt Rising: The Politics of Space, Place, and Region*, eds. Michelle Nickerson and Darren Dochuk (Philadelphia: University of Pennsylvania Press, 2011), 217–39, 222–23.

93. Richard A. McGee, *Prisons and Politics* (Lexington, MA: Lexington, 1981), 121–22.

94. Ibid., 122.

95. Vivien M. L. Miller, *Hard Labor and Hard Time: Florida's "Sunshine Prison" and Chain Gangs* (Gainesville: University Press of Florida, 2012), especially 193–97.

96. Ibid., 111–14; 146–47.

97. Ibid., 197–98.

98. Ibid., 197–200.

99. Ibid., 199.

100. Ibid., 200.

101. Ibid., 147.

102. In the 1940s, when the state created its first system of parole and its first formal parole board, there was still virtually no actual supervision of parolees; the board did not even meet face to face with prisoners. Thus, while the state adopted the *language* of rehabilitation in its discussions of parole, in reality in the 1940s and 1950s it continued to operate simply as a system of early release (Miller, *Hard Labor and Hard Time*, 87–88).

103. Ibid., especially 188–239.

104. Leonard H. Roberts, "A History of Inmate Rehabilitation through Education in the Florida State Correctional System, 1868–1980" (PhD dissertation, University of Florida, 1981), 49–52.

105. Miller, *Hard Labor and Hard Time*, 207–208.

106. Ibid., 256.

107. Ibid., 271.

108. Ibid., 272. Similarly, a January 1939 memorandum written by J. O. Gates, a Florida state inspector whose job it was to monitor conditions in prison camps along state and county roads, reported: "State [road prison] camps are equipped with all modern conveniences. The food compares favorably with that of the army or the C.C.C. camps" (Twenty-Fifth Biennial Prison Report, 1937–1938, 13, as cited in Miller, 175).

109. Miller, *Hard Labor and Hard Time*, especially 159–87.

110. Ibid., 159–87.

111. Ibid., 104.

112. Ibid., 46–71. On similar heel slashing in Texas (which occurred in even-greater numbers), see Perkinson, *Texas Tough*, 215–17.

113. Heather Schoenfeld, "The Politics of Prison Growth: From Chain Gangs to Work Release Centers and Supermax Prisons, Florida, 1955–2000" (PhD dissertation, Northwestern University, 2009), 137–39.

114. Elizabeth Hinton, *From the War on Poverty to the War on Crime: The Making of Mass Incarceration in America* (Cambridge, MA: Harvard University Press, 2016), 2.

115. Schoenfeld, "The Politics of Prison Growth," 149. Note that while the eventual scale back of the road prisons can be understood as part of a broader struggle to modernize and centralize punishment in Florida, the state operated road prisons long past when most other states stopped using prisoners' labor to build and maintain roads. Schoenfeld explains that Florida's road prisons continued to exist because they were politically useful (a way for state legislators to maintain connections to local politicians) and because they provided a ready and cheap labor force (Schoenfeld, "The Politics of Prison Growth," 117). One can also speculate that some politicians in Florida may have valued the road prisons precisely *because of* stories of austere, even-brutal conditions; maintaining support for the road prisons was perhaps a way to signal a commitment to fiscal austerity and tough, "southern justice."

116. Miller, *Hard Labor and Hard Time*, 197–200, 290.

117. Ibid., 43.

118. Ibid., 200.

119. Ibid., 251 and 271.

120. This shell filling (so to speak) allows penal administrators, prisoners, guards, and others to debate within and among themselves about the proper meaning and content of the notion of "rehabilitation"—which has long been about some core commitment to the belief that those who commit crime can, and should, be encouraged to change their ways, but how that change ought to occur and who is responsible for making it happen varies over time (and from place to place) (Philip Goodman, "'Another Second Chance': Rethinking Rehabilitation through the Lens of California's Prison Fire Camps," *Social Problems* 59, no. 4 (2012a): 437–58.

121. Tom O'Connor, "Donn Pearce: Mini Biography," *Internet Movie Database*, http://www.imdb.com/name/nm0668914/bio (accessed June 29, 2016).

122. Richard L. Pangburn, "Friday's Forgotten Book: Cool Hand Luke by Donn Pearce," *Little Known Gems: Reviews and Interpretations Blog* (September 14, 2012), http://trackofthecat.blogspot.ca/2012/09/tuesdays-forgotten-film-cool-hand-luke.html (accessed June 29, 2016).

123. American Film Institute, "AFI's 100 Greatest Movie Quotes of All Time," *AFI.com* (June 21, 2005), http://www.afi.com/100Years/quotes.aspx (accessed June 29, 2016); *CafePress*, "Movie Quotes What We Have Here Is Failure to Communicate Gifts & Merchandise," http://www.cafepress.ca/+movie-quotes-what-we-have-here-is-failure-to-communicate+gifts (accessed June 29, 2016).

124. Thompson, "Blinded by a 'Barbaric' South," 74–75.
125. Murray Edelman, *Political Language: Words That Succeed and Policies That Fail* (New York: Academic Press, 1977), especially 57–76 and 119–40.
126. Garland, *The Culture of Control*.

CHAPTER 5

1. Marie Gottschalk, *The Prison and the Gallows: The Politics of Mass Incarceration in America* (New York: Cambridge University Press, 2006), 1.
2. Sourcebook of Criminal Justice Statistics Online, "Number and Rate (per 100,000 Resident Population in Each Group) of Sentenced Prisoners under Jurisdiction of State and Federal Correctional Authorities on December 31" (2013), http://www.albany.edu/sourcebook/pdf/t6282012.pdf (accessed June 24, 2015).
3. Pew Center on the States, *One in 31: The Long Reach of American Corrections* (Washington, DC: Pew Charitable Trusts, 2009).
4. Michelle Alexander, *The New Jim Crow: Mass Incarceration in the Age of Colorblindness* (New York: New Press, 2010); Radley Balko, *Rise of the Warrior Cop: The Militarization of America's Police Forces* (New York: PublicAffairs, 2013); Mary Louise Frampton, Ian Haney Lopez, and Jonathan Simon (eds.), *After the War on Drugs: Race, Democracy, and a New Reconstruction* (New York: New York University Press, 2008); David Garland, *Peculiar Institution: America's Death Penalty in an Age of Abolition* (Cambridge, MA: Belknap Press of Harvard University Press, 2010); and Elizabeth Hinton, *From the War on Poverty to the War on Crime: The Making of Mass Incarceration in America* (Cambridge, MA: Harvard University Press, 2016).
5. For introductions, see John Pratt, David Brown, Mark Brown, Simon Hallsworth, and Wayne Morrison (eds.), *The New Punitiveness: Trends, Theories, Perspectives* (Cullompton, UK: Willan, 2005); John Pratt, *Penal Populism* (London: Routledge, 2007).
6. David Garland, *The Culture of Control: Crime and Social Order in Contemporary Society* (Chicago: University of Chicago Press, 2001), 9.
7. See especially Katherine Beckett, *Making Crime Pay: Law and Order in Contemporary American Politics* (New York: Oxford University Press, 1997).
8. See, e.g., Alexander, *The New Jim Crow*; and Garland, *The Culture of Control*. Some critics refer to these approaches as "criminologies of catastrophe." See, e.g., Steven Hutchinson, "Countering Catastrophic Criminology: Reform, Punishment, and the Modern Liberal Compromise," *Punishment & Society* 8, no. 4 (2006): 443–67; and Pat O'Malley, "Criminologies of Catastrophe? Understanding Criminal Justice on the Edge of the New Millennium," *Australian & New Zealand Journal of Criminology* 33, no. 2 (2000): 153–67.
9. Mary Bosworth, "Penal Moderation in the United States? Yes We Can," *Criminology & Public Policy* 10, no. 2 (2011): 335–43.

10. Carl Hulse, "On Criminal Justice, the Right and Left Meet in the Center," *New York Times*, February 19, 2015, A1. Rachel Weiner, "Va. Bills That Would Curtail Police Powers Create a 'Weird Alliance,'" *Washington Post* (February 18, 2015), https://www.washingtonpost.com/local/virginia-politics/va-legislation-that-would-curtail-police-powers-create-a-weird-alliance/2015/02/18/0cf88450-b77e-11e4-9423-f3d0a1ec335c_story.html (accessed June 27, 2016).

11. E. Ann Carson and Daniela Golinelli, *Prisoners in 2012: Trends in Admissions and Releases, 1991–2012* (Washington, DC: Bureau of Justice Statistics, 2013).

12. Garland, *The Culture of Control*, 81.

13. Katherine S. Newman, *No Shame in My Game: The Working Poor in the Inner City* (New York: A. A. Knopf and Russell Sage Foundation, 1999), especially xi–xv.

14. Garland, *The Culture of Control*, 82.

15. As Elizabeth Hinton puts it: "When issues of crime control, sentencing, and confinement moved to the center of domestic policy, the strategies federal policymakers adopted for the urban intervention yielded new possibilities for supervision in the halls of urban schools, in the elevators of housing projects, and in the reception rooms of welfare offices. . . . Born from the fusion of law enforcement and the community action, job training, and public housing programs within the Great Society, this network metastasized into the modern carceral state" (Hinton, *From the War on Poverty to the War on Crime*, 13–14). See, more generally, Jonathan Simon, *Governing through Crime: How the War on Crime Transformed American Democracy and Created a Culture of Fear* (New York: Oxford University Press, 2007); Joe Soss, Richard C. Fording, and Sanford F. Schram, *Disciplining the Poor: Neoliberal Paternalism and the Persistent Power of Race* (Chicago: University of Chicago Press, 2011); Loïc Wacquant, *Punishing the Poor: The Neoliberal Government of Social Insecurity* (Durham, NC: Duke University Press, 2009); and Bruce Western, *Punishment and Inequality in America* (New York: Russell Sage Foundation, 2006).

16. See especially Alexander, The New Jim Crow; Victor M. Rios, Punished: Policing the Lives of Black and Latino Boys (New York: New York University Press, 2011); Western, Punishment and Inequality in America; and Loïc Wacquant, Urban Outcasts: A Comparative Sociology of Advanced Marginality (Malden, MA: Polity, 2008b).

17. Ruth D. Peterson and Lauren J. Krivo, Divergent Social Worlds: Neighborhood Crime and the Racial-Spatial Divide (New York: Russell Sage Foundation, 2010). New research, however, suggests that much of the increase in violent crime rates (especially rape and aggravated assault) during the 1970s and 1980s was due to better police reporting rather than increased victimization rates (Janet L. Lauritsen, Maribeth L. Rezey, and Karen Heimer, "When Choice of Data Matters: Analyses of U.S. Crime Trends, 1973–2012," *Journal of Quantitative Criminology* 32, no. 3 (2016): 335–55).

18. Hinton, From the War on Poverty to the War on Crime, 6–7.

19. Beckett, *Making Crime Pay.*

20. Vesla M. Weaver, "Frontlash: Race and the Development of Punitive Crime Policy," *Studies in American Political Development* 21, no. 2 (2007): 230–65. See also Beckett, *Making Crime Pay*; and Katherine Beckett and Theodore Sasson, *The Politics of Injustice: Crime and Punishment in America* (2d ed.) (Thousand Oaks, CA: SAGE, 2004).

21. Weaver, "Frontlash," 240–42.

22. Beckett, *Making Crime Pay.*

23. Naomi Murakawa, *The First Civil Right: How Liberals Built Prison America* (New York: Oxford University Press, 2014). See also Hinton, *From the War on Poverty to the War on Crime*; Lisa Miller, "What's Violence Got to Do with It? Inequality, Punishment, and State Failure in US Politics," *Punishment & Society* 17, no. 2 (2015): 184–210; and Khalil Gibran Muhammad, *The Condemnation of Blackness: Race, Crime, and the Making of Modern Urban America* (Cambridge, MA: Harvard University Press, 2010).

24. Hinton, *From the War on Poverty to the War on Crime*, 57–62.

25. Elizabeth Hinton, "'A War within Our Own Boundaries': Lyndon Johnson's Great Society and the Rise of the Carceral State," *Journal of American History* 102, no. 1 (2015): 100–12, 101.

26. In this manner, the Omnibus Crime Control Act greatly intensified and facilitated the development of aggressive, militarized urban police forces—a trend that has if anything grown even stronger in the wake of 9/11. Radley Balko reminds us that while we have become accustomed to the idea of police forces utilizing tanks and other military gear in the heart of American cities, such practices would have been virtually imaginable a century ago (Balko, *Rise of the Warrior Cop*).

27. Joshua Page, "Why Punishment Is Purple," *Society Pages* (September 26, 2012), https://thesocietypages.org/papers/purple-punishment (accessed June 27, 2016).

28. Beckett, *Making Crime Pay.*

29. Beth Schwartzapfel and Bill Keller, "Willie Horton Revisited," *Marshall Project* (May 13, 2015), https://www.themarshallproject.org/2015/05/13/willie-horton-revisited#.FO7s4JyxH (accessed April 28, 2016).

30. For more on the rise of sex offender laws, see Chrysanthi S. Leon, *Sex Fiends, Perverts, and Pedophiles: Understanding Sex Crime Policy in America* (New York: New York University Press, 2011).

31. Michael C. Campbell and Heather Schoenfeld, "The Transformation of America's Penal Order: A Historicized Political Sociology of Punishment," *American Journal of Sociology* 118, no. 5 (2013): 1375–1423; Lisa L. Miller, *The Perils of Federalism: Race, Poverty, and the Politics of Crime Control* (New York: Oxford University Press, 2008).

32. William J. Stuntz, *The Collapse of American Criminal Justice* (Cambridge, MA: Belknap Press of Harvard University Press, 2011); and John F. Pfaff, *Locked*

*In: The True Causes of Mass Incarceration—and How to Achieve Real Reform* (New York: Basic Books, 2017).

33. E. Ann Carson, *Prisoners in 2014* (Washington, DC: Bureau of Justice Statistics, 2015).

34. Sourcebook of Criminal Justice Statistics Online, "Table 2.1.2012: Attitudes toward the Most Important Problem Facing the Country," http://www.albany.edu/sourcebook/pdf/t212012.pdf (accessed March 3, 2016).

35. David B. Holian, "He's Stealing My Issues! Clinton's Crime Rhetoric and the Dynamics of Issue Ownership," *Political Behavior* 26, no. 2 (2004): 95–124.

36. US Department of Justice, "Violent Crime Control and Law Enforcement Act of 1994," Fact Sheet (October 24, 1994), https://www.ncjrs.gov/txtfiles/billfs.txt (accessed March 3, 2016).

37. Murakawa, *The First Civil Right*, 115–28.

38. Mark D. Ramirez, "Punitive Sentiment," *Criminology* 51, no. 2 (2013): 329–64; Angela J. Thielo, Francis T. Cullen, Derek M. Cohen, and Cecilia Chouhy, "Rehabilitation in a Red State: Public Support for Correctional Reform in Texas," *Criminology & Public Policy* 15, no. 1 (2016): 137–70.

39. Sari Horwitz and Juliet Eilperin, "Obama Commutes Sentences of 46 Nonviolent Drug Offenders," *Washington Post* (July 13, 2015), https://www.washingtonpost.com/world/national-security/obama-commutes-sentences-of-46-non-violent-drug-offenders/2015/07/13/b533f61e-2974-11e5-a250-42bd812efc09_story.html (accessed March 3, 2016).

40. Ari Melber, "Obama Bans the Box," *MSNBC* (November 2, 2015), http://www.msnbc.com/msnbc/obama-bans-the-box (accessed April 28, 2016).

41. Juliet Eilperin, "Obama Bans Solitary Confinement for Juveniles in Federal Prisons," *Washington Post* (January 26, 2016), https://www.washingtonpost.com/politics/obama-bans-solitary-confinement-for-juveniles-in-federal-prisons/2016/01/25/056e14b2-c3a2-11e5-9693-933a4d31bcc8_story.html (accessed March 3, 2016).

42. Beth Schwartzapfel, "Obama Is Reinstating Pell Grants for Prisoners," *Marshall Project* (July 30, 2015), https://www.themarshallproject.org/2015/07/30/obama-is-reinstating-pell-grants-for-prisoners (accessed March 3, 2016); Steven W. Thrasher, "Finally, the Obama I Fell in Love With," *The Guardian* (July 17, 2015), http://www.theguardian.com/commentisfree/2015/jul/17/obama-love-reforms (accessed March 3, 2016).

43. Peter Baker, "Obama Calls for Effort to Fix a 'Broken System' of Criminal Justice," *New York Times* (July 14, 2015), http://www.nytimes.com/2015/07/15/us/politics/obama-calls-for-effort-to-fix-a-broken-system-of-criminal-justice.html?_r=0 (accessed June 27, 2016).

44. Bill Keller, "Congress Prepares to Deliver (a Little) Criminal Justice Reform," *Marshall Project* (October 21, 2015), https://www.themarshallproject.org/2015/10/21/congress-prepares-to-deliver-a-little-criminal-justice-reform#.7TUrfnT9T (accessed March 29, 2016).

45. Bill Keller, "Justice Reform, RIP?," *Marshall Project* (February 12, 2016), https://www.themarshallproject.org/2016/02/12/justice-reform-rip (accessed June 27, 2016).

46. For a complementary perspective on the interactions between national and state-level developments, see Campbell and Schoenfeld, "The Transformation of America's Penal Order."

47. For source references, see figure 5.1.

48. Volker Janssen, "Sunbelt Lock-Up: Where the Suburbs Met the Super-Max," in *Sunbelt Rising: The Politics of Space, Place, and Region*, eds. Michelle Nickerson and Darren Dochuk (Philadelphia: University of Pennsylvania Press, 2011), 217–39.

49. Don Chaddock (California Department of Corrections and Rehabilitation), "Unlocking History: Deuel Vocational Institution Can Trace Roots to WWII Air Field," *Inside CDCR* (August 31, 2015), http://www.insidecdcr.ca.gov/2015/08/unlocking-history-deuel-vocational-institution-can-trace-roots-to-wwii-air-field (accessed May 25, 2016). In a 1983 interview, Procunier claimed that McGee was "a genius," but also complained that McGee was too liberal, especially during his last decades as director (Gabrielle Morris, "The Art of Corrections Management, California, 1967–1974" [Berkeley: Bancroft Library, Regional Oral History Office, University of California, 1984], http://archive.org/stream/artcorrectionsoomorr-rich/artcorrectionsoomorrrich_djvu.txt [accessed May 4, 2016]).

50. Page, *The Toughest Beat*, 29.

51. Heather Jane McCarty, "From Con-Boss to Gang Lord: The Transformation of Social Relations in California Prisons, 1943–1983" (PhD dissertation, University of California, Berkeley, 2004), 255.

52. Michael Campbell, "The Emergence of Penal Extremism in California: A Dynamic View of Institutional Structures and Political Processes," *Law & Society Review* 48, no. 2 (2014): 377–409.

53. For an explanation of declining imprisonment rates under Governor Reagan, see Rosemary Gartner, Anthony N. Doob, and Franklin E. Zimring, "The Past as Prologue? Decarceration in California Then and Now," *Criminology & Public Policy* 10, no. 2 (2011): 291–325.

54. Page, *The Toughest Beat*; Vanessa Barker, *The Politics of Imprisonment: How the Democratic Process Shapes the Way America Punishes Offenders* (New York: Oxford University Press, 2009); and Ruth Wilson Gilmore, *Golden Gulag: Prisons, Surplus, Crisis, and Opposition in Globalizing California* (Berkeley: University of California Press, 2007).

55. Mona Lynch, *Sunbelt Justice: Arizona and the Transformation of American Punishment* (Stanford, CA: Stanford University Press, 2009). In Texas, another punitive exemplar, high imprisonment rates also came late and were driven by a complex mix of factors (including prisoner rights' litigation). For a complementary account comparing California's and Texas's imprisonment trajectories, see Michael Campbell, *Agents of Change: Law Enforcement, Prisons, and Politics in Texas and*

*California* (PhD dissertation, University of California, Irvine, 2009). See also Michael C. Campbell, "Politics, Prisons, and Law Enforcement: An Examination of the Emergence of 'Law and Order' Politics in Texas," *Law & Society Review* 45, no. 3 (2011): 631–65.

56. Lynch, *Sunbelt Justice*, 59.

57. Ibid., 53–84.

58. Ibid., 107.

59. Jeff Biggers, *State Out of the Union: Arizona and the Final Showdown over the American Dream* (New York: Nation Books, 2012), 101–105.

60. Lynch, *Sunbelt Justice*, 107–108.

61. Lisa Guenther, *Solitary Confinement: Social Death and Its Afterlives* (Minneapolis: University of Minnesota Press, 2013).

62. Keramet Reiter, *23/7: Pelican Bay Prison and the Rise of Long-Term Solitary* (New Haven, CT: Yale University Press, 2016). Brett Story argues that the modern use of solitary confinement inside prisons is deeply intertwined with efforts to limit social solidarity and prisoners' power, especially by those on the margins of society ("The Prison Inside: A Genealogy of Solitary Confinement as Counter-resistance," in *Historical Geographies of Prisons: Unlocking the Usable Carceral Past*, eds. Karen M. Morin and Dominique Moran (Abingdon, UK: Routledge, 2015), 34–50.

63. Robert Martinson, "What Works?—Questions and Answers about Prison Reform," *Public Interest* 35 (1974): 22–54, 25. This article was based on a larger collaborative research project (Douglas Lipton, Robert Martinson, and Judith Wilks, *The Effectiveness of Correctional Treatment: A Survey of Treatment Evaluation Studies* [New York: Praeger, 1975]).

64. According to one of Martinson's contemporaries writing in 1975, nearly half the examined evaluations showed *some* indication of a successful intervention (Ted Palmer, "Martinson Revisited," *Journal of Research in Crime and Delinquency* 12, no. 2 (1975): 133–52). For context on Martinson and the impact of his 1974 article, see Michelle Brown, *The Culture of Punishment: Prison, Society, and Spectacle* (New York: New York University Press, 2009), 153–89; Francis T. Cullen, "The Twelve People Who Saved Rehabilitation: How the Science of Criminology Made a Difference," *Criminology* 43, no. 1 (2005): 1–42; and Francis T. Cullen and Karen E. Gilbert, *Reaffirming Rehabilitation* (2d ed.) (New York: Routledge, 2013).

65. *60 Minutes* (Norman Gorin, producer), "It Doesn't Work" (1975).

66. On the myriad ways in which the article became a rallying cry, see Cullen, "The Twelve People Who Saved Rehabilitation"; and Garland, *The Culture of Control*, 60–63.

67. A 1983 Senate report on the proposed legislation noted: "Recent studies suggest that this [rehabilitation] approach has failed [citing Martinson and others in a footnote], and most sentencing judges as well as the Parole Commission agree that the rehabilitation model is not an appropriate basis for sentencing decisions"

(US Senate Report No. 98–225 [August 4, 1983], http://www.fd.org/docs/select-topics---sentencing/SRA-Leg-History.pdf (accessed June 25, 2015).

68. *Mistretta v. United States*, 488 U.S. 361 (1989), 365.

69. American Friends Service Committee, *Struggle for Justice: A Report on Crime and Punishment in America* (New York: Hill & Wang, 1971).

70. Garland, *The Culture of Control*, 55–61.

71. This dissatisfaction with indeterminate sentencing led to the adoption of determinate sentencing schemes in states across the United States, which stripped discretion from judges while increasing the power of prosecutors, whose "aggressiveness" contributed extensively to the expansion of the carceral state. See, more generally, John F. Pfaff, "The War on Drugs and Prison Growth: Limited Importance, Limited Legislative Options," *Harvard Journal on Legislation* 52, no. 1 (2015): 173–220.

72. See, e.g., Palmer, "Martinson Revisited."

73. See, e.g., Mark W. Lipsey and David B. Wilson, "The Efficacy of Psychological, Educational, and Behavioral Treatment: Confirmation from Meta-analysis," *American Psychologist* 48, no. 12 (1993): 1181–1209; Mark W. Lipsey and Francis T. Cullen, "The Effectiveness of Correctional Rehabilitation: A Review of Systematic Reviews," *Annual Review of Law and Social Science* 3 (2007): 297–320; and Cullen, "The Twelve People Who Saved Rehabilitation."

74. See, e.g., Donald A. Andrews and James Bonta, *The Psychology of Criminal Conduct* (2d ed.) (Cincinnati: Anderson, 1998).

75. Cecelia Klingele, "The Promises and Perils of Evidence-Based Corrections," *Notre Dame Law Review* 91, no. 2 (2016): 537–84.

76. Trenchant critiques include that risks and needs are in practice indistinguishable, that actuarial instruments are used in a manner that often disproportionately harms women or visible minorities, that many prison "treatment" programs are coercive in nature, and that such approaches can facilitate criminal justice expansion. See, e.g., Klingele, "The Promises and Perils of Evidence-Based Corrections"; Dawn Moore and Kelly Hannah-Moffat, "The Liberal Veil: Revisiting Canadian Penality," in *The New Punitiveness: Trends, Theories, Perspectives*, eds. John Pratt et al. (Cullompton, UK: Willan, 2005), 85–100; Kelly Hannah-Moffat, "Criminogenic Needs and the Transformative Risk Subject: Hybridizations of Risk/Need in Penality," *Punishment & Society* 7, no. 1 (2005): 29–51; and Paula Maurutto and Kelly Hannah-Moffat, "Assembling Risk and the Restructuring of Penal Control," *British Journal of Criminology* 46, no. 3 (2006): 438–54.

77. In Canada, the risk-needs-responsivity framework was not only popular but was nearly hegemonic throughout the late twentieth century (and remains so today) (Moore and Hannah-Moffat, "The Liberal Veil").

78. For a similar argument in the context of the 2010s, see, for example, John Halushka, "Managing Rehabilitation: Accountability, Discipline, and 'Defensive

Institutionalism' at the Frontlines of Reentry Service Provision" (working paper presented at the "Penal Boundaries" workshop, University of Toronto, 2016).

79. See, e.g., Philip Goodman, "'Another Second Chance': Rethinking Rehabilitation through the Lens of California's Prison Fire Camps," *Social Problems* 59, no. 4 (2012a): 437–58; Lynne A. Haney, *Offending Women: Power, Punishment, and the Regulation of Desire* (Berkeley: University of California Press, 2010); Jill A. McCorkel, *Breaking Women: Gender, Race, and the New Politics of Imprisonment* (New York: New York University Press, 2013); and Rebecca Tiger, *Judging Addicts: Drug Courts and Coercion in the Justice System* (New York: New York University Press, 2012).

80. For additional context, see Shelley Johnson Listwan, Cheryl Lero Jonson, Francis T. Cullen, and Edward Latessa, "Cracks in the Penal Harm Movement: Evidence from the Field," *Criminology & Public Policy* 7, no. 3 (2008): 423–65.

81. There was also a group of researchers who focused on "career criminals" and other groups of "offenders" believed to be responsible for a large amount of crime (and hard to "cure"). This line of research, argues John Hagan, was especially influential in facilitating the buildup of mass incarceration (John Hagan, *Who Are the Criminals? The Politics of Crime Policy from the Age of Roosevelt to the Age of Reagan* [Princeton, NJ: Princeton University Press, 2010]).

82. Michelle S. Phelps, "Rehabilitation in the Punitive Era: The Gap between Rhetoric and Reality in U.S. Prison Programs," *Law & Society Review* 45, no. 1 (2011): 33–68, 49.

83. Ibid., 49–50.

84. Ibid., 53–54.

85. This includes life-skills programs, community readjustment training programs, and other prerelease programs such as finance planning, job application training, and anger management (Phelps, "Rehabilitation in the Punitive Era," 54–55).

86. In keeping with our story of variation across place, the downscaling of prison programs was relative: prisons in the Northeast had a higher ratio of treatment-oriented staff relative to the number of prisoners in the first decade of the twenty-first century than states in the South in the 1980s (Michelle S. Phelps, "The Place of Punishment: Variation in the Provision of Inmate Services Staff across the Punitive Turn," *Journal of Criminal Justice* 40, no. 5 (2012): 348–57).

87. Philip Goodman, "Hero or Inmate, Camp or Prison, Rehabilitation or Labor Extraction: A Multi-level Study of California's Prison Fire Camps" (PhD dissertation, University of California, Irvine, 2010), 59–150. See also Volker Janssen, "From the Inside Out: Therapeutic Penology and Political Liberalism in Postwar California," *Osiris* 22, no. 1 (2007): 116–34.

88. For a useful, if somewhat histrionic, introduction to the early decades of the conservation camp program, see Lloyd Thorpe, *Men to Match the Mountains* (Seattle, WA: Met, 1972).

89. A copy of the speech can be found in the California State Archives (F3717: 438).

90. In terms of the nature of prisoners' labor, there are continuities dating back even earlier. In California's prison highway camps (which the state operated from 1915 to 1974), prisoners used a variety of hand tools to grade the land (but for the purpose of building a road, not fighting a fire). Indeed, even today, prisoners and staff in the fire camps refer to those camp prisoners who fight fires as "on the grade," or "grade eligible," terms that presumably date back to the highway camps. Furthermore, and unlike Florida's road prisons (discussed in chapter 4), California considered highway camp prisoners "honor prisoners," and they enjoyed many of the same relative liberties as those housed in the fire camps, and somewhat more comfortable living conditions (Goodman, "Hero or Inmate, Camp or Prison, Rehabilitation or Labor Extraction," 66–88).

91. Goodman, "Another Second Chance."

92. Goodman, "Hero or Inmate, Camp or Prison, Rehabilitation or Labor Extraction," 59–150.

93. Michelle S. Phelps, "Mass Probation: Toward a More Robust Theory of State Variation in Punishment," *Punishment & Society* OnlineFirst (May 10, 2016).

94. Jonathan Simon, "Punishment and the Political Technologies of the Body," in *The SAGE Handbook of Punishment and Society*, eds. Jonathan Simon and Richard Sparks (London: SAGE, 2013), 60–89.

95. Phelps, "Mass Probation," 7–8.

96. Michelle S. Phelps, "The Paradox of Probation: Community Supervision in the Age of Mass Incarceration," *Law & Policy* 35, no. 1–2 (2013): 51–80.

97. On the new discourses more generally, and the role of community supervision, see Malcolm M. Feeley and Jonathan Simon, "The New Penology: Notes on the Emerging Strategy of Corrections and Its Implications," *Criminology* 30, no. 4 (1992): 449–74.

98. For recent analyses of these trends, see Marie Gottschalk, *Caught: The Prison State and the Lockdown of American Politics* (Princeton, NJ: Princeton University Press, 2015); Hadar Aviram, *Cheap on Crime: Recession-Era Politics and the Transformation of American Punishment* (Berkeley: University of California Press, 2015); David A. Green, "US Penal-Reform Catalysts, Drivers, and Prospects," *Punishment & Society* 17, no. 3 (2015): 271–98; Katherine Beckett, Anna Reosti, and Emily Knaphus, "The End of an Era? Understanding the Contradictions of Criminal Justice Reform," *ANNALS of the American Academy of Political and Social Science* 664, no. 1 (2016): 238–59; Heather Schoenfeld, "A Research Agenda on Reform: Penal Policy and Politics across the States," *ANNALS of the American Academy of Political and Social Science* 664, no. 1 (2016): 155–74; and Todd R. Clear and Natasha A. Frost, *The Punishment Imperative: The Rise and Failure of Mass Incarceration in America* (New York: New York University Press, 2013). See also Michelle S. Phelps, "Possibilities and Contestation in Twenty-First-Century US Criminal Justice Downsizing," *Annual Review of Law & Social Science* 12 (2017), for an account that applies the agonistic perspective and expands on the themes of this chapter.

99. Carson and Golinelli, *Prisoners in 2012*.

100. Sentencing Project, *U.S. Prison Population Trends: Broad Variation among States in Recent Years* (Washington, DC: Sentencing Project, 2015). These declines allowed many states to close down entire prisons and reduce correctional costs (Susan F. Turner, Lois M. Davis, Terry Fain, Helen Braithwaite, Theresa Lavery, Wayne Choinski, and George Camp, "A National Picture of Prison Downsizing Strategies," *Victims & Offenders* 10, no. 4 (2015): 401–19). However, on the complexities of reducing correctional costs, see John F. Pfaff, "The Complicated Economics of Prison Reform," *Michigan Law Review* 114, no. 6 (2016): 951–81.

101. Jessica M. Eaglin, "Against Neorehabilitation," *SMU Law Review* 66, no. 1 (2013): 189–226; David A. Green, "Penal Optimism and Second Chances: The Legacies of American Protestantism and the Prospects for Penal Reform," *Punishment & Society* 15, no. 2 (2013): 123–46; and Shannon M. Graves, "Correctional Mission Statements as Indicators of the Criminal Justice Policy Environment: A Research Note," *Criminal Justice Policy Review* 26, no. 5 (2015): 488–99.

102. Gottschalk, *Caught*.

103. David Dagan and Steven M. Teles, "The Social Construction of Policy Feedback: Incarceration, Conservatism, and Ideological Change," *Studies in American Political Development* 29, no. 2 (2015): 127–53.

104. Sara Steen and Rachel Bandy, "When the Policy Becomes the Problem: Criminal Justice in the New Millennium," *Punishment & Society* 9, no. 1 (2007): 5–26.

105. Aviram, *Cheap on Crime*.

106. Josh Sanburn, "Murders in U.S. Cities Reach Record Lows Again," *Time*, January 2, 2014.

107. Green, "US Penal-Reform Catalysts, Drivers, and Prospects."

108. See, e.g., Sentencing Project, *Fewer Prisoners, Less Crime: A Tale of Three States* (Washington, DC: Sentencing Project, 2015).

109. Schoenfeld, "A Research Agenda on Reform."

110. Margo Schlanger, "Civil Rights Injunctions over Time: A Case Study of Jail and Prison Court Orders," *New York University Law Review* 81, no. 2 (2006): 550–630.

111. Jonathan Simon, *Mass Incarceration on Trial: A Remarkable Court Decision and the Future of Prisons in America* (New York: New Press, 2014).

112. Cf. Listwan et al., "Cracks in the Penal Harm Movement."

113. Lynch, *Sunbelt Justice*, 206–207.

114. Ibid., 187. For a similar argument in Florida, see Heather Schoenfeld, "Mass Incarceration and the Paradox of Prison Conditions Litigation," *Law & Society Review* 44, no. 3–4 (2010): 731–68.

115. Lynch, *Sunbelt Justice*, 189–91.

116. American Civil Liberties Union, "Arizona Agrees to Major Improvements in Prison Health Care, Crucial Limits on Solitary Confinement in Landmark Settlement," press release, (October 14, 2014), https://www.aclu.org/news/

arizona-agrees-major-improvements-prison-health-care-crucial-limits-solitary-confinement (accessed June 23, 2016).

117. Although we focus here on solitary confinement, there have been other recent legal victories, such as a 2014 settlement in which Arizona agreed to completely overhaul its prison health system.

118. Keramet Reiter, "The Most Restrictive Alternative: A Litigation History of Solitary Confinement in U.S. Prisons, 1960–2006," *Studies in Law, Politics, and Society* 57 (2012), 71–124.

119. Marie Gottschalk, "Staying Alive: Reforming Solitary Confinement in U.S. Prisons and Jails," *Yale Law Journal Forum* 125 (2016): 253–66, 256.

120. Reiter, "The Most Restrictive Alternative."

121. Guenther, *Solitary Confinement.*

122. For a review of this literature, see American Civil Liberties Union, *Briefing Paper: The Dangerous Overuse of Solitary Confinement in the United States* (New York: American Civil Liberties Union, 2014).

123. American Civil Liberties Union, *Briefing Paper*, 4.

124. Atul Gawande, "Hellhole: The United States Holds Tens of Thousands of Inmates in Long-Term Solitary Confinement: Is This Torture?," *New Yorker* (March 30, 2009), http://www.newyorker.com/magazine/2009/03/30/hellhole (accessed June 27, 2016).

125. One the role of prisoners, more generally, in shaping and critiquing the carceral state through litigation, see Robert T. Chase, "We Are Not Slaves: Rethinking the Rise of Carceral States through the Lens of the Prisoners' Rights Movement," *Journal of American History* 102, no. 1 (2015): 73–86.

126. Keramet Reiter, "The Pelican Bay Hunger Strike: Resistance within the Structural Constraints of a US Supermax Prison," *South Atlantic Quarterly* 113, no. 3 (2014): 579–611.

127. David Cole, "Solitary Confinement: The Beginning of the End?," *New York Review of Books* (September 10, 2015), http://www.nybooks.com/daily/2015/09/10/solitary-confinement-beginning-end (accessed March 3, 2016); Paige St. John, "California Agrees to Move Thousands of Inmates Out of Solitary Confinement," *Los Angeles Times* (September 1, 2015), http://www.latimes.com/local/lanow/la-me-ln-california-will-move-thousands-of-inmates-out-of-solitary-20150901-story.html (accessed March 3, 2016).

128. Eilperin, "Obama Bans Solitary Confinement for Juveniles in Federal Prisons."

129. Dagan and Teles, "The Social Construction of Policy Feedback," 142.

130. Green, "Penal Optimism and Second Chances."

131. Jeremy Travis, "Reflections on the Reentry Movement," *Federal Sentencing Reporter* 20, no. 2 (2007): 84–87.

132. Sara Steen, Traci Lacock, and Shelby McKinzey, "Unsettling the Discourse of Punishment? Competing Narratives of Reentry and the Possibilities for Change," *Punishment & Society* 14, no. 1 (2012): 29–50; Eaglin, "Against Neorehabilitation."

133. Klingele, "The Promises and Perils of Evidence-Based Corrections."

134. Carson and Golinelli, *Prisoners in 2012*, 2.

135. Jim Parsons, Qing Wei, Christian Henrichson, Ernest Drucker, and Jennifer Trone, *End of an Era? The Impact of Drug Law Reform in New York City* (New York: Vera Institute, 2015).

136. Julilly Kohler-Hausmann, "'The Attila the Hun Law': New York's Rockefeller Drug Laws and the Making of a Punitive State," *Journal of Social History* 44, no. 1 (2010): 71–95.

137. Barker, *The Politics of Imprisonment*, 146–50.

138. Ibid., 144; Julilly Kohler-Hausmann, "'The Attila the Hun Law,'" 76; Michael Javen Fortner, *Black Silent Majority: The Rockefeller Drug Laws and the Politics of Punishment* (Cambridge, MA: Harvard University Press, 2015), 129–30.

139. Marie Gottschalk, *The Prison and the Gallows*, 180–82; and Lauritsen, Rezey, and Heimer, "When Choice of Data Matters."

140. Heather Ann Thompson, *Blood in the Water: The Attica Prison Uprising of 1971 and Its Legacy* (New York: Pantheon, 2016).

141. Vanessa Barker, *The Politics of Imprisonment*, 149.

142. The votes were 41 to 14 in the Senate and 80 to 65 in the assembly (Barker, *The Politics of Imprisonment*, 149).

143. For other examples and discussions of black elite support for punitive crime policy, see James Forman Jr., "Racial Critiques of Mass Incarceration: Beyond the New Jim Crow," *New York University Law Review* 87, no. 1 (2012): 101–46; and Gottschalk, *Caught*, 149–58.

144. Barker, *The Politics of Imprisonment*, 151.

145. Donna Murch, "Who's to Blame for Mass Incarceration?," *Boston Review* (October 16, 2015), https://bostonreview.net/books-ideas/donna-murch-michael-javen-fortner-black-silent-majority (accessed March 2, 2016); Marc Parry, "Defending Their Homes: How Crime-Terrorized African-Americans Helped Spur Mass Incarceration," *Chronicle of Higher Education* (August 3, 2015), http://chronicle.com/article/Black-Silent-Majority/231983 (accessed June 22, 2016).

146. Regarding a similar debate over black support for the 1994 crime bill, Elizabeth Hinton, Julilly Kohler-Hausmann, and Vesla Weaver argue that this process can be understood as *selective hearing*: "Policy makers pointed to black support for greater punishment and surveillance, without recognizing accompanying demands to redirect power and economic resources to low-income minority communities. When blacks ask for *better* policing, legislators tend to hear *more* instead" ("Did Blacks Really Endorse the 1994 Crime Bill?," *New York Times* [April 13, 2016], A25, http://www.nytimes.com/2016/04/13/opinion/did-blacks-really-endorse-the-1994-crime-bill.html [accessed September 14, 2016]).

147. Barker, *The Politics of Imprisonment*, 126. See also Bert Useem, "Right-Sizing Corrections in New York," *Justice Research and Policy* 12, no. 1 (2010): 89–112.

148. Fortner, *Black Silent Majority*.

149. Michael Javen Fortner, "The Carceral State and the Crucible of Black Politics: An Urban History of the Rockefeller Drug Laws," *Studies in American Political Development* 27, no. 1 (2013): 14–35, 28.

150. Max H. Seigel, "Lindsay Assails Governor's Plan to Combat Drugs," *New York Times* (January 10, 1973, p. 1), as quoted in Kohler-Hausmann, "'The Attila the Hun Law,'" 81.

151. Joseph E. Persico, *The Imperial Rockefeller: A Biography of Nelson A. Rockefeller* (New York: Simon and Schuster, 1982), as summarized in Jennifer Gonnerman, *Life on the Outside: The Prison Odyssey of Elaine Bartlett* (New York: Picador, 2005), 52.

152. Fortner, *Black Silent Majority*, 193.

153. Kohler-Hausmann, "'The Attila the Hun Law,'" 85; John F. Pfaff, "The War on Drugs and Prison Growth," figure 7.

154. David F. Weiman and Christopher Weiss, "The Origins of Mass Incarceration in New York State: The Rockefeller Drug Laws and the Local War on Drugs," in *Do Prisons Make Us Safer? The Benefits and Costs of the Prison Boom*, eds. Steven Raphael and Michael A. Stoll (New York: Russell Sage Foundation, 2009), 73–116, 95.

155. Kohler-Hausmann, "'The Attila the Hun Law,'" 85–86.

156. Craig Reinarman and Harry G. Levine, *Crack in America: Demon Drugs and Social Justice* (Berkeley: University of California Press, 1997); Donna Murch, "Crack in Los Angeles: Crisis, Militarization, and Black Response to the Late Twentieth-Century War on Drugs," *Journal of American History* 102, no. 1 (2015): 162–73.

157. Quoted in Gottschalk, *Caught*, 264.

158. For the classic statement on broken windows policing, see James Q. Wilson and George L. Kelling, "Broken Windows: The Police and Neighborhood Safety," *Atlantic Monthly* 249, no. 3 (1982): 29–38.

159. Neil Smith, "Giuliani Time: The Revanchist 1990s," *Social Text* 57 (Winter 1998), 1–20.

160. Weiman and Weiss, "The Origins of Mass Incarceration in New York State," 95.

161. Barker, *The Politics of Imprisonment*, 153; Jan M. Chaiken, *Correctional Populations in the United States, 1997* (Washington, DC: Bureau of Justice Statistics, 2000).

162. Barker, *The Politics of Imprisonment*, 152.

163. Ernest Drucker, "Population Impact of Mass Incarceration under New York's Rockefeller Drug Laws: An Analysis of Years of Life Lost," *Journal of Urban Health: Bulletin of the New York Academy of Medicine* 79, no. 3 (2002), 434–35.

164. Franklin E. Zimring, *The City That Became Safe: New York's Lessons for Urban Crime and Its Control* (New York: Oxford University Press, 2012), 6.

165. Zimring, *The City That Became Safe*, 51.

166. In fact, scholars continue to debate the causes of the crime decline—which emerged in cities across the country—and there is no evidence that the "war on drugs" propelled this success. At best, overall increases in incarceration played a

small role in crime reductions in the 1990s (Alfred Blumstein and Joel Wallman [eds.], *The Crime Drop in America* [rev. ed.] [New York: Cambridge University Press, 2006]).

167. To fund this work, Kunstler established the William Moses Kunstler Fund for Racial Justice, a charitable organization that continues to organize protests around New York's drug laws today. Kunstler, it is worth noting, also played a key role in representing the inmates involved in the Attica Prison riots. For more information, see http://kunstler.org/about.html (accessed March 28, 2015).

168. This group included Elaine Bartlett, who received a sentence of 20 years to life for her minor role in the sale of four ounces of cocaine in upstate New York. Bartlett played the starring role in a number of articles and a popular book by journalist Jennifer Gonnerman (*Life on the Outside*).

169. Judith Greene and Marc Mauer, *Downscaling Prisons: Lessons from Four States* (Washington, DC: Sentencing Project, 2010), 13.

170. Marc Mauer, *The Changing Racial Dynamics of the War on Drugs* (Washington, DC: Sentencing Project, 2009), 16–17.

171. Correctional Association of New York, "Letter from the Director," (April 1, 2003), http://www.correctionalassociation.org/news/letter-from-the-director (accessed March 28, 2015).

172. Amanda B. Cissner, Michael Rempel, Allyson Walker Franklin, John Roman, Samuel Bieler, Robyn L. Cohen and Carolyn R. Cadoret, *A Statewide Evaluation of New York's Adult Drug Courts: Identifying Which Policies Work Best*, (New York: Center for Court Innovation, 2013).

173. Tiger, *Judging Addicts*. For a Canadian study of specialized courts (including drug courts) making a similar point, see Kelly Hannah-Moffat and Paula Maurutto, "Shifting and Targeted Forms of Penal Governance: Bail, Punishment, and Specialized Courts," *Theoretical Criminology* 16, no. 2 (2012): 201–19.

174. Greene and Mauer, *Downscaling Prisons*, 11–12.

175. Ibid., 14–15.

176. Ibid., 7.

177. Barker, *The Politics of Imprisonment*, 164; Useem, "Right-Sizing Corrections in New York."

178. Barker, *The Crisis of Imprisonment*, 161; Greene and Mauer, *Downscaling Prisons*, 16–17.

179. Barker, *The Politics of Imprisonment*, 165; Greene and Mauer, *Downscaling Prisons*, 17.

180. Greene and Mauer, *Downscaling Prisons*, 18.

181. Barker, *The Politics of Imprisonment*, 165–66.

182. New York Civil Liberties Union, "Hundreds Rally at Governor's NYC Office, Demand End of Rockefeller Drug Laws" (March 25, 2009), http://www.nyclu.org/node/2313 (accessed March 28, 2015).

183. Greene and Mauer, *Downscaling Prisons*, 24–25.

184. These include eliminating the remaining barriers for diversion (individuals convicted of the most-serious offenses or with a violent felony conviction in the last 10 years are still excluded), basing sentences on individuals' *role* in the drug trade rather than the *amount* of drugs, and addressing the cases of currently incarcerated drug offenders (Correctional Association of New York, "Analysis of Rockefeller Drug Law Reform Bill," May 1, 2009, http://www.correctiona-lassociation.org/resource/analysis-of-rockefeller-drug-law-reform-bill [accessed March 28, 2015]).

185. Greene and Mauer, *Downscaling Prisons*, 21–22; Parsons et al., *End of an Era?* The reductions in racial disparities are also reflective of a national shrinking of the racial gap in incarceration rates, as black incarceration rates decline while those for whites increase (Mauer, *The Changing Racial Dynamics of the War on Drugs*).

186. Issa Kohler-Hausmann, "Jumping Bunnies and Legal Rules: The Organizational Sociologist and the Legal Scholar Should Be Friends," in *The New Criminal Justice Thinking*, eds. Sharon Dolovich and Alexandra Natapoff (New York: New York University Press, in press), figures 1 and 2. See also Pfaff, "The War on Drugs and Prison Growth," figure 7. Ironically, the decline in prison sentences for drug offenses was in part a consequence of Bratton's infamous policing strategy to focus on low-level arrest, which resulted in fewer felony arrests being brought to the courts (James Austin and Michael P. Jacobson, *How New York City Reduced Mass Incarceration: A Model for Change?* [New York: Vera Institute of Justice, 2013], 22–24).

187. Ram Subramanian and Ruth Delaney, "Playbook for Change? States Reconsider Mandatory Sentences," *Federal Sentencing Reporter* 26, no. 3 (2014): 198–211.

188. Carson and Golinelli, *Prisoners in 2012*, 2.

189. Matt Ferner and Nick Wing, "GOP Congressman's Bill Would Subject Heroin Dealers To The Death Penalty," *Huffington Post* (September 29, 2016), http://www.huffingtonpost.com/entry/heroin-dealers-death-penalty_us_57ec4051e4b024a52d2cc053 (accessed October 4, 2016).

CHAPTER 6

1. As we mentioned in the introduction, our use of this agonistic perspective focuses almost exclusively on prisons, probation, and parole (with special attention to prisons). However, we think that the agonistic framework could be profitably employed to analyze other criminal justice arenas (such as policing), and potentially other spheres of public policy. And although we limited our focus herein to the United States, we hope our perspective will prove useful to those working outside the American penal context.

2. Herbert Blumer, "What Is Wrong with Social Theory?," *American Sociological Review* 19, no. 1 (1954): 3–10. As Blumer writes, sensitizing concepts give "the user a general sense of reference and guidance in approaching empirical instances" (p. 7).

3. Marie Gottschalk, "The Folly of Neoliberal Prison Reform," *Boston Review* (June 8, 2015), http://bostonreview.net/books-ideas/marie-gottschalk-neoliberal-prison-reform-caught (accessed June 15, 2015).

4. Marc Mauer and David Cole, "How to Lock Up Fewer People," *New York Times* (May 23, 2015), http://www.nytimes.com/2015/05/24/opinion/sunday/how-to-lock-up-fewer-people.html (accessed June 1, 2016).

5. Bill Keller, "Congress Prepares to Deliver (a Little) Criminal Justice Reform," *Marshall Project* (October 21, 2015), https://www.themarshallproject.org/2015/10/21/congress-prepares-to-deliver-a-little-criminal-justice-reform#.7TUrfnT9T (accessed March 29, 2016).

6. Dan Friedman, "Top Former Law Enforcement Officials Buck Bipartisan Calls for Sentencing Reform," *Washington Examiner* (December 10, 2015), http://www.washingtonexaminer.com/top-former-law-enforcement-officials-buck-bipartisan-calls-for-sentencing-reform/article/2578116#.Vm9J2pJls1Q.twitter (accessed March 29, 2016).

7. Steven H. Cook, written statement for the United States Senate Committee on the judiciary hearing on "The Sentencing Reform and Corrections Act of 2015" (October 19, 2015), http://www.judiciary.senate.gov/imo/media/doc/10-19-15%20Cook%20Testimony.pdf (accessed March 29, 2016).

8. Jeff Sessions, Tom Cotton, David Vitter, and David Perdue, "'Dear Colleague' letter to the United States Senate" (February 9, 2016), https://t.co/QkKNBlyvTv (accessed March 29, 2016).

9. Bill Keller, "Justice Reform, RIP?," *Marshall Project* (February 12, 2016), https://www.themarshallproject.org/2016/02/12/justice-reform-rip?utm_medium=email&utm_campaign=newsletter&utm_source=opening-statement&utm_term=newsletter-20160212-383#.QgvFCgAU7 (accessed March 29, 2016).

10. For example, opposition to New York governor Andrew Cuomo's plans to provide college courses for prisoners, the struggle against the Minnesota Sentencing Guideline Commission's efforts to reduce sentences for drug offenses (a modified version of which passed in May 2016), support for tougher mandatory sentences in Louisiana, and the return of mandatory minimums for drug offenses in Indiana (Thomas Kaplan, "Cuomo Drops Plan to Use State Money to Pay for College Classes for Inmates," *New York Times* (April 2, 2014), A23; Andy Mannix, "Legislator Moves to Block Landmark Drug Overhaul," *Star Tribune* (February 23, 2016), http://www.startribune.com/legislators-move-to-block-landmark-drug-overhaul/369746641 (accessed March 30, 2016); Julia O'Donoghue, "Lawmakers Continue Tougher Mandatory Sentences for Violent Crimes," *NOLA.com* (March 29, 2016), http://www.nola.com/politics/index.ssf/2016/03/mandatory_minimum_violent_crim.html (accessed May 18, 2016); Nick Wing, Roque Planas, and Ryan Grim, "Drug Warriors Say 'Bring Back the War on Drugs Because It Totally Worked," *Huffington Post* (September 10, 2015), http://www.huffingtonpost.com/entry/drug-war-william-bennett-john-walters_us_55f1ae50e4b03784e27840fb (accessed

March 30, 2016); and Dan Carden, "Pence Reinstates Mandatory Minimum Prison Terms for Some Drug Crimes," *Northwest Indiana Times* (March 21, 2016), http://www.nwitimes.com/news/local/govt-and-politics/pence-reinstates-mandatory-minimum-prison-terms-for-some-drug-crimes/article_7438d356-3c54-54aa-b68a-8b0b7c3c640e.html (accessed June 6, 2016).

11. Simone Weichselbaum, "Top Cops and Prosecutors Form Alliance to Battle Crime and Prison Crowding," *Marshall Project* (October 10, 2015), https://www.themarshallproject.org/2015/10/21/top-cops-and-prosecutors-form-alliance-to-battle-crime-and-prison-crowding#.72RdUjCrB (accessed March 29, 2016).

12. Timothy Williams, "Police Leaders Join Call to Cut Prison Rosters," *New York Times* (October 20, 2015), http://mobile.nytimes.com/2015/10/21/us/police-leaders-join-call-to-cut-prison-rosters.html?referer=https://t.co/OLfOHLsFHH&_r=4 (accessed March 30, 2016).

13. Joshua Page, *The Toughest Beat: Politics, Punishment, and the Prison Officers Union in California* (New York: Oxford University Press, 2011); Jonathan Simon, *Governing through Crime: How the War on Crime Transformed American Democracy and Created a Culture of Fear* (New York: Oxford University Press, 2007); David Garland, *The Culture of Control: Crime and Order in Contemporary Society* (Chicago: University of Chicago Press, 2001); and Katherine Beckett and Theodore Sasson, *The Politics of Injustice: Crime and Punishment in America* (2d ed.) (Thousand Oaks, CA: SAGE, 2004). On the concept of "moral capital," see Jennifer Sherman, "Coping with Rural Poverty: Economic Survival and Moral Capital in Rural America," *Social Forces* 85, no. 2 (2006): 891–913; and Mariana Valverde, "Moral Capital," *Canadian Journal of Law & Society* 9, no. 1 (1994): 213–32.

14. Mark Obbie, "Can a New Victims Advocacy Movement Break Cycles of Violence?," *Al Jazeera America* (January 13, 2006), http://america.aljazeera.com/articles/2016/1/13/a-new-advocacy-movements-breaks-cycle-of-victimization-and-violence.html (accessed May 30, 2016).

15. See, for example, Californians for Safety and Justice, *California Crime Victims' Voices: Findings from the First-Ever Survey of California Crime Victims and Survivors* (2013), http://www.courts.ca.gov/documents/BTB_XXII_IIIE_3.pdf (accessed June 10, 2016).

16. Given the counterdoxic position of these groups, it should not come as a surprise that the leader of CVUC says about such organizations as CSJ: "I think it's very misleading for a crime victims' group to say, 'We're representing victims, yet we're weakening our laws and lessening protection for the most vulnerable in our society.' . . . I really wouldn't say that they are crime victim advocates." There is now a symbolic struggle to determine who gets to speak as (and for) crime victims—and what constitutes acceptable positions for crime victim advocates' to take (Mark Obbie, "Can a New Victims Advocacy Movement Break Cycles of Violence?," *Aljazeera America* (January 13, 2016), http://america.aljazeera.com/articles/2016/1/13/

a-new-advocacy-movements-breaks-cycle-of-victimization-and-violence.html (accessed June 24, 2016).

17. Totals calculated using the online *New York Times* archive on October 3, 2016, with the search term "incarceration OR imprisonment."

18. Editorial Board, "End Mass Incarceration Now," *New York Times* (May 24, 2014), http://www.nytimes.com/2014/05/25/opinion/sunday/end-mass-incarceration-now.html (accessed September 14, 2016).

19. Robert Mann, "David Vitter Is a Cheap Political Prostitute: Even Louisiana Racists Smell the Desperation in His Foul New Campaign Ad," *Salon* (October 28, 2015), http://www.salon.com/2015/10/28/david_vitter_is_a_cheap_political_prostitute_even_louisiana_racists_smell_the_desperation_in_his_foul_new_campaign_ad (accessed March 30, 2016); Carl Hulse, "Bipartisan Criminal Justice Overhaul Is Haunted by Willie Horton," *New York Times* (January 4, 2016), http://www.nytimes.com/2016/01/05/us/politics/bipartisan-criminal-justice-overhaul-is-haunted-by-willie-horton.html?_r=0 (accessed March 30, 2016); David Weigel, "David Vitter Ad Stokes Fear of 'Dangerous Thugs' Freed by Criminal Justice Reform," *Washington Post* (October 28, 2015), https://www.washingtonpost.com/news/post-politics/wp/2015/10/28/david-vitter-ad-stokes-fear-of-dangerous-thugs-freed-by-criminal-justice-reform (accessed March 30, 2016).

20. See, e.g., Editorial Board, "Obama Must Push for Reforms at Nation's Police Departments," *Boston Globe* (December 3, 2014), https://www.bostonglobe.com/opinion/editorials/2014/12/03/obama-must-push-for-reforms-nation-police-departments/ec1iDaBb3MEF30EzAAlUMN/story.html (accessed June 6, 2016).

21. Maurice Chammah, "The Dissenters: Not Everybody Is Aboard the Criminal Justice Reform Bandwagon; Here's Why," *Marshall Project* (November 6, 2015), https://www.themarshallproject.org/2015/11/06/the-dissenters#.Fc93j6GKo (accessed June 23, 2016).

22. Barry Latzer, "The Myth of Mass Incarceration," *Wall Street Journal* (February 22, 2016), http://www.wsj.com/article_email/the-myth-of-mass-incarceration-1456184736-lMyQjAxMTA2NDIyMzEyNDM4Wj (accessed March 30, 2016).

23. Friedman, "Top Former Law Enforcement Officials Buck Bipartisan Calls for Sentencing Reform."

24. Carl Takei, "From Mass Incarceration to Mass Control, and Back Again: How Bipartisan Criminal Justice Reform May Lead to a For-Profit Nightmare," *University of Pennsylvania Journal of Law and Social Change* 20 (forthcoming).

25. For an international perspective on how the concept of justice might reinvigorate penal reform, see Stephen Farrall, Barry Goldson, Ian Loader, and Anita Dockley (eds.), *Justice and Penal Reform: Re-shaping the Penal Landscape* (New York: Routledge, 2016).

26. James Forman Jr., "Racial Critiques of Mass Incarceration: Beyond the New Jim Crow," *New York University Law Review* 87, no. 1 (2012), 101–46; Marie Gottschalk,

*Caught: The Prison State and the Lockdown of American Politics* (Princeton, NJ: Princeton University Press, 2015).

27. E. Ann Carson, *Prisoners in 2013* (Washington, DC: Bureau of Justice Statistics, 2014).

28. James Austin, Eric Cadora, Todd R. Clear, Kara Dansky, Judith Greene, Vanita Gupta, Marc Mauer, Nicole Porter, Susan Tucker, and Malcolm C. Young, *Ending Mass Incarceration: Charting a New Justice Reinvestment* (Washington, DC: Sentencing Project, 2013).

29. Christopher Seeds, "Bifurcation Nation: Strategy in Contemporary American Punishment," SSRN Scholarly Paper (2015); Katherine Beckett, Anna Reosti, and Emily Knaphus, "The End of an Era? Understanding the Contradictions of Criminal Justice Reform," *ANNALS of the American Academy of Political and Social Science* 664, no. 1 (2016): 238–59; and Gottschalk, *Caught*.

30. Gottschalk, *Caught*.

31. Hadar Aviram, "The Correctional Hunger Games: Understanding Realignment in the Context of the Great Recession," *ANNALS of the American Academy of Political and Social Science* 664, no. 1 (2016): 260–79.

32. Marie Gottschalk, "Sentenced to Life: Penal Reforms and the Most Severe Sanctions," *Annual Review of Law and Social Science* 9 (2013), 353–82, 354.

33. See, e.g., California's recent decision to loosen housing restrictions for some sex offenders (Kate Mather and Victoria Kim, "California Eases Jessica's Law Restrictions for Some Sex Offenders," *Los Angeles Times* (March 26, 2015), http://www.latimes.com/local/crime/la-me-jessica-law-20150327-story.html#page=1 (accessed June 14, 2016).

34. See, e.g., Jonathan Simon, "Reconsidering the Punishment of Violent Crime," *PrawfsBlawg* (July 9, 2009), http://prawfsblawg.blogs.com/prawfsblawg/2009/07/reconsidering-the-punishment-of-violent-crime.html (accessed June 5, 2016); Mauer and Cole, "How to Lock Up Fewer People"; and Gottschalk, *Caught*.

35. John F. Pfaff, *Locked In: The True Causes of Mass Incarceration—and How to Achieve Real Reform* (New York: Basic Books, 2017); Gottschalk, *Caught*, 266–68.

36. Morning Consult and Vox. National Tracking Poll (Project 160812), https://cdn3.vox-cdn.com/uploads/chorus_asset/file/7052001/160812_topline_Vox_vi_AP.0.pdf (accessed October 3, 2016).

37. Pew Charitable Trusts, *Public Opinion on Sentencing and Corrections Policy in America* (Washington DC: Pew Charitable Trusts, 2012).

38. Gottschalk, *Caught*; Sara Steen, Traci Lacock, and Shelby McKinzey, "Unsettling the Discourse of Punishment? Competing Narratives of Reentry and the Possibilities for Change," *Punishment & Society* 14, no. 1 (2012): 29–50; and Cecelia Klingele, "The Promises and Perils of Evidence-Based Corrections," *Notre Dame Law Review* 91, no. 2 (2016): 537–84.

39. James Kilgore, "Opposing Mass Incarceration Is 'Trendy,' but Can We Stop the Train of Piecemeal Reform?," *Truthout* (June 3, 2016), http://www.truth-out.org/opinion/

item/36277-opposing-mass-incarceration-is-trendy-but-can-we-stop-the-train-of-piecemeal-reform (accessed June 5, 2016); Nicole D. Porter, "Unfinished Project of Civil Rights in the Era of Mass Incarceration and the Movement for Black Lives," *Wake Forest Journal of Law & Policy* 6, no. 1 (2016): 1–34; Keeanga-Yamahtta Taylor, *From #BlackLivesMatter to Black Liberation* (Chicago: Haymarket, 2016); Amy E. Lerman and Vesla M. Weaver, "Protest Is Democracy at Work," *Slate* (December 23, 2014), http://www.slate.com/articles/news_and_politics/jurisprudence/2014/12/police_brutality_protesters_history_of_civil_rights_women_s_suffrage_child. html (accessed March 5, 2016); and Deva Woodly, "Black Lives Matter: The Politics of Race and Movement in the 21st Century," *Public Seminar* (January 18, 2016), http://www.publicseminar.org/2016/01/black-lives-matter-the-politics-of-race-and-movement-in-the-21st-century/#.V1Rg1pMrJBz (accessed March 5, 2016).

40. Gottschalk argues that this social-structural argument is correct; however, she warns against insisting on social-structural reform as a condition for criminal justice reform. There are many policy changes that can be made to shrink the carceral state without simultaneously reducing structural inequality (Gottschalk, *Caught*, 277–79).

41. Keramet Reiter, "The Pelican Bay Hunger Strike: Resistance within the Structural Constraints of a US Supermax Prison," *South Atlantic Quarterly* 113, no. 3 (2014): 579–611.

42. "Alabama Prison Strike Organizer Speaks from Behind Bars: We Are Engaged in a Struggle for Our Lives," *Democracy Now!* (May 13, 2016), http://www.democracynow.org/2016/5/13/alabama_prison_strike_organizer_speaks_from (accessed May 29, 2016).

43. Beth Schwartzappfel, "A Primer on the Nationwide Prisoners' Strike," *The Marshall Project* (September 27, 2016), https://www.themarshallproject.org/2016/09/27/a-primer-on-the-nationwide-prisoners-strike#.1WW5BjfFi (accessed October 4, 2016).

44. See especially Francis Fox Piven, *Challenging Authority: How Ordinary People Change America* (Lanham, MD: Rowman & Littlefield, 2006).

45. Kim Bell, "Trump Blames Gangs of Illegal Immigrants for Woes in Ferguson, St. Louis," *St. Louis Dispatch* (August 26, 2015), http://www.stltoday.com/news/local/govt-and-politics/trump-blames-gangs-of-illegal-immigrants-for-woes-in-ferguson/article_ab07521a-1426-5799-9908-00e3eeb5398b.html (accessed June 11, 2016).

46. Piven, *Challenging Authority*.

47. See, e.g., David Garland, *The Culture of Control: Crime and Social Order in Contemporary Society* (Chicago: University of Chicago Press, 2001); and Loïc Wacquant, *Punishing the Poor: The Neoliberal Government of Social Insecurity* (Durham, NC: Duke University Press, 2009).

48. See, e.g., Michelle Alexander, *The New Jim Crow: Mass Incarceration in the Era of Colorblindness* (New York: New Press, 2012); and Loïc Wacquant, "Deadly Symbiosis: When Ghetto and Prison Meet and Mesh," *Punishment & Society* 3, no. 1 (2001): 95–133.

49. Andres F. Rengifo and Don Stemen, "The Impact of Drug Treatment on Recidivism: Do Mandatory Programs Make a Difference? Evidence from Kansas's Senate Bill 123," *Crime & Delinquency* 59, no. 6 (2013): 930–50.

50. Mark H. Bergstrom and Joseph Sabino Mistick, "Danger and Opportunity: Making Public Safety Job One in Pennsylvania's Indeterminate Sentencing System," *Justice Research and Policy* 12, no. 1 (2010): 73–88.

51. Jessica M. Eaglin, "Against Neorehabilitation," *SMU Law Review* 66 (2013): 189–226.

52. Aviram, "The Correctional Hunger Games."

53. Keeanga-Yamahtta Taylor, *From #BlackLivesMatter to Black Liberation.*

54. See, e.g., Aamer Madhani, "Several Big U.S. Cities See Homicide Rates Surge," *USA Today* (July 10, 2015), http://www.usatoday.com/story/news/2015/07/09/us-cities-homicide-surge-2015/29879091 (accessed March 30, 2016).

55. Heather MacDonald, "The New Nationwide Crime Wave," *Wall Street Journal* (May 29, 2015), http://www.wsj.com/articles/the-new-nationwide-crime-wave-1432938425 (accessed March 30, 2016); Matt Desmond, Andrew V. Papachristos, and David S. Kirk. "Police Violence and Citizen Crime Reporting in the Black Community." *American Sociological Review* 81, no. 5 (2016): 857–76; and Matthew Friedman, Nicole Fortier, and James Cullen, *Crime in 2015: A Preliminary Analysis* (New York: Brennan Center for Justice, 2016).

56. Alyssa Davis, "In U.S., Concern about Crime Climbs to 15-Year High," *Gallup* (April 6, 2016), http://www.gallup.com/poll/190475/americans-concern-crime-climbs-year-high.aspx? (accessed April 10, 2016).

57. Tierney Sneed, "How Donald Trump Threatens to Blow Up Bipartisan Criminal Justice Reform," *Talking Points Memo* (September 10, 2015), http://talkingpoints-memo.com/livewire/criminal-justice-reform-gop-primary (accessed March 30, 2016). These examples also highlight the importance of elections as routine events that affect the nature, timing, and outcome of struggle.

58. Eli Hager, "Scott Walker on Crime and Punishment: Back to the '90s," *Marshall Project* (June 26, 2015), https://www.themarshallproject.org/2015/06/26/scott-walker-on-crime-and-punishment-back-to-the-90s?ref=hp-2-121 (accessed June 27, 2015); Jacob Sullum, "Ted Cruz Abandons Criminal Justice Reform on His Way to the White House," *Forbes* (January 28, 2016), http://www.forbes.com/sites/jacobsullum/2016/01/28/ted-cruz-abandons-criminal-justice-reform-on-his-way-to-the-white-house/#1cae43626e13 (accessed June 6, 2016).

59. Jonathan Simon, "A Summer Classic: Moral Panic over a Pier Shooting," *Governing through Crime* (July 8, 2015), http://governingthroughcrime.blogspot.com/2015/07/a-summer-classic-moral-panic-over-pier.html (accessed June 10, 2016).

60. Gottschalk, *Caught*, 217–18.

61. Hadar Aviram, *Cheap on Crime: Recession-Era Politics and the Transformation of American Punishment* (Berkeley: University of California Press, 2015); Marie

Gottschalk, "Cell Blocks & Red Ink: Mass Incarceration, the Great Recession & Penal Reform," *Daedalus* 139, no. 3 (2010): 62–73.

62. Aviram, *Cheap on Crime*; Gottschalk, *Caught*.

63. Eli Stokols, "Trump's Politics of Fear," *Politico* (June 14, 2016), http://www.polit-ico.com/story/2016/06/donald-trump-orlando-strategy-fear-224292 (accessed June 14, 2016).

64. See also David Garland, "Beyond the Culture of Control," *Critical Review of International Social and Political Philosophy* 7, no. 2 (2004): 160–89.

65. On "presentism" as an epistemological obstacle, see Pierre Bourdieu and Loïc Wacquant, *An Invitation to Reflexive Sociology* (Chicago: University of Chicago Press, 1992).

66. Ian Loader and Richard Sparks, "For an Historical Sociology of Crime Policy in England and Wales since 1968," *Critical Review of International Social and Political Philosophy* 7, no. 2 (2004): 5–32, 12.

67. Vanessa Barker, *The Politics of Imprisonment: How the Democratic Process Shapes the Way America Punishes Offenders* (New York: Oxford University Press, 2009).

68. International comparative research affirms the importance of mapping out political and legal institutions. Scholars demonstrate, for example, that the United States' institutional armature promotes intense struggles over criminal justice at national, local, and state levels, while the institutional characteristics of other countries (especially in western Europe) dampen or ameliorate this political contestation. This is particularly clear with the example of the death penalty (David Garland, *Peculiar Institution: America's Death Penalty in the Age of Abolition* [Cambridge, MA: Belknap Press of Harvard University Press, 2010], 164). However, see this alternative account of Italy as a "contested state" (Zelia A. Gallo, "Punishment, Authority and Political Economy: Italian Challenges to Western Punitiveness," *Punishment & Society* 17, no. 5 [2015]: 598–623). See also Joachim J. Savelsberg, "Knowledge, Domination, and Criminal Punishment," *American Journal of Sociology* 99, no. 4 (1994): 911–43; and James Q. Whitman, *Harsh Justice: Criminal Punishment and the Widening Divide between America and Europe* (New York: Oxford University Press, 2005).

69. Gail Super, "Punishment and the Body in the 'Old' and 'New' South Africa: A Story of Punitivist Humanism," *Theoretical Criminology* 15, no. 4 (2011b): 427–43; Gail Super, "'Like Some Rough Beast Slouching towards Bethlehem to Be Born': A Historical Perspective on the Institution of the Prison in South Africa, 1976–2004," *British Journal of Criminology* 51, no. 1 (2011a): 201–21.

70. Office of the Correctional Investigator (2013), "Backgrounder: Aboriginal Offenders—a Critical Situation," http://goo.gl/CKRSME (accessed May 5, 2015); Leah Sakala, "Breaking Down Mass Incarceration in the 2010 Census: State-by-State Incarceration Rates by Race/Ethnicity," *prisonpolicy.org* (May 28, 2014), http://www.prisonpolicy.org/reports/rates.html (accessed June 9, 2016).

See also Nancy Macdonald, "Canada's Prisons Are the 'New Residential Schools,'" *Maclean's* (February 18, 2016), http://www.macleans.ca/news/canada/canadas-prisons-are-the-new-residential-schools/(accessed June 9, 2016).

71. Loïc Wacquant, "Suitable Enemies: Foreigners and Immigrants in the Prisons of Europe," *Punishment & Society* 1, no. 2 (1999): 215–22.

72. We share with O'Malley the belief that attending to concrete political struggles over criminal justice shows the persistence of resistance and possibilities for different (less catastrophic) futures (Pat O'Malley, "Criminologies of Catastrophe? Understanding Criminal Justice on the Edge of the New Millennium," *Australian & New Zealand Journal of Criminology* 33, no. 2 [2000]: 153–67).

73. Steven Hutchinson, "Countering Catastrophic Criminology: Reform, Punishment, and the Modern Liberal Compromise," *Punishment & Society* 8, no. 4 (2010): 443–67, 447. It seems telling that critics such as O'Malley and Hutchinson have spent much of their careers researching punishment in commonwealth nations such as Australia, Canada, and England.

74. David A. Green, "Penal Optimism and Second Chances: The Legacies of American Protestantism and the Prospects for Penal Reform," *Punishment & Society* 15, no. 2 (2013): 123–46, 124.

75. On assemblages, see especially Paula Maurutto and Kelly Hannah-Moffat, "Assembling Risk and the Restructuring of Penal Control," *British Journal of Criminology* 46, no. 3 (2006): 438–54.

# Selected Bibliography

Alexander, Michelle. *The New Jim Crow: Mass Incarceration in the Age of Colorblindness.* New York: New Press, 2010.

Allen, Francis A. "Criminal Justice, Legal Values and the Rehabilitative Ideal." *Journal of Criminal Law, Criminology & Police Science* 50, no. 3 (1959), 226–32.

American Friends Service Committee. *A Struggle for Justice: A Report on Crime and Punishment in America.* New York: Hill & Wang, 1971.

Andrews, Donald A., and James Bonta. *The Psychology of Criminal Conduct.* 2d ed. Cincinnati: Anderson, 1998.

Annison, Harry. *Dangerous Politics: Risk, Political Vulnerability, and Penal Policy.* Oxford: Oxford University Press, 2015.

Appier, Janis. *Policing Women: The Sexual Politics of Law Enforcement and the LAPD.* Philadelphia: Temple University Press, 1998.

Austin, James, Eric Cadora, Todd R. Clear, Kara Dansky, Judith Greene, Vanita Gupta, Marc Mauer, Nicole Porter, Susan Tucker, and Malcolm C. Young. *Ending Mass Incarceration: Charting a New Justice Reinvestment.* Washington, DC: Sentencing Project, 2013.

Austin, James, and Michael P. Jacobson. *How New York City Reduced Mass Incarceration: A Model for Change?* New York: Vera Institute of Justice, 2013.

Aviram, Hadar. *Cheap on Crime: Recession-Era Politics and the Transformation of American Punishment.* Berkeley: University of California Press, 2015.

———. "The Correctional Hunger Games: Understanding Realignment in the Context of the Great Recession." *ANNALS of the American Academy of Political and Social Science* 664, no. 1 (2016), 260–79.

Ayers, Edward L. *Vengeance and Justice: Crime and Punishment in the 19th-Century American South.* New York: Oxford University Press, 1984.

Balko, Radley. *Rise of the Warrior Cop: The Militarization of America's Police Forces.* New York: PublicAffairs, 2013.

Barker, Vanessa. *The Politics of Imprisonment: How the Democratic Process Shapes the Way America Punishes Offenders.* New York: Oxford University Press, 2009.

Baumgartner, Frank R., Bryan D. Jones, and Peter B. Mortensen. "Punctuated Equilibrium Theory: Explaining Stability and Change in Public Policymaking." In *Theories of the Policy Process*, edited by Paul A. Sabatier and Christopher M. Weible, pp. 59–104. 3d ed. Boulder, CO: Westview, 2014.

Beckett, Katherine. *Making Crime Pay: Law and Order in Contemporary American Politics*. New York: Oxford University Press, 1997.

Beckett, Katherine, Anna Reosti, and Emily Knaphus. "The End of an Era? Understanding the Contradictions of Criminal Justice Reform." *ANNALS of the American Academy of Political and Social Science* 664, no. 1 (2016), 238–59.

Beckett, Katherine, and Theodore Sasson. *The Politics of Injustice: Crime and Punishment in America*. 2d ed. Thousand Oaks, CA: SAGE, 2004.

Berger, Dan. *Captive Nation: Black Prison Organizing in the Civil Rights Era*. Chapel Hill: University of North Carolina Press, 2014.

Bergstrom, Mark H., and Joseph Sabino Mistick. "Danger and Opportunity: Making Public Safety Job One in Pennsylvania's Indeterminate Sentencing System." *Justice Research and Policy* 12, no. 1 (2010), 73–88.

Biggers, Jeff. *State Out of the Union: Arizona and the Final Showdown over the American Dream*. New York: Nation Books, 2012.

Blackmon, Douglas A. *Slavery by Another Name: The Re-enslavement of Black Americans from the Civil War to World War II*. New York: Anchor, 2009.

Blue, Ethan. *Doing Time in the Depression: Everyday Life in Texas and California Prisons*. New York: New York University Press, 2012.

Blumer, Herbert. "What Is Wrong with Social Theory?" *American Sociological Review* 19, no. 1 (1954), 3–10.

Blumstein, Alfred, and Joel Wallman, eds. *The Crime Drop in America*. Rev. ed. New York: Cambridge University Press, 2006.

Bosworth, Mary. *Engendering Resistance: Agency and Power in Women's Prisons*. Aldershot, UK: Ashgate, 1999.

———. "Penal Moderation in the United States? Yes We Can." *Criminology & Public Policy* 10, no. 2 (2011), 335–43.

Bourdieu, Pierre, and Loïc J. D. Wacquant. *An Invitation to Reflexive Sociology*. Chicago: University of Chicago Press, 1992.

Bowler, Anne E., Chrysanthi S. Leon, and Terry G. Lilley. "'What Shall We Do with the Young Prostitute? Reform Her or Neglect Her?': Domestication as Reform at the New York State Reformatory for Women at Bedford, 1901–1913." *Journal of Social History* 47, no. 2 (2013), 458–81.

Bright, Charles. *The Powers That Punish: Prison and Politics in the Era of the "Big House," 1920–1955*. Ann Arbor: University of Michigan Press, 1996.

Brown, Michelle. *The Culture of Punishment: Prison, Society, and Spectacle*. New York: New York University Press, 2009.

Campbell, Michael C. "Agents of Change: Law Enforcement, Prisons, and Politics in Texas and California." PhD dissertation, University of California, Irvine, 2009.

————. "Politics, Prisons, and Law Enforcement: An Examination of the Emergence of 'Law and Order' Politics in Texas." *Law & Society Review* 45, no. 3 (2011), 631–65.

————. "Ornery Alligators and Soap on a Rope: Texas Prosecutors and Punishment Reform in the Lone Star State." *Theoretical Criminology* 16, no. 3 (2012), 289–311.

————. "The Emergence of Penal Extremism in California: A Dynamic View of Institutional Structures and Political Processes." *Law & Society Review* 48, no. 2 (2014), 377–409.

Campbell, Michael C., and Heather Schoenfeld. "The Transformation of America's Penal Order: A Historicized Political Sociology of Punishment." *American Journal of Sociology* 118, no. 5 (2013), 1375–1423.

Carleton, Mark T. *Politics and Punishment: The History of the Louisiana State Penal System.* Baton Rouge: Louisiana State University Press, 1971.

Chambers, John Whiteclay, II. *The Tyranny of Change: America in the Progressive Era, 1890–1920.* 2d ed. New Brunswick, NJ: Rutgers University Press, 2000.

Chase, Robert T. "We Are Not Slaves: Rethinking the Rise of Carceral States through the Lens of the Prisoners' Rights Movement." *Journal of American History* 102, no. 1 (2015), 73–86.

Cissner, Amanda B., Michael Rempel, Allyson Walker Franklin, John Roman, Samuel Bieler, Robyn L. Cohen, and Carolyn R. Cadoret. *A Statewide Evaluation of New York's Adult Drug Courts: Identifying Which Policies Work Best.* New York: Center for Court Innovation, 2013.

Clear, Todd R., and Natasha A. Frost. *The Punishment Imperative: The Rise and Failure of Mass Incarceration in America.* New York: New York University Press, 2013.

Clemmer, Donald. *The Prison Community.* Boston: Christopher, 1940.

Cole, Simon A. *Suspect Identities: A History of Fingerprinting and Criminal Identification.* Cambridge, MA: Harvard University Press, 2001.

Conover, Ted. *Newjack: Guarding Sing Sing.* New York: Vintage, 2001.

Cullen, Francis T. "The Twelve People Who Saved Rehabilitation: How the Science of Criminology Made a Difference." *Criminology* 43, no. 1 (2005), 1–42.

Cullen, Francis T. "Rehabilitation: Beyond Nothing Works." In *Crime and Justice in America, 1975–2025,* edited by Michael Tonry, pp. 299–376. Chicago: University of Chicago Press, 2013.

Cullen, Francis T., and Karen E. Gilbert. *Reaffirming Rehabilitation.* 2d ed. New York: Routledge, 2013.

Cummins, Eric. *The Rise and Fall of California's Radical Prison Movement.* Stanford, CA: Stanford University Press, 1994.

Dagan, David, and Steven M. Teles. "The Social Construction of Policy Feedback: Incarceration, Conservatism, and Ideological Change." *Studies in American Political Development* 29, no. 2 (2015), 127–53.

Davidson, R. Theodore. *Chicano Prisoners: The Key to San Quentin.* New York: Holt, Rinehart and Winston, 1974.

Desmond, Matt, Andrew V. Papachristos, and David S. Kirk. "Police Violence and Citizen Crime Reporting in the Black Community." *American Sociological Review* 81, no. 5 (2016), 857–76.

Dix, Dorothea. *Remarks on Prisons and Prison Discipline in the United States* (1845). Whitefish, MT: Kessinger, 2008.

Drucker, Ernest. "Population Impact of Mass Incarceration under New York's Rockefeller Drug Laws: An Analysis of Years of Life Lost." *Journal of Urban Health: Bulletin of the New York Academy of Medicine* 79, no. 3 (2002), 434–35.

Du Bois, W. E. B. "The Spawn of Slavery: The Convict-Lease System in the South." In *African American Classics in Criminology and Criminal Justice*, edited by Shaun L. Gabbidon, Helen Taylor Greene, and Vernetta D. Young, pp. 81–88. Thousand Oaks, CA: SAGE, 2002.

Durkheim, Émile. *The Division of Labor in Society*. Translated by W. D. Halls. New York: Free Press, 1997.

Eaglin, Jessica M. "Against Neorehabilitation." *SMU Law Review* 66, no. 1 (2013), 189–226.

Edelman, Murray. *Political Language: Words That Succeed and Policies That Fail.* New York: Academic Press, 1977.

Emirbayer, Mustafa, and Victoria Johnson. "Bourdieu and Organizational Analysis." *Theory and Society* 37, no. 1 (2008), 1–44.

Farrall, Stephen, Barry Goldson, Ian Loader, and Anita Dockley, eds. *Justice and Penal Reform: Re-shaping the Penal Landscape.* New York: Routledge, 2016.

Feeley, Malcolm M., and Jonathan Simon. "The New Penology: Notes on the Emerging Strategy of Corrections and Its Implications." *Criminology* 30, no. 4 (1992), 449–74.

Fligstein, Neil, and Doug McAdam. "Toward a General Theory of Strategic Action Fields." *Sociological Theory* 29, no.1 (2011), 1–26.

Forman, James, Jr. "Racial Critiques of Mass Incarceration: Beyond the New Jim Crow." *New York University Law Review* 87, no. 1 (2012), 101–46.

Fortner, Michael Javen. "The Carceral State and the Crucible of Black Politics: An Urban History of the Rockefeller Drug Laws." *Studies in American Political Development* 27, no. 1 (2013), 14–35.

———. *Black Silent Majority: The Rockefeller Drug Laws and the Politics of Punishment.* Cambridge, MA: Harvard University Press, 2015.

Foucault, Michel. *Discipline and Punish: The Birth of the Prison.* 2d Vintage ed. Translated by Alan Sheridan. New York: Vintage, 1995.

Frampton, Mary Louise, Ian Haney Lopez, and Jonathan Simon, eds. *After the War on Drugs: Race, Democracy, and a New Reconstruction.* New York: New York University Press, 2008.

Freedman, Estelle B. *Their Sisters' Keepers: Women's Prison Reform in America, 1830–1930.* Ann Arbor: University of Michigan Press, 1981.

Friedman, Lawrence M. *Crime and Punishment in American History.* New York: Basic Books, 1993.

Friedman, Matthew, Nicole Fortier, and James Cullen. *Crime in 2015: A Preliminary Analysis*. New York: Brennan Center for Justice, 2016.

Frost, Natasha A. "The Mismeasure of Punishment: Alternative Measures of Punitiveness and Their (Substantial) Consequences." *Punishment & Society* 10, no. 3 (2008), 277–300.

Gallo, Zelia A. "Punishment, Authority and Political Economy: Italian Challenges to Western Punitiveness." *Punishment & Society* 17, no. 5 (2015), 598–623.

Garfinkel, Harold. *Studies in Ethnomethodology.* Englewood Cliffs, NJ: Prentice-Hall, 1967.

Garland, David. *Punishment and Welfare: A History of Penal Strategies*. Aldershot, UK: Gower, 1985.

———. *Punishment and Modern Society: A Study in Social Theory*. Chicago: University of Chicago Press, 1990.

———. *The Culture of Control: Crime and Social Order in Contemporary Society*. Chicago: University of Chicago Press, 2001.

———. "Beyond the Culture of Control." *Critical Review of International Social and Political Philosophy* 7, no. 2 (2004), 160–89.

———. "Penal Excess and Surplus Meaning: Public Torture Lynchings in Twentieth-Century America." *Law & Society Review* 39, no. 4 (2005), 793–833.

———. *Peculiar Institution: America's Death Penalty in an Age of Abolition*. Cambridge, MA: Belknap Press of Harvard University Press, 2010.

Gartner, Rosemary, Anthony N. Doob, and Franklin E. Zimring. "The Past as Prologue? Decarceration in California Then and Now." *Criminology & Public Policy* 10, no. 2 (2011), 291–325.

Garvey, Stephen P. "Freeing Prisoners' Labor." *Stanford Law Review* 50, no. 2 (1998), 339–98.

Getis, Victoria. *The Juvenile Court and Progressives*. Urbana: University of Illinois Press, 2000.

Gildemeister, Glen A. *Prison Labor and Convict Competition with Free Workers in Industrializing America, 1840–1890*. New York: Garland, 1987.

Gilmore, Ruth Wilson. *Golden Gulag: Prisons, Surplus, Crisis, and Opposition in Globalizing California*. Berkeley: University of California Press, 2007.

Glaser, Daniel. *Preparing Convicts for Law-Abiding Lives: The Pioneering Penology of Richard A. McGee*. Albany: State University of New York Press, 1995.

Gonnerman, Jennifer. *Life on the Outside: The Prison Odyssey of Elaine Bartlett*. New York: Picador, 2005.

Goodman, Philip. "Hero or Inmate, Camp or Prison, Rehabilitation or Labor Extraction: A Multi-level Study of California's Prison Fire Camps." PhD dissertation, University of California, Irvine, 2010.

———. "'Another Second Chance': Rethinking Rehabilitation through the Lens of California's Prison Fire Camps." *Social Problems* 59, no. 4 (2012a), 437–58.

———. "Hero *and* Inmate: Work, Prisons, and Punishment in California's Fire Camps." *Working USA: The Journal of Labor & Society* 15, no. 3 (2012b), 353–76.

Goodman, Philip, Joshua Page, and Michelle Phelps. "The Long Struggle: An Agonistic Perspective on Penal Development." *Theoretical Criminology* 19, no. 3 (2015), 315–35.

Gottschalk, Marie. *The Prison and the Gallows: The Politics of Mass Incarceration in America*. New York: Cambridge University Press, 2006.

———. "Cell Blocks & Red Ink: Mass Incarceration, the Great Recession & Penal Reform." *Daedalus* 139, no. 3 (2010), 62–73.

———. "Sentenced to Life: Penal Reforms and the Most Severe Sanctions." *Annual Review of Law and Social Science* 9 (2013), 353–82.

———. *Caught: The Prison State and the Lockdown of American Politics*. Princeton, NJ: Princeton University Press, 2015.

———. "Staying Alive: Reforming Solitary Confinement in U.S. Prisons and Jails." *Yale Law Journal Forum* 125 (2016), 253–66.

Graves, Shannon M. "Correctional Mission Statements as Indicators of the Criminal Justice Policy Environment: A Research Note." *Criminal Justice Policy Review* 26, no. 5 (2015), 488–99.

Green, David A. "Penal Optimism and Second Chances: The Legacies of American Protestantism and the Prospects for Penal Reform." *Punishment & Society* 15, no. 2 (2013), 123–46.

———. "US Penal-Reform Catalysts, Drivers, and Prospects." *Punishment & Society* 17, no. 3 (2015), 271–98.

Greene, Judith, and Marc Mauer. *Downscaling Prisons: Lessons from Four States*. Washington, DC: Sentencing Project, 2010.

Guenther, Lisa. *Solitary Confinement: Social Death and Its Afterlives*. Minneapolis: University of Minnesota Press, 2013.

Gusfield, Joseph R. *Symbolic Crusade: Status Politics and the American Temperance Movement*. Urbana: University of Illinois Press, 1963.

Hagan, John. *Who Are the Criminals? The Politics of Crime Policy from the Age of Roosevelt to the Age of Reagan*. Princeton, NJ: Princeton University Press, 2010.

Halushka, John. "Managing Rehabilitation: Accountability, Discipline, and 'Defensive Institutionalism' at the Frontlines of Reentry Service Provision." Working paper, presented at the "Penal Boundaries" workshop, University of Toronto, 2016.

Haney, Lynne A. *Offending Women: Power, Punishment, and the Regulation of Desire*. Berkeley: University of California Press, 2010.

Hannah-Moffat, Kelly. "Criminogenic Needs and the Transformative Risk Subject: Hybridizations of Risk/Need in Penality." *Punishment & Society* 7, no. 1 (2005), 29–51.

Hannah-Moffat, Kelly, and Paula Maurutto. "Shifting and Targeted Forms of Penal Governance: Bail, Punishment, and Specialized Courts." *Theoretical Criminology* 16, no. 2 (2012), 201–19.

Hess, Kären Matison, and Christine Hess Orthmann. *Introduction to Law Enforcement and Criminal Justice*. 10th ed. Belmont, CA: Delmar, Cengage Learning, 2012.

Hicks, Cheryl D. "'Bright and Good Looking Colored Girl': Black Women's Sexuality and 'Harmful Intimacy' in Early-Twentieth-Century New York." In *The Punitive*

*Turn: New Approaches to Race and Incarceration*, edited by Deborah E. McDowell, Claudrena N. Harold, and Juan Battle, pp. 73–107. Charlottesville: University of Virginia Press, 2013.

Hindus, Michael S. *Prison and Plantation: Crime, Justice, and Authority in Massachusetts and South Carolina, 1767–1878*. Chapel Hill: University of North Carolina Press, 2012.

Hinton, Elizabeth. "'A War within Our Own Boundaries': Lyndon Johnson's Great Society and the Rise of the Carceral State." *Journal of American History* 102, no. 1 (2015), 100–12.

———. *From the War on Poverty to the War on Crime: The Making of Mass Incarceration in America*. Cambridge, MA: Harvard University Press, 2016.

Holian, David B. "He's Stealing My Issues! Clinton's Crime Rhetoric and the Dynamics of Issue Ownership." *Political Behavior* 26, no. 2 (2004), 95–124.

Hornblum, Allen M. *Acres of Skin: Human Experiments at Holmesburg Prison; A True Story of Abuse and Exploitation in the Name of Medical Science*. New York: Routledge, 1999.

Hutchinson, Steven. "Countering Catastrophic Criminology: Reform, Punishment, and the Modern Liberal Compromise." *Punishment & Society* 8, no. 4 (2006), 443–67.

Irwin, John. *The Felon*. Englewood Cliffs, NJ: Prentice-Hall, 1970.

———. *Prisons in Turmoil*. Boston: Little, Brown, 1980.

Jacobs, David, and Ronald Helms. "Collective Outbursts, Politics, and Punitive Resources: Toward a Political Sociology of Spending on Crime Control." *Social Forces* 77, no. 4 (1999), 1497–1523.

Jacobs, James B. *Stateville: The Penitentiary in Mass Society*. Chicago: University of Chicago Press, 1977.

Jacobson, Michael. *Downsizing Prisons: How to Reduce Crime and End Mass Incarceration*. New York: New York University Press, 2005.

Janssen, Volker. "From the Inside Out: Therapeutic Penology and Political Liberalism in Postwar California." *Osiris* 22, no. 1 (2007), 116–34.

———. "Sunbelt Lock-Up: Where the Suburbs Met the Super-Max." In *Sunbelt Rising: The Politics of Space, Place, and Region*, edited by Michelle Nickerson and Darren Dochuk, pp. 217–39. Philadelphia: University of Pennsylvania Press, 2011.

Keve, Paul W. *Prisons and the American Conscience: A History of U.S. Federal Corrections*. Carbondale: Southern Illinois University Press, 1991.

Klingele, Cecelia. "The Promises and Perils of Evidence-Based Corrections." *Notre Dame Law Review* 91, no. 2 (2016), 537–84.

Kohler-Hausmann, Issa. "Misdemeanor Justice: Control without Conviction." *American Journal of Sociology* 119, no. 2 (2013), 351–93.

———. "Jumping Bunnies and Legal Rules: The Organizational Sociologist and the Legal Scholar Should Be Friends." In *The New Criminal Justice Thinking*, edited by Sharon Dolovich and Alexandra Natapoff. New York: New York University Press, in press.

Kohler-Hausmann, Julilly. "'The Attila the Hun Law': New York's Rockefeller Drug Laws and the Making of a Punitive State." *Journal of Social History* 44, no. 1 (2010), 71–95.

Kruttschnitt, Candace, and Rosemary Gartner. *Marking Time in the Golden State: Women's Imprisonment in California.* Cambridge, UK: Cambridge University Press, 2005.

Kunzel, Regina G. *Criminal Intimacy: Prison and the Uneven History of Modern American Sexuality.* Chicago: University of Chicago Press, 2008.

Lauritsen, Janet L., Maribeth L. Rezey, and Karen Heimer. "When Choice of Data Matters: Analyses of U.S. Crime Trends, 1973–2012." *Journal of Quantitative Criminology* 32, no. 3 (2016), 335–55.

LeFlouria, Talitha L. "'Under the Sting of the Lash': Gendered Violence, Terror, and Resistance in the South's Convict Camps." *Journal of African American History* 100, no. 3 (2015a), 366–84.

———. *Chained in Silence: Black Women and Convict Labor in the New South.* Chapel Hill: University of North Carolina Press, 2015b.

Leon, Chrysanthi S. *Sex Fiends, Perverts, and Pedophiles: Understanding Sex Crime Policy in America.* New York: New York University Press, 2011.

Leonard, Thomas C. "Retrospectives: Eugenics and Economics in the Progressive Era." *Journal of Economic Perspectives* 19, no. 4 (2005), 207–24.

Lerman, Paul. *Community Treatment and Social Control: A Critical Analysis of Juvenile Correctional Policy.* Chicago: University of Chicago Press, 1975.

Lewis, W. David. *From Newgate to Dannemora: The Rise of the Penitentiary in New York, 1796–1848.* Ithaca, NY: Cornell University Press, 1965.

Lichtenstein, Alex. *Twice the Work of Free Labor: The Political Economy of Convict Labor in the New South.* New York: Verso, 1996.

Lipsey, Mark W., and Francis T. Cullen. "The Effectiveness of Correctional Rehabilitation: A Review of Systematic Reviews." *Annual Review of Law and Social Science* 3 (2007), 297–320.

Lipsey, Mark W., and David B. Wilson. "The Efficacy of Psychological, Educational, and Behavioral Treatment: Confirmation from Meta-analysis." *American Psychologist* 48, no. 12 (1993), 1181–1209.

Lipton, Douglas, Robert Martinson, and Judith Wilks. *The Effectiveness of Correctional Treatment: A Survey of Treatment Evaluation Studies.* New York: Praeger, 1975.

Listwan, Shelley Johnson, Cheryl Lero Jonson, Francis T. Cullen, and Edward J. Latessa. "Cracks in the Penal Harm Movement: Evidence from the Field." *Criminology & Public Policy* 7, no. 3 (2008), 423–65.

Loader, Ian, and Richard Sparks. "For an Historical Sociology of Crime Policy in England and Wales since 1968." *Critical Review of International Social and Political Philosophy* 7, no. 2 (2004), 5–32.

Lynch, Mona. "Rehabilitation as Rhetoric: The Ideal of Reformation in Contemporary Parole Discourse and Practices." *Punishment & Society* 2, no. 1 (2000), 40–65.

———. *Sunbelt Justice: Arizona and the Transformation of American Punishment*. Palo Alto, CA: Stanford University Press, 2009.

Mancini, Matthew J. *One Dies, Get Another: Convict Leasing in the American South, 1866–1928*. Columbia: University of South Carolina Press, 1996.

Martinson, Robert. "What Works?—Questions and Answers about Prison Reform." *Public Interest* 35 (1974), 22–54.

Mauer, Marc. *The Changing Racial Dynamics of the War on Drugs*. Washington, DC: Sentencing Project, 2009.

Maurutto, Paula, and Kelly Hannah-Moffat. "Assembling Risk and the Restructuring of Penal Control." *British Journal of Criminology* 46, no. 3 (2006), 438–54.

McAfee, Ward M. "A History of Convict Labor in California." *Southern California Quarterly* 72, no. 1 (1990), 19–40.

McCarty, Heather Jane. "From Con-Boss to Gang Lord: The Transformation of Social Relations in California Prisons, 1943–1983." PhD dissertation, University of California, Berkeley, 2004.

McCorkel, Jill A. *Breaking Women: Gender, Race, and the New Politics of Imprisonment*. New York: New York University Press, 2013.

McGee, Richard A. *Prisons and Politics*. Lexington, MA: Lexington, 1981.

McGerr, Michael. *A Fierce Discontent: The Rise and Fall of the Progressive Movement in America, 1870–1920*. New York: Oxford University Press, 2003.

McGirr, Lisa. *The War on Alcohol: Prohibition and the Rise of the American State*. New York: W. W. Norton, 2016.

McLennan, Rebecca M. *The Crisis of Imprisonment: Protest, Politics, and the Making of the American Penal State, 1776–1941*. New York: Cambridge University Press, 2008.

McNeill, Fergus, Nicola Burns, Simon Halliday, Neil Hutton, and Cyrus Tata. "Risk, Responsibility and Reconfiguration: Penal Adaptation and Misadaptation." *Punishment & Society* 11, no. 4 (2009), 419–42.

Melossi, Dario, and Massimo Pavarini. *The Prison and the Factory: Origins of the Penitentiary System*. Translated by Glynis Cousin. New York: Macmillan, 1981.

Meranze, Michael. *Laboratories of Virtue: Punishment, Revolution, and Authority in Philadelphia, 1760–1835*. Chapel Hill: University of North Carolina Press, 1996.

Miller, Lisa L. *The Perils of Federalism: Race, Poverty, and the Politics of Crime Control*. New York: Oxford University Press, 2008.

———. "What's Violence Got to Do with It? Inequality, Punishment, and State Failure in US Politics." *Punishment & Society* 17, no. 2 (2015), 184–210.

Miller, Vivien M. L. *Hard Labor and Hard Time: Florida's "Sunshine Prison" and Chain Gangs*. Gainesville: University Press of Florida, 2012.

Mitford, Jessica. *Kind and Usual Punishment: The Prison Business*. New York: Knopf, 1973.

Moore, Dawn, and Kelly Hannah-Moffat. "The Liberal Veil: Revisiting Canadian Penality." In *The New Punitiveness: Trends, Theories, Perspectives*, edited by John Pratt, David Brown, Mark Brown, Simon Hallsworth, and Wayne Morrison, pp. 85–100. Cullompton, UK: Willan, 2005.

Muhammad, Khalil Gibran. *The Condemnation of Blackness: Race, Crime, and the Making of Modern Urban America*. Cambridge, MA: Harvard University Press, 2010.

Muller, Christopher. "Northward Migration and the Rise of Racial Disparity in American Incarceration, 1880–1950." *American Journal of Sociology* 118, no. 2 (2012), 281–326.

Murakawa, Naomi. *The First Civil Right: How Liberals Built Prison America*. New York: Oxford University Press, 2014.

Murch, Donna. "Crack in Los Angeles: Crisis, Militarization, and Black Response to the Late Twentieth-Century War on Drugs." *Journal of American History* 102, no. 1 (2015), 162–73.

Muth, William R., and Thom Gehring. "The Correctional Education / Prison Reform Link: 1913–1940 and Conclusion." *Journal of Correctional Education* 37, no. 1 (1986), 14–17.

Myers, Martha A. *Race, Labor, and Punishment in the New South*. Columbus: Ohio State University Press, 1998.

Nelken, David. *Comparative Criminal Justice: Making Sense of Difference*. Los Angeles: SAGE, 2010.

Newman, Katherine S. *No Shame in My Game: The Working Poor in the Inner City*. New York: A. A. Knopf and Russell Sage Foundation, 1999.

O'Malley, Pat. "Volatile and Contradictory Punishment." *Theoretical Criminology* 3, no. 2 (1999), 175–96.

———. "Criminologies of Catastrophe? Understanding Criminal Justice on the Edge of the New Millennium." *Australian & New Zealand Journal of Criminology* 33, no. 2 (2000), 153–67.

Osborne, Geraint B. "Scientific Experimentation on Canadian Inmates, 1955 to 1975." *Howard Journal of Criminal Justice* 45, no. 3 (2006), 284–306.

Oshinsky, David M. *Worse Than Slavery: Parchman Farm and the Ordeal of Jim Crow Justice*. New York: Free Press, 1996.

Page, Joshua. *The Toughest Beat: Politics, Punishment, and the Prison Officers Union in California*. New York: Oxford University Press, 2011.

———. "Punishment and the Penal Field." In *The SAGE Handbook of Punishment and Society*, edited by Jonathan Simon and Richard Sparks, pp. 152–65. Los Angeles: SAGE, 2013.

Palmer, Ted. "Martinson Revisited." *Journal of Research in Crime and Delinquency* 12, no. 2 (1975), 133–52.

Parsons, Jim, Qing Wei, Christian Henrichson, Ernest Drucker, and Jennifer Trone. *End of an Era? The Impact of Drug Law Reform in New York City*. New York: Vera Institute, 2015.

Perkinson, Robert. *Texas Tough: The Rise of America's Prison Empire*. New York: Metropolitan, 2010.

Petersilia, Joan. *When Prisoners Come Home: Parole and Prisoner Reentry*. New York: Oxford University Press, 2003.

Peterson, Ruth D., and Lauren J. Krivo. *Divergent Social Worlds: Neighborhood Crime and the Racial-Spatial Divide.* New York: Russell Sage Foundation, 2010.

Pfaff, John F. "The War on Drugs and Prison Growth: Limited Importance, Limited Legislative Options." *Harvard Journal on Legislation* 52, no. 1 (2015), 173–220.

———. "The Complicated Economics of Prison Reform." *Michigan Law Review* 114, no. 6 (2016), 951–81.

———. *Locked In: The True Causes of Mass Incarceration—and How to Achieve Real Reform.* New York: Basic Books, 2017.

Phelps, Michelle S. "Rehabilitation in the Punitive Era: The Gap between Rhetoric and Reality in U.S. Prison Programs." *Law & Society Review* 45, no. 1 (2011), 33–68.

———. "The Place of Punishment: Variation in the Provision of Inmate Services Staff across the Punitive Turn." *Journal of Criminal Justice* 40, no. 5 (2012), 348–57.

———. "The Paradox of Probation: Community Supervision in the Age of Mass Incarceration." *Law & Policy* 35, no. 1–2 (2013), 51–80.

———. "Mass Probation: Toward a More Robust Theory of State Variation in Punishment." *Punishment & Society* OnlineFirst (May 10, 2016).

———. "Possibilities and Contestation in Twenty-First-Century US Criminal Justice Downsizing." *Annual Review of Law & Social Science* 12 (2017).

Pierson, Paul. "When Effect Becomes Cause: Policy Feedback and Political Change." *World Politics* 45, no. 4 (1993), 595–628.

Pisciotta, Alexander W. *Benevolent Repression: Social Control and the American Reformatory-Prison Movement.* New York: New York University Press, 1994.

Piven, Frances Fox. "Deviant Behavior and the Remaking of the World." *Social Problems* 28, no. 5 (1981), 489–508.

———. *Challenging Authority: How Ordinary People Change America.* Lanham, MD: Rowman & Littlefield, 2006.

Platt, Anthony M. *The Child Savers: The Invention of Delinquency.* 2d ed. Chicago: University of Chicago Press, 1977.

Porter, Nicole D. "Unfinished Project of Civil Rights in the Era of Mass Incarceration and the Movement for Black Lives." *Wake Forest Journal of Law & Policy* 6, no. 1 (2016), 1–34.

Powelson, Harvey, and Reinhard Bendix. "Psychiatry in Prison." *Psychiatry* 14, no. 1 (1951), 73–86.

Pratt, John, David Brown, Mark Brown, Simon Hallsworth, and Wayne Morrison, eds. *The New Punitiveness: Trends, Theories, Perspectives.* Cullompton, UK: Willan, 2005.

———. *Penal Populism.* London: Routledge, 2007.

Rafter, Nicole Hahn. *Partial Justice: Women, Prisons, and Social Control.* 2d ed. New Brunswick, NJ: Transaction, 1990.

———. *Creating Born Criminals.* Urbana: University of Illinois Press, 1997.

Ramirez, Mark D. "Punitive Sentiment." *Criminology* 51, no. 2 (2013), 329–64.

Reinarman, Craig, and Harry G. Levine, eds. *Crack in America: Demon Drugs and Social Justice.* Berkeley: University of California Press, 1997.

Reiter, Keramet. "The Most Restrictive Alternative: A Litigation History of Solitary Confinement in U.S. Prisons, 1960–2006." *Studies in Law, Politics and Society* 57 (2012), 71–124.

———. "The Pelican Bay Hunger Strike: Resistance within the Structural Constraints of a US Supermax Prison." *South Atlantic Quarterly* 113, no. 3 (2014), 579–611.

———. *23/7: Pelican Bay Prison and the Rise of Long-Term Solitary*. New Haven, CT: Yale University Press, 2016.

Rengifo, Andres F., and Don Stemen. "The Impact of Drug Treatment on Recidivism: Do Mandatory Programs Make a Difference? Evidence from Kansas's Senate Bill 123." *Crime & Delinquency* 59, no. 6 (2013), 930–50.

Rhine, Edward E., Tina L. Mawhorr, and Evalyn C. Parks. "Implementation: The Bane of Effective Correctional Programs." *Criminology & Public Policy* 5, no. 2 (2006), 347–58.

Rios, Victor M. *Punished: Policing the Lives of Black and Latino Boys*. New York: New York University Press, 2011.

Roberts, Leonard H. "A History of Inmate Rehabilitation through Education in the Florida State Correctional System, 1868–1980." PhD dissertation, University of Florida, 1981.

Robinson, Gwen. "Late-Modern Rehabilitation: The Evolution of a Penal Strategy." *Punishment & Society* 10, no. 4 (2008), 429–45.

Rothman, David J. "Perfecting the Prison: United States, 1789–1865." In *The Oxford History of the Prison: The Practice of Punishment in Western Society*, edited by Norval Morris and David J. Rothman, pp. 100–16. New York: Oxford University Press, 1995.

———. *Conscience and Convenience: The Asylum and Its Alternatives in Progressive America*. Rev. ed. New York: Aldine de Gruyter, 2002a.

———. *The Discovery of the Asylum: Social Order and Disorder in the New Republic*. Rev. ed. New York: Aldine de Gruyter, 2002b.

Rubin, Ashley T. "Institutionalizing the Pennsylvania System: Organizational Exceptionalism, Administrative Support, and Eastern State Penitentiary, 1829–1875." PhD dissertation, University of California, Berkeley, 2013.

———. "Resistance or Friction: Understanding the Significance of Prisoners' Secondary Adjustments." *Theoretical Criminology* 19, no. 1 (2015a), 23–42.

———. "A Neo-institutional Account of Prison Diffusion." *Law & Society Review* 49, no. 2 (2015b), 365–400.

———. "Penal Change as Penal Layering: A Case Study of Proto-prison Adoption and Capital Punishment Reduction, 1785–1822." *Punishment & Society* 18, no. 4 (2016), 420–41.

Rusche, Georg, and Otto Kirchheimer. *Punishment and Social Structure*. New Brunswick, NJ: Transaction, 2003.

Rutherford, Andrew. *Transforming Criminal Policy: Spheres of Influence in the United States, the Netherlands, and England and Wales during the 1980s*. Winchester, UK: Waterside, 1996.

Ryan, Mick. *Penal Policy and Political Culture in England and Wales: Four Essays on Policy and Process*. Winchester, UK: Waterside, 2003.

Savelsberg, Joachim J. "Law That Does Not Fit Society: Sentencing Guidelines as a Neoclassical Reaction to the Dilemmas of Substantivized Law." *American Journal of Sociology* 97, no. 5 (1992), 1346–81.

———. "Knowledge, Domination, and Criminal Punishment." *American Journal of Sociology* 99, no. 4 (1994), 911–43.

Schattschneider, Elmer Eric. *The Semisovereign People: A Realist's View of Democracy in America*. Boston: Cengage Learning, 1975.

Schlanger, Margo. "Civil Rights Injunctions over Time: A Case Study of Jail and Prison Court Orders." *New York University Law Review* 81, no. 2 (2006), 550–630.

Schlossman, Michael B. "Less Interest, Less Treatment: Mexican-American Youth and the Los Angeles Juvenile Court in the Great Depression Era." *Punishment & Society* 14, no. 2 (2012), 193–216.

Schlossman, Steven, and Stephanie Wallach. "The Crime of Precocious Sexuality: Female Juvenile Delinquency in the Progressive Era." *Harvard Educational Review* 48, no. 1 (1978), 65–94.

Schneiderhan, Erik. *The Size of Others' Burdens: Barack Obama, Jane Addams, and the Politics of Helping Others*. Stanford, CA: Stanford University Press, 2015.

Schoenfeld, Heather. "The Politics of Prison Growth: From Chain Gangs to Work Release Centers and Supermax Prisons, Florida, 1955–2000." PhD dissertation, Northwestern University, 2009.

———. "Mass Incarceration and the Paradox of Prison Conditions Litigation." *Law & Society Review* 44, no. 3–4 (2010), 731–68.

———. "The Delayed Emergence of Penal Modernism in Florida." *Punishment & Society* 16, no. 3 (2014), 258–84.

———. "A Research Agenda on Reform: Penal Policy and Politics across the States." *ANNALS of the American Academy of Political and Social Science* 664, no. 1 (2016), 155–74.

Seeds, Christopher. "Bifurcation Nation: Strategy in Contemporary American Punishment." *Punishment & Society* (2016).

Shapiro, Karin A. *A New South Rebellion: The Battle against Convict Labor in the Tennessee Coalfields, 1871–1896*. Chapel Hill: University of North Carolina Press, 1998.

Sherman, Jennifer. "Coping with Rural Poverty: Economic Survival and Moral Capital in Rural America." *Social Forces* 85, no. 2 (2006), 891–913.

Simon, Jonathan. *Poor Discipline: Parole and the Social Control of the Underclass, 1890–1990*. Chicago: University of Chicago Press, 1993.

———. *Governing through Crime: How the War on Crime Transformed American Democracy and Created a Culture of Fear*. New York: Oxford University Press, 2007.

———. "Punishment and the Political Technologies of the Body." In *The SAGE Handbook of Punishment and Society*, edited by Jonathan Simon and Richard Sparks, pp. 60–89. London: SAGE, 2013.

————. *Mass Incarceration on Trial: A Remarkable Court Decision and the Future of Prisons in America*. New York: New Press, 2014.

Simon, Jonathan, and Richard Sparks. "Punishment and Society: The Emergence of an Academic Field." In *The SAGE Handbook of Punishment and Society*, edited by Jonathan Simon and Richard Sparks, pp. 1–20. London: SAGE, 2013.

Smith, Neil. "Giuliani Time: The Revanchist 1990s." *Social Text* 57 (Winter 1998), 1–20.

Smith, Philip. *Punishment and Culture*. Chicago: University of Chicago Press, 2008.

Soss, Joe, Richard C. Fording, and Sanford F. Schram. *Disciplining the Poor: Neoliberal Paternalism and the Persistent Power of Race*. Chicago: University of Chicago Press, 2011.

Stanley, Leo L. "Tuberculosis in San Quentin." *California and Western Medicine* 49, no. 6 (1938), 436–39.

Steen, Sara, and Rachel Bandy. "When the Policy Becomes the Problem: Criminal Justice in the New Millennium." *Punishment & Society* 9, no. 1 (2007), 5–26.

Steen, Sara, Traci Lacock, and Shelby McKinzey. "Unsettling the Discourse of Punishment? Competing Narratives of Reentry and the Possibilities for Change." *Punishment & Society* 14, no. 1 (2012), 29–50.

Story, Brett. "The Prison Inside: A Genealogy of Solitary Confinement as Counter-resistance." In *Historical Geographies of Prisons: Unlocking the Usable Carceral Past*, edited by Karen M. Morin and Dominique Moran, pp. 34–50. Abingdon, UK: Routledge, 2015.

Stromquist, Shelton. *Reinventing "The People": The Progressive Movement, the Class Problem, and the Origins of Modern Liberalism*. Urbana: University of Illinois Press, 2006.

Studt, Elliot, Sheldon L. Messinger, and Thomas P. Wilson. *C-unit: Search for Community in Prison*. New York: Russell Sage Foundation, 1968.

Stuntz, William J. *The Collapse of American Criminal Justice*. Cambridge, MA: Belknap Press of Harvard University Press, 2011.

Subramanian, Ram, and Ruth Delaney. "Playbook for Change? States Reconsider Mandatory Sentences." *Federal Sentencing Reporter* 26, no. 3 (2014), 198–211.

Sullivan, Larry E. *The Prison Reform Movement: Forlorn Hope*. Boston: Twayne, 1990.

Super, Gail. "'Like Some Rough Beast Slouching towards Bethlehem to Be Born': A Historical Perspective on the Institution of the Prison in South Africa, 1976–2004." *British Journal of Criminology* 51, no. 1 (2011a), 201–21.

————. "Punishment and the Body in the 'Old' and 'New' South Africa: A Story of Punitivist Humanism." *Theoretical Criminology* 15, no. 4 (2011b), 427–43.

Sutton, John R. "Imprisonment and Social Classification in Five Common-Law Democracies, 1955–1985." *American Journal of Sociology* 106, no. 2 (2000), 350–86.

Sykes, Gresham M. *The Society of Captives: A Study of a Maximum Security Prison* (1958). Princeton, NJ: Princeton University Press, 2007.

Takei, Carl. "From Mass Incarceration to Mass Control, and Back Again: How Bipartisan Criminal Justice Reform May Lead to a For-Profit Nightmare." *University of Pennsylvania Journal of Law and Social Change* 20 (forthcoming).

Tanenhaus, David S. *Juvenile Justice in the Making*. New York: Oxford University Press, 2004.

Tarrow, Sydney. *Power in Movement: Social Movements, Collective Action and Politics*. New York: Cambridge University Press, 1994.

Taylor, Keeanga-Yamahtta. *From #BlackLivesMatter to Black Liberation*. Chicago: Haymarket, 2016.

Taylor, Verta. "Social Movement Continuity: The Women's Movement in Abeyance." *American Sociological Review* 54, no. 5 (1989), 761–75.

Teeters, Negley K. *The Cradle of the Penitentiary: The Walnut Street Jail at Philadelphia, 1773–1835*. Philadelphia: Temple University Press, 1955.

Thielo, Angela J., Francis T. Cullen, Derek M. Cohen, and Cecilia Chouhy. "Rehabilitation in a Red State: Public Support for Correctional Reform in Texas." *Criminology & Public Policy* 15, no. 1 (2016), 137–70.

Thompson, Heather Ann. "Blinded by a 'Barbaric' South: Prison Horrors, Inmate Abuse, and the Ironic History of American Penal Reform." In *The Myth of Southern Exceptionalism*, edited by Matthew D. Lassiter and Joseph Crespino, pp. 74–98. Oxford: Oxford University Press, 2010.

———. *Blood in the Water: The Attica Prison Uprising of 1971 and Its Legacy*. New York: Pantheon, 2016.

Thorpe, Lloyd. *Men to Match the Mountains*. Seattle, WA: Met, 1972.

Tiger, Rebecca. *Judging Addicts: Drug Courts and Coercion in the Justice System*. New York: New York University Press, 2012.

Tonry, Michael. *Thinking about Crime: Sense and Sensibility in American Penal Culture*. New York: Oxford University Press, 2004.

Travis, Jeremy. "Reflections on the Reentry Movement." *Federal Sentencing Reporter* 20, no. 2 (2007), 84–87.

Turner, Susan F., Lois M. Davis, Terry Fain, Helen Braithwaite, Theresa Lavery, Wayne Choinski, and George Camp. "A National Picture of Prison Downsizing Strategies." *Victims & Offenders* 10, no. 4 (2015), 401–19.

Uggen, Christopher, Mike Vuolo, Sarah Lageson, Ebony Ruhland, and Hilary K. Whitham. "The Edge of Stigma: An Experimental Audit of the Effects of Low-Level Criminal Records on Employment." *Criminology* 52, no. 4 (2014), 627–54.

Useem, Bert. "Right-Sizing Corrections in New York." *Justice Research and Policy* 12, no. 1 (2010), 89–112.

Valverde, Mariana. "Moral Capital." *Canadian Journal of Law & Society* 9, no. 1 (1994), 213–32.

Vaughan, Diane. "Bourdieu and Organizations: The Empirical Challenge." *Theory and Society* 37, no. 1 (2008), 65–81.

Verma, Anjuli. "The Law-Before: Legacies and Gaps in Penal Reform." *Law & Society Review* 49, no. 4 (2015), 847–82.

Von Drehle, David. *Triangle: The Fire That Changed America*. New York: Grove, 2003.

Wacquant, Loic. "'Suitable Enemies': Foreigners and Immigrants in the Prisons of Europe." *Punishment & Society* 1, no. 2 (1999), 215–22.

Wacquant, Loïc. "Deadly Symbiosis: When Ghetto and Prison Meet and Mesh." *Punishment & Society* 3, no. 1 (2001), 95–133.

———. "Pierre Bourdieu." In *Key Sociological Thinkers*, edited by Rob Stones, pp. 261–77. 2d ed. New York: Palgrave Macmillan, 2008a.

———. *Urban Outcasts: A Comparative Sociology of Advanced Marginality*. Malden, MA: Polity, 2008b.

———. *Punishing the Poor: The Neoliberal Government of Social Insecurity*. Durham, NC: Duke University Press, 2009.

Walker, Samuel. *Popular Justice: A History of American Criminal Justice*. 2d ed. New York: Oxford University Press, 1998.

Ward, Geoff K. *The Black Child-Savers: Racial Democracy and Juvenile Justice*. Chicago: University of Chicago Press, 2012.

Ward, Robert David, and William Warren Rogers. *Alabama's Response to the Penitentiary Movement, 1829–1865*. Gainesville: University Press of Florida, 2003.

Weaver, Vesla M. "Frontlash: Race and the Development of Punitive Crime Policy." *Studies in American Political Development* 21, no. 2 (2007), 230–65.

Weiman, David F., and Christopher Weiss. "The Origins of Mass Incarceration in New York State: The Rockefeller Drug Laws and the Local War on Drugs." In *Do Prisons Make Us Safer? The Benefits and Costs of the Prison Boom*, edited by Steven Raphael and Michael A. Stoll, pp. 73–116. New York: Russell Sage Foundation, 2009.

Western, Bruce. *Punishment and Inequality in America*. New York: Russell Sage Foundation, 2006.

Whitman, James Q. *Harsh Justice: Criminal Punishment and the Widening Divide between America and Europe*. New York: Oxford University Press, 2005.

Wilkinson, William Richard. *Prison Work: A Tale of Thirty Years in the California Department of Corrections*. Edited by John C. Burnham and Joseph F. Spillane. Columbus: Ohio State University Press, 2005.

Wilson, James Q., and George L. Kelling. "Broken Windows: The Police and Neighborhood Safety." *Atlantic Monthly* 249, no. 3 (1982), 29–38.

Wright, Erik Olin. *The Politics of Punishment: A Critical Analysis of Prisons in America*. New York: Harper & Row, 1973.

Yaley, Barbara Jeanne. "Habits of Industry: Labor and Penal Policy in California, 1849–1940." PhD dissertation, University of California, Santa Cruz, 1980.

Zimmerman, Jane. "The Penal Reform Movement in the South during the Progressive Era, 1890–1917." *Journal of Southern History* 17, no. 4 (1951), 462–92.

Zimring, Franklin E. *The City That Became Safe: New York's Lessons for Urban Crime and Its Control*. New York: Oxford University Press, 2012.

Zimring, Franklin E., and Gordon Hawkins. *The Scale of Imprisonment*. Chicago: University of Chicago Press, 1991.

———. *Incapacitation: Penal Confinement and the Restraint of Crime.* Oxford: Oxford University Press, 1995.

Zimring, Franklin E., Gordon Hawkins, and Sam Kamin. *Punishment and Democracy: Three Strikes and You're Out in California.* New York: Oxford University Press, 2001.

# Index

*Note*: The letter *f* following a page number denotes a figure.